FINANCIAL CRISES

Institutions and Markets in a Fragile Environment

Edited by

EDWARD I. ALTMAN
and
ARNOLD W. SAMETZ

A WILEY-INTERSCIENCE PUBLICATION

JOHN WILEY & SONS
NEW YORK • LONDON • SYDNEY • TORONTO

Copyright © 1977 by John Wiley & Sons, Inc.

All rights reserved. Published simultaneously in Canada.

No part of this book may be reproduced by any means,
nor transmitted, nor translated into a machine language
without the written permission of the publisher.

This publication is designed to provide accurate and authoritative information in regard to the subject matter covered. It is sold with the understanding that the publisher is not engaged in rendering
legal, accounting, or other professional service. If legal advice or other expert assistance is required,
the services of a competent professional person should be sought.

*From a Declaration of Principles jointly adopted by a Committee of the American Bar Association
and a Committee of Publishers.*

Library of Congress Cataloging in Publication Data:

Main entry under title:

Financial crises.

  Papers presented at a conference held at New York
University May 20–21, 1976.
  "A Wiley-Interscience publication."
  Includes bibliographies and index.
  1. Finance—United States—Congresses. 2. Financial
institutions—United States—Congresses. 3. Finance—
Congresses. I. Altman, Edward I., 1941– II. Sam-
etz, Arnold W.

HG181.F58   332′.0973   77-2308
ISBN 0-471-02685-9

Printed in the United States of America

10 9 8 7 6 5 4 3 2 1

Contributors

Anthony F. Aloi, President, Lasser Brothers, Inc., New York, New York

Edward I. Altman, Professor of Finance, New York University, New York, New York

George J. Benston, Professor of Finance, Graduate School of Management and Center for the Study of Financial Institutions and Markets, University of Rochester, Rochester, New York

Ernest Bloch, Professor of Finance, New York University, New York, New York

Marc P. Blum, Associate at Gordon, Feinblatt, Rothman, Hoffberger, and Hollander, Baltimore, Maryland

Barry Bosworth, Research Associate, Brookings Institution, Washington, D.C.

Jesse Burkhead, Professor of Economics, Maxwell School, Syracuse University, Syracuse, New York

Alan K. Campbell, Dean, Maxwell School, Syracuse University, Syracuse, New York

Edward B. Deakin, Assistant Professor of Accounting, University of Texas, Austin, Texas

Robert A. Eisenbeis, Assistant to the Director, Division of Research and Statistics, Board of Governors of the Federal Reserve System, Washington, D.C.

Karen Gerard, Vice President, Chase Manhattan Bank, New York, New York

Jack Guttentag, Professor of Finance, Wharton School, University of Pennsylvania, Philadelphia, Pennsylvania

George H. Hempel, Professor of Finance, Washington University, St. Louis, Missouri, and Project Director, Advisory Committee on Intergovernmental Relations, Washington, D.C.

Warren C. Hutchins, Chief Executive Officer and Managing Director, Merrill Lynch International Bank, Ltd., London, England

Henry Kaufman, Partner and Member of the Executive Committee, Salomon Brothers, New York, New York

Roger Klein, Vice President and Director of Economic Research, Securities Industry Association, New York, New York

Leon Korobow, Assistant Vice President, Bank Supervision and Relations Function, Federal Reserve Bank of New York, New York, New York

Robert Lindsay, Professor of Finance, New York University, New York, New York

John Lintner, Gund Professor of Economics and Business Administration, Harvard University, Boston, Massachusetts

H. Jack Lissenden, Director of Finance, City of Richmond, Virginia

Daniel Martin, Senior Banking Research Analyst, Banking Studies Department, Federal Reserve Bank of New York, New York, New York

James D. McWilliams, Vice President of Trust Investment, Continental Illinois National Bank and Trust Company of Chicago, Chicago, Illinois

Hyman P. Minsky, Professor of Economics, Washington University, St. Louis, Missouri

Robert A. Mullin, Deputy Comptroller for Special Surveillance, Office of Comptroller of the Currency, Washington, D.C.

Guy E. Noyes, Senior Vice President and Economist, Morgan Guarantee Trust Company, New York, New York

John Petersen, Executive Director, Municipal Finance Officers Association, Washington, D.C.

Arnold W. Sametz, Professor of Finance and Director, Salomon Brothers Center for the Study of Financial Institutions, New York University, New York, New York

Eugene J. Sherman, Vice President and Director of Research, Merrill Lynch Government Securities, Inc., New York, New York.

Allen Sinai, Director of Financial Economics, Data Resources, Inc., and Visiting Associate Professor of Economics and Finance, Sloan School, Massachusetts Institute of Technology, Cambridge, Massachusetts

Joseph F. Sinkey, Jr., Associate Professor of Banking and Finance, University of Georgia, Athens, Georgia

Thomas M. Timlen, Executive Vice President, Federal Reserve Bank of New York, New York, New York

David P. Stuhr, Economist, Banking Studies Department, Federal Reserve Bank of New York, and Associate Professor of Finance, Rutgers University, New Brunswick, New Jersey

George M. von Furstenberg, Professor of Economics, Indiana University, Lafayette, Indiana

Henry C. Wallich, Member, Board of Governors of the Federal Reserve System, Washington, D.C.

Albert M. Wojnilower, Senior Vice President and Director, First Boston Corporation, New York, New York

Kenneth M. Wright, Vice President and Chief Economist, American Life Insurance Association, Washington, D.C.

Foreword

To the post-World War II generation the words "financial crisis" had a historical but not contemporary meaning for quite a long time. For two decades following the great war the world of business and finance behaved in classical cyclical fashion. No major excesses were committed. Memories of the great crash became blurred, and few were able to recall the panic of 1907. It seemed that modern economics had found ways to prevent the crises and panics that had hit most earlier generations at least once in their lifetime. There was much that was assuring besides the reasonable economic performance of the 1950s and early 1960s. The monitoring of economics and finance intensified with the frequent collection of many new data. The advent of econometrics held forth great promise of expanding our understanding of economic behavior. Even the language of economists contained great assurance. More economists spoke convincingly about objectives and made bold predictions about future stability.

When a financial crisis finally struck, it was not of the old-fashioned kind. It was rather mild. It was called the credit crunch of 1966. "Crunch" was too harsh a label, but like any crisis it was a surprise to the postwar generation, and for a while it laid seige to the savings deposit institutions. The subsequent crises, however, were of increasing intensity. During their most intense moments, they contained all the ingredients that had fueled the financial debacles of old. How close we came to disaster in 1970, and then again in 1974 and early 1975, no one will ever accurately record. It was a frightening period with rapidly rising interest rates, some spectacular business failures, spiralling preferences for high credit quality and liquidity, and doubts about the strength of some of the largest and most prominent financial institutions.

In light of these events, it is fitting to do now what we failed to do a decade or so ago, namely, to examine and study the whys and wherefores of financial crises and methods of preventing their occurrence.

Henry Kaufman
General Partner
Salomon Brothers

New York, New York
February 1977

Preface

During the most recent economic recession (1973–1975) the nation's financial markets and institutions were faced with pressures and strains not experienced since the 1930s. The commercial banking sector was severely shaken in this period with 4 bank failures in 1974, 13 in 1975, and 10 in the first 6 months of 1976. The stability and financial integrity of the industry was a subject of concern. The nation's regulatory agencies for commercial banks, particularly the Office of the Comptroller of Currency and the FDIC, came under severe pressure to strengthen and make public their respective efforts to identify and rehabilitate banks that were potential failures. Bankers and regulators alike, were asked to testify before Congress on the soundness of the banking system. The failures of the Unted States National Bank of San Diego (1973) and the Franklin National Bank of New York (1974) were stunning, and there were growing fears that additional billion-dollar banks might fail.

During this same severe recession the number of failures in the business sector increased sharply, and the liabilities involved reached record dollar levels. Short-term failure liabilities rose from $1.9 billion in 1970 to $3.1 billion in 1974 and $4.4 billion in 1975. The number of large-firm failures increased dramatically with the much publicized W. T. Grant Co. bankruptcy in 1975, the most outstanding because of its size. Large enterprises can no longer be assumed to be immune from financial insolvency.

The nation's money and capital markets have also been under extreme pressure in recent years, with the result that overall capital flows have been restricted and particular sectors subjected to severe curtailment and even conditions best described as financial crises. Municipal and public agency markets all but dried up for a time, the problems in these markets being most evident in the Northeast, particularly in New York City. Short-term markets for debt were struck by a commercial paper crisis that developed from the Penn Central bankruptcy, and there were other scares in the Eurocurrency, and short-term municipal markets and other rollover situations.

The question whether our financial market system as a whole was endangered, during this period, as a result of its fragility and increasing instability led economists and financial experts to ask the more general question whether the financial system, as we now know it, is resilient enough to handle future shocks to the environment such as those experienced in 1974 and 1975. And if it is not so adaptable, how might it be made so.

The aforementioned events, and our interest in capital markets and financial institutions in general, motivated the organization of a special conference on financial crises by the Salomon Brothers Center for the Study of Financial Institutions, at New York University's Graduate School of Business Administration. The conference was held on May 20–21, 1976, at New York University, and the 2-day session was attended by over 400 individuals from the government, financial institutions, private business, and the academic sector. Forty-three distinguished economists and financial experts from the private and public sectors as well as from academic institutions throughout the country made presentations which addressed the issues noted above.

The discussions were organized to treat both micro- and macroeconomic issues related to financial crises. The sessions were as follows:

Session 1: Early Warning Systems for Problem Financial Institutions
Session 2: Failure Models for Nonfinancial Institutions
Session 3: The American Financial Environment—Fragile or Resilient?
Session 4: Endangered Financial Markets

We have included in this volume the most important papers from these sessions and are grateful to the participants and to those who helped organize the sessions for their professional efforts. We are especially delighted that the presentations were so well received by those attending and expect that this volume will form an important reference for understanding the dynamics of our financial system. The information and analysis presented and the experiences exchanged should help in coping with future financial crises and may help to prevent or mitigate their potentially devastating effects.

In addition to the individuals whose papers or critiques are included in this volume, we would like to express our appreciation to the others who participated in the conference in a meaningful way. These include Ken Garbade, William Silber, and George Sorter from New York University, Warren Marcus from Salomon Brothers, Richard Platt, then Director of the FSLIC, and Katherine Schipper of Carnegie-Mellon University.

The administrative efforts of Phoebe Hoban and P. Narayanan are appreciated. Finally, we are indebted to Kathy Alamo for her outstanding organizational efforts. She ran the conference from behind the scenes and made our own tasks that much easier.

EDWARD I. ALTMAN
ARNOLD W. SAMETZ

New York, New York
February 1977

Contents

xiii

PART ONE

Identifying Financial Problems of Institutions in Today's Economy

Early Warning Systems for Problem Financial Institutions

EDWARD I. ALTMAN

At the conference on *financial crises*, one of the most controversial topics was the development and implementation of early warning systems for detecting potential problem financial institutions in the United States. Such systems are of interest to financial institutions, their investors, depositors, and other creditors, and to the regulatory agencies established to protect the financial integrity of the industry they are charged to regulate. In addition to the regulators, complementary organizations have been established to insure depositors or customers of the institutions against loss due to failure of the firm. The latter include the Federal Deposit Insurance Corporation (FDIC) for commercial and mutual savings banks, the Federal Savings and Loan Insurance Corporation (FSLIC) for savings and loan associations, and the Securities Investor Protection Corporation (SIPC) for brokers and dealers in securities.

Representatives from the three primary agencies charged with regulating the *commercial banking industry* were asked to present their latest work with respect to developing early warning systems for the banks under their jurisdiction. It is interesting to note that there were concurrent efforts at the three commercial bank agencies, that is, the Federal Reserve Bank of New York, the FDIC, and the office of the Comptroller of Currency, and little or no interaction between them. One of the objectives of the conference and this group of

3

papers is to bring—for the first time as far as we can tell—the three agencies together and to present a forum for information exchange and future cooperation. For reasons discussed at a later point, the results of this forum and potential future cooperation may take a different form than contemplated.

Three of the papers are given in this part of the book. The first chapter dealing with commercial banks utilizes a statistical methodology known as discriminant analysis to predict and/or classify financial institutions into relative healthy or unhealthy categories; various financial characteristics of the institutions are analyzed on a simultaneous basis. In this way, objectively weighted measures are combined to arrive at an overall score or rating for each member of the population being investigated. The other two papers also utilize comparative scoring techniques based on peer group analysis. The studies differ, however, in several ways. The reader should scrutinize the sampling techniques, the structure of the comparative analysis, the types of variables selected, and finally the conclusions and implications specified.

Korobow, Stuhr, and Martin present their latest in a series of papers on "A Probabilistic Approach to Early Warning of Changes in Bank Financial Condition." They are careful to point out that the measures of interest to them are those of commercial bank vulnerability, using data routinely reported to bank regulatory agencies rather than the conditions of banks that have already deteriorated. Their scoring, peer group process—based on group averages and standard deviations—was very efficient in correctly indicating banks that received low supervisory ratings in some period subsequent to that used to calculate the data. The authors are encouraged that such a system, which is still being tested, will bring added efficiency to bank examinations.

Sinkey, presents a summary of his extensive empirical research on early warning systems for problem or failed banks. He discusses questions involving what a problem bank is, whether bank failures can be predicted, and how bank examiners identify unhealthy situations. As in prior works, Sinkey utilizes quadratic discriminant analysis to identify banks of a problem nature. Again, we recommend careful reading of the exact groups used. In addition, Sinkey presents an alternative to the traditional two-or-more group discriminant analysis called the "outlier technique." This technique, which is basically a multivariate, peer group analysis, holds good promise for future work in the field. Finally, Sinkey presents a scenario of what he believes would be the most effective way to organize and implement the supervision and examination of commercial banks. He is careful to point out that these recommendations are his and not those of the FDIC.

In the third paper dealing with commercial banks Mullin outlines the National Bank Surveillance System of the Office of the Comptroller of the Currency in terms of its development, the personnel involved, the reports created by the system, and the various subsystems within the overall effort. While its approach is more traditional in nature than the rigorous statistical techniques utilized in the other studies, it does rely on both computerized reports generated on a quarterly basis as well as the specification of the dynamics involved with respect to actions taken by supervisory personnel. This system, while still not totally operational, probably stands a greater chance of implementation, in its present form, than the aforementioned systems of the other agencies.

Following these three papers, a distinguished panel of discussants critically analyzed the efforts of the regulatory agencies. Guttentag (Pennsylvania) and Benston (Rochester) are generally suspicious of the ability of these systems to capture the essence of commercial bank problems, but both comment that their efforts are useful and of credit to the proponents. Both discussants recommend alternative procedures or elaborations to make the systems more effective. Elsenbels also discusses the papers, but more in terms of putting these efforts in perspective. He presents what he believes to be the present state of the art of early warning systems for financial institutions as well as directions for future work.

SOME INTERESTS NOT REPRESENTED

When discussing the implications of early warning systems for financial institutions—particularly commercial banks—one may reflect on the parties that could assist in the overall understanding of the problem. Two parties that we considered for inclusion in the conference were members of the U.S. Congress and representatives of the banking industry itself. We attempted to invite both groups but, for one reason or another, leading individuals in the U.S. Senate and the House of Representatives could not attend, and the top bankers we approached chose not to participate. It is worthwhile to note what these parties could have added to the discussion.

At the time we were planning the conference, among the hottest pieces of legislation being discussed in Congress were the new financial institution acts in both the Senate and the House. In the fall of 1975, both bills contained sections on bringing the three commercial bank regulatory agencies under one roof with respect to examination and surveillance. These particular sections of the bills seemed particularly relevant, since it was our feeling that wasteful, duplicative, and noncooperative efforts were going on in at least three of the interested agencies and that perhaps the best efforts of the three could be combined into a system for the entire banking industry. No doubt, the behavioral and organizational complexities involved in dealing with three agencies make such cooperation currently impractical, but, if there were one overall authority, such an endeavor might be worth pursuing. For many reasons, however (some not completely explained by Congress), the relevant sections of both the House and Senate bills were dropped in the spring of 1976.

We expect, however, that one of the important results of this conference was to bring the leading researchers and the most relevant administrators into closer contact and communication.

The banking industry is large and varied, and to select a representative to speak on problem banks clearly presented a potentially uncomfortable assignment for any member of the industry willing to accept such a challenge. In addition, since the major papers discussed efforts to develop early warning systems, comment from the banking industry would have to be in the form of a discussion rather than of a principal paper. We believe these constraints, and perhaps a few others, were responsible for the lack of direct participation by bankers in the conference.

PROSPECTS FOR EARLY WARNING SYSTEM IMPLEMENTATION

There are at least four major ingredients for successful implementation of a statistical early warning system for financial institutions developed at a regulatory agency:

1. An efficient and understandable system
2. Understanding and cooperation among the developer, the administrator, and existing surveillance personnel
3. Support from the top of the regulatory agency
4. Continuity of key personnel.

Usually when a regulatory agency decides to go ahead and investigate the efficiency of a system for detecting problem organizations, some individual section of the agency has the initial responsibility to develop it. This section may be the economic research, or examination and/or surveillance division, or some special deputy of the agency chairperson. The system is usually developed with assistance from outside, but this is not always the case. Unless the effort has the understanding and support from the top, however (point 3), it is doomed to failure. Needless to say, if the developed system does not test out efficiently, implementation will not be attempted (point 1). Careful education of all relevant parties about the adopted system, and how it will be utilized once it is implemented, is vital to its acceptance throughout the agency (point 2). Researchers that we know report that one of the most difficult aspects of establishing any sophisticated system is the "selling" of its merits and its potential to the individuals presently responsible for surveillance.

The final constraint (point 4)—continuity of key personnel—is rarely considered until an individual leaves an organization. There are usually several key persons whose continued employment by the regulatory agency is critical to the implementation of the system. If the developer(s) of the system are internal employees, they certainly are in a crucial position. Their immediate supervisor, who no doubt supported the system's development in discussions with top personnel, is also important. Finally, the head of the organization must usually be perpetuated especially if he, and some of his key subordinates, are political appointees. Let me illustrate the dynamics of these statements with reference to several individuals who took part in the conference on financial crises.

The current efforts at the FDIC are unfortunately less likely now to be implemented because of personnel changes. Both Sinkey and his immediate supervisor, Eisenbeis, are no longer with the agency. In addition, the FDIC has made a recent change in administration at all levels, including the chairman; usually what follows major reorganizations is "throwing out the old and working on developing the new." Officials at the FDIC, however, believe that past efforts will be pursued, despite the fact that some key individuals are no longer there. Ironically, the change in personnel noted above may lead to increased cooperation and a chance of success at another bank regulatory agency, namely, the Federal Reserve. Korobow et al. represent the Federal Reserve Bank of New York only, and their efforts are not formally connected with the Board of Governors of the Federal Reserve in Washington. Eisenbeis joined the board of governors in July 1976 and brings to his new position a rich background and sympathy with the techniques and interest in developing early warning systems. Perhaps the communication fostered at the conference and by these papers will add to internal communication within the Federal Reserve system.

It is difficult to estimate at this point what will happen at the comptroller's office. In July 1976 the Comptroller of the Currency, James Smith, announced his resignation. Even if there were support at the top before, there is no guarantee that it will continue.

At the FHLBB, efforts to implement an early warning system are being complicated by the resignation of the director of the FSLIC (the office that developed the system) and the presidential elections of November 1976. A new president in the White House will appoint a new chairperson of the FHLBB (the job is vacant now) who may in turn choose to change some of the key positions and individuals important to the continued testing and eventual implementation of their system. Probably by the time this book is published, answers to these questions will be known.

We do expect efforts to construct and implement efficient early warning systems for our nation's financial institutions to continue and to be successful in the near future. We hope that the papers presented in this section of the book will help in this endeavor.

1.
A Probabilistic Approach to Early Warning of Changes in Bank Financial Condition

LEON KOROBOW,
DAVID P. STUHR,
AND DANIEL MARTIN*

The subject of early warning is one that challenges our understanding of the nation's financial system. In the perspective of the strains imposed on banks by virulent inflation and severe recession during the past few years, it is clear that improved methods of early detection of financial weaknesses in our banking system could help bank regulatory authorities to anticipate and mitigate future problems. An effective early warning system could make a substantial contribution to a more smoothly functioning financial system.

The Federal Reserve Bank of New York has for several years had under study statistical techniques to assist in the supervision of banks in the Second Federal Reserve District. This research has been aimed at the development of

* The authors acknowledge the many helpful comments made by their colleagues at the Federal Reserve Bank of New York, but accept full responsibility for this paper. This article also appears in the July 1976 issue of the Federal Reserve Bank of New York *Monthly Review*.

early warning indicators from financial reports that banks file routinely with regulatory agencies. The results thus far strongly suggest that substantial improvements in the allocation of supervisory resources could be achieved by focusing attention primarily on banks designated vulnerable by the criteria set forth in the early warning procedures. These procedures also can provide estimates of the probability, under varying economic circumstances, that any single bank will develop severe financial weakness at some future date. Earlier investigations have been described in the September 1974 and July 1975 issues of the Federal Reserve Bank of New York *Monthly Review.* This article brings those reports up to date and comments more broadly on the role that early warning research can play in improving bank supervision.

EARLY WARNING AS AN AID TO SUPERVISION

The financial turbulence of the early 1970s clearly highlighted an important new dimension of the problem of bank supervision. The failure of the United States National Bank of San Diego, the Franklin National Bank, and the Security National Bank dramatized the consequences of high risks and imprudent management, if not fraud, even for large institutions. Each of these banks had assets in excess of $1 billion. While failures on this scale have been relatively few, the general problems that have surfaced in banking in recent years clearly indicate that large banks are not immune to failure and that improved techniques of spotting financial deterioration at an early stage could make an important contribution to the stability of our financial system.

Many of the problems that have affected banks in recent years are the direct result of the twin shocks, severe inflation and recession. In some cases, a willingness to extend the normal limits of risk taking for the sake of enhanced profits during the late 1960s and early 1970s contributed to a degree of risk exposure which, in retrospect, proved to be unwise. Clearly, banks must be prepared to take risks if they are to serve the financial needs of the nation's economy, but these risks must be tempered by the public's interest in a sound and stable banking system, since the potential costs of widespread instability in banking extend far beyond the banks directly concerned.

The achievement of an appropriate balance between risk taking and the preservation of comfortable margins of safety with respect to earnings, capital, and liquidity is a goal that both bankers and bank supervisors have a vital stake in pursuing. From this point of view, it is important to recognize what bank supervisors have always known: On-site examinations provide accurate insight into developing, as well as actual, financial problems at banks. The experience of supervisors and the results of financial research indicate that financial deterioration typically does not occur overnight. A decline in earnings, capital, liquidity, and asset quality, and inadequate management as reflected in poor internal controls and auditing procedures, usually develop over a period of time. Thus regularly scheduled bank examinations normally uncover these adverse developments.

Regular examinations not only probe a bank's financial condition but also provide valuable information on whether or not banks are complying with regulatory policies and procedures. An on-site examination has strong precautionary and psychological influences on a bank and is the major cutting edge of supervisory policy.

There are, nonetheless, several factors that make an effective statistical early warning system important for responsive and efficient bank supervision. First, significant changes in a bank's management policies and financial condition can occur between examinations. Second, an on-site examination is a lengthy and expensive process and not always the most cost-effective method of tracking small, but important, changes in a bank's financial condition. Third, although examiners generally are sensitive to developing trends that indicate potential future management or financial problems and normally comment on such matters in their reports, they must necessarily emphasize their findings concerning the actual condition of the bank rather than the estimated impact of potential problems. Fourth, an examiner's findings are part of the official record and could provide the basis for enforcement or other supervisory actions. In contrast, statistical early warning measures can be informal, affording the opportunity for experiments with techniques to uncover financial weakness at its earliest stages.

In short, early warning analysis can be a valuable adjunct to the process of bank examination and supervision. By providing accurate and timely information on changes in a bank's financial condition between examinations, it can make possible a more efficient use of supervisory resources. Moreover, an efficient early warning system can be a useful tool of analysis in the ongoing appraisal of a bank's financial condition.

DETECTING POTENTIAL DETERIORATION

Early-warning research at the Federal Reserve Bank of New York has recently focused on the problem of detecting potential financial deterioration in banks rather than on studying the characteristics of banks that have already undergone severe deterioration. This emphasis on measuring vulnerability to future problems rather than the currect condition required a substantial modification of the methodology employed in the earliest stages of the project.[1]

Measures of vulnerability were investigated, using financial data reported routinely to bank regulatory agencies, so that the condition of banks could be closely monitored in periods between scheduled on-site examinations. Since overall economic conditions have a substantial impact on a bank's ability to withstand unexpected shocks or strains, the analysis was structured to take into account the expected external environment.

Several financial variables were selected for testing. These were variables that experience had indicated were closely associated with sustained financial strength or weakness. The objective was to combine the smallest set of variables into a single measure of vulnerability that would indicate early signs of financial deterioration. To find this measure we computed the average and standard deviation of each variable. Then for each bank we compared its set of values for the variables to the respective averages and divided the resulting differences by the standard deviations of each of the variables. These "standardized deviations" were added algebraically, according to their expected contribution to vulnerability, to form an overall bank score. In general, the higher a bank's score the more resistant to adverse economic or financial developments it is expected to be, while the lower the score the greater its expected vulnerability. The resulting performance measure provided an indication of financial strength or weakness for all member banks in the Second Federal Reserve District.

The 350 or so member banks comprising this group included banks that varied widely in size, scope of banking business, and propensity for taking risks. Among these banks were a large number whose management policies were known to be conservative and whose balance sheets and income statements would lead most observers to conclude that they had a low tolerance for risk. The overall group also included several larger banks, as well as many that were active practitioners of liability management. We rejected performance comparisons based on banks that were similar in size and scope of banking

---

[1] See Leon Korobow and David P. Stuhr, "Toward Early Warning of Changes in Banks' Financial Condition: A Progress Report," Federal Reserve Bank of New York, *Monthly Review*, July 1975. See also David P. Stuhr and Robert Van Wicklen, "Rating the Financial Condition of Banks: A Statistical Approach to Aid Bank Supervision," Federal Reserve Bank of New York, *Monthly Review* September 1974, pp. 233–238; Joseph F. Sinkey, Jr., and David A. Walker, "Problem Banks: Identification and Characteristics," Bank Administration Institute, *Journal of Bank Research,* Winter 1975; Joseph F. Sinkey, Jr., "A Multivariate Statistical Analysis of the Character of Problem Banks," American Finance Association, *The Journal of Finance,* March 1975; Joseph F. Sinkey, Jr., "Early-Warning System: Some Preliminary Predictions of Problem Commercial Banks," *Proceedings of a Conference on Bank Structure and Competition,* Federal Reserve Bank of Chicago, May 1975, pp. 85–91.

activities. The risk exposure in a group of similarly situated banks may be uniformly high or low and thus be misleading as a basis for determining the degree to which a particular bank may be vulnerable to economic and financial strains.

MEASURING EFFICIENCY

The scoring approach provides a means for comparing and tracking bank financial performance over varying periods of time. However, one of the main problems in applying these procedures to the supervisory process is the need for a link between a bank's scores and an independent measure of its soundness. In other words, it is important to know the significance of a low score and the degree of vulnerability indicated by lower standings on the list of scores.

One measure of the effectiveness of the procedures is suggested by the role of the bank score as an aid to bank supervision. This measure is the extent to which bank scores in a base year provide an accurate indication of banks that deteriorated seriously in subsequent years, as evidenced by the receipt of low ratings from supervisory personnel.

If the scoring procedure accurately identifies banks that will subsequently receive low ratings, improvements in efficiency could be achieved by concentrating supervisory resources on such banks. It is convenient to divide the banks into two groups—resistant and vulnerable—according to their scores. The dividing line can be selected with the aid of a cost function which minimizes the cost of two types of error, that is, drawing the line too high and examining more banks than necessary, and drawing the line too low, thus failing to identify banks that are likely to deteriorate or fail.

The cost of the first type of error for a given bank is based on the size of the bank, since the cost of examining a large bank usually far exceeds the cost of examining a small bank. The cost of the second type of error is assumed to be a large multiple of the cost of examining the bank and reflects the high costs of failing to identify and to examine a bank that subsequently undergoes substantial deterioration.[2] The optimal dividing line between resistant and vulnerable banks is one that minimizes these costs. The gain in efficiency represents the reduction in examination expenses, less the cost of failing to identify correctly banks that subsequently deteriorate. In this article, the gain is expressed as the percentage reduction in costs from examining only banks

[2] We assumed that the cost of correct classification is zero. This implies that the examination costs associated with designating as vulnerable and, therefore, examining banks that deteriorated seriously is matched by the benefits of identifying the source of, and possibly arresting, the deterioration. See Korobow and Stuhr, *op. cit.*, pp. 160–163.

designated vulnerable, compared with the costs of examining all banks annually, as at present. In the comparison, total costs are comprised of the costs of the two types of errors described above.[3]

AN EARLY WARNING FUNCTION

Using the cost function, it was possible to compare alternative sets of variables in terms of their value in identifying as vulnerable banks that would be given a low supervisory ratings in a subsequent period. The set of variables that yielded the most efficient allocation of supervisory resources was selected after experimentation with many different combinations. A set of 6 variables was found to be more efficient than any other combination tested, including the 12-variable combination employed in the July 1975 report. The 6 variables are shown in Table 1, where their contributions to resistance and vulnerability are indicated by plus and minus signs, respectively.

The first variable, total operating expenses/total operating revenues, is a measure of a bank's ability to generate revenues from normal banking operations and to control total expenses in an efficient manner.[4] The aspect of this variable that seems to account for its better performance compared with measures of income or rate of return, which proved less efficient, is that it reflects the limits on bank revenues imposed by market competition and emphasizes the importance of internal cost control as a means of maintaining or increasing operating efficiency.

The next two variables—total loans/total assets and commercial and industrial loans/total loans—measure the risk of loss inherent in business lending. The inclusion of both variables is in effect a means of emphasizing the

---

[3] The total cost of the two types of errors can be expressed:

$$TC = \sum_{i=1}^{m} (\text{cost } r{:}w)_i + \sum_{j=1}^{n} (\text{cost } v{:}s)_j$$

where TC = total cost

  m = number of banks receiving low summary ratings classified as resistant

(cost $r{:}w)_1$ = cost of classifying as resistant the ith bank when it receives a low summary rating

  n = number of banks with high or intermediate summary ratings classified as vulnerable.

 (cost $v{:}s)_j$ = cost of classifying as vulnerable the jth bank when it retains a high or intermediate summary rating.

The optimal cutoff point is found by calculating the total cost of the errors associated with every possible dividing line, ranging from classifying all banks as vulnerable to classifying all banks as resistant.

[4] Operating expenses include all costs except securities losses and extraordinary items.

Table 1　Six Early Warning Variables

Variable	Sign[a]
Total operating expenses/total operating revenues	−
Total loans/total assets	−
Commercial and industrial loans/total loans	−
Provision for loss/total loans and investments	−
Net liquid assets/total assets[b]	+
Gross capital/risk assets[c]	+

[a] A plus sign means that an increase in the value of the variable is indicative of strength; a minus sign means that an increase in the variable is indicative of weakness.

[b] Net liquid assets are defined as: U.S. Treasury securities maturing in less than 1 year plus federal funds sold plus loans to brokers and dealers minus federal funds purchased minus other liabilities for borrowed money.

[c] Gross capital = equity capital plus capital notes and debentures plus loss reserves; risk assets = total assets minus cash and due from banks minus U.S. Treasury securities.

several important aspects of the bank's loan portfolio. Two of the six—provision for loss/total loans and investments and net liquid assets/total assets—are new variables. The former represents a measure of prospective losses envisioned by bank management in relation to the bank's overall loans and investments; the latter measures the bank's ability to meet potential requirements for liquidity. Finally, the ratio of gross capital/risk assets is a modified version of an earlier measure of bank capital and is included as an indicator of the ability of banks to cushion losses.

The efficiency of these six variables in classifying banks as resistant or vulnerable is indicated in Table 2. Two separate periods are shown: (1) base year 1969, identifying vulnerable banks in 1970–1972, and (2) base year 1971, identifying vulnerable banks in 1972–1974. In the first period, the inflationary boom in the economy generated a high level of loan activity and sustained many borrowers whose underlying financial position was not strong. Many banks therefore showed good financial results. In the latter period, severe financial strain and recession presented a stringent test of financial staying power for borrowers and lenders alike.

In each estimation period, the calculation to determine the most efficient cutoff score involved the comparison of each bank's score for the base year with its supervisory rating in the subsequent 3-year period. A comparison was made

Table 2 Analysis of Gains in Efficiency from Classification of Banks into Resistant and Vulnerable Groups on the Basis of the Scoring Procedure

Cutoff Bank Score Based on:	Base Year 1969: Estimation Period 1970–1972		Base Year 1971: Estimation Period 1972–1974	
	Percent of Banks Having Low Supervisory Ratings Correctly Identified	Gain in Efficiency (%)	Percent of Banks Having Low Supervisory Ratings Correctly Identified	Gain in Efficiency (%)
Optimal cutoff point	86.8	47.2	92.9	42.2
Naive forecast 1[a]	26.3	11.9	26.8	−75.4
Naive forecast 2[b]	89.5	31.7	75.0	7.6

[a] All banks with low supervisory ratings in the base year 1969 or 1971 are assumed to retain these ratings in the subsequent 3 years, and no other banks receive low ratings.
[b] All banks with low or intermediate supervisory ratings as of 1969 or 1971 are assumed to be vulnerable in the next three years. Banks with high ratings in 1969 or 1971 are assumed to be resistant.

of the gains and losses at various cutoff points.[5] At the optimal cutoff point, which gives the highest gain in efficiency, the six-variable early warning function produced a 47 percent increase in efficiency in the 1970–1972 period and a 42 percent increase in 1972–1974. Moreover, about 87 percent of the banks that received low supervisory ratings in 1970–1972 and 93 percent in 1972–1974 were correctly identified as vulnerable in the respective base years.

These gains are well in excess of any gains that could be expected from following several naive decision rules for allocating supervisory resources. For example, naive forecast 1 in Table 2 is based on the assumption that bank supervisory ratings will not change over the estimation period. This assumption gave rise to a decision rule that banks with high or intermediate supervisory ratings would not be examined annually. Only low-rated banks in the base year would be subject to annual examinations. This rule yielded a small gain in efficiency in 1970–1972 and a substantial loss in 1972–1974.[6]

Naive forecast 2 is a broader rule which exempted from annual on-site examination banks having the highest supervisory ratings. All banks with intermediate or low supervisory ratings in the base year would be examined annually. In this case, the gain in efficiency was much lower than the gain achieved using the optimal decision rule of the early warning function estimated over the period 1970–1972 and was negligible over the period 1972–1974. Thus the early warning function developed from the six variables possesses a significantly greater capacity to isolate banks that will receive low ratings than either of the naive decision rules. Of course, the value of early warning procedures in improving the efficiency of bank supervision depends on the applicability of the cutoff points, developed from past estimation periods, to the economic conditions expected in the future. Research conducted thus far indicates a good degree of stability.

A PROBABILITY INTERPRETATION OF THE SCORING PROCEDURE

While the division of banks into resistant and vulnerable groups was useful in appraising the efficiency of alternative early warning functions, it made no distinction as to the likelihood that individual banks would deteriorate or fail in each group. A study of the bank scores for various base years indicated that many of the banks at the low range of scores subsequently deteriorated,

---

[5] A bank was considered to have had a low supervisory rating if it received a low rating in at least one of the three years subsequent to the base year, although it may not have received a low rating in all three years. In general, approximately three-quarters of the banks that received low supervisory ratings during the periods studied had high or intermediate ratings in the base years.

[6] About three out of five of the banks receiving low ratings during the next 3 years are not correctly identified by this rule.

although some did not, and a few that ranked high met difficulty. The outcome owed much to the composition of each bank's loan portfolio, the economic influences affecting the bank's borrowers, as well as its investments, capital, and liquidity, and the capacity of bank management to adjust its financial position quickly and effectively to a changing economic environment. While these factors are reflected in the indicators of financial vulnerability employed, it must be emphasized that we are dealing with probabilistic events in the sense that many of the management initiatives that can strongly affect the soundness and future condition of both resistant and vulnerable banks cannot be forecast reliably.

Nonetheless, a study of bank scores and the location in the listing of banks that received low supervisory ratings in the period subsequent to the base year clearly indicates a high concentration of low-rated banks at the bottom of the list. This observation confirms the direct relationship between the vulnerability of a bank and its financial performance as measured by supervisory ratings. It also suggests that regression analysis can be used to translate bank scores into a probability estimate of the likelihood of a bank receiving a low supervisory rating given a specific economic environment.

In estimating the probability of banks receiving a low supervisory rating as a function of their scores, we constructed an "observed probability" for each member bank in the Second Federal Reserve District. These probabilities were obtained by determining for banks whose scores were within a selected interval in the base year the proportion that received low supervisory ratings over the estimation period subsequent to the base year.[7] This proportion was taken to be a proxy for the given bank's probability of receiving a low supervisory rating. The observed probabilities were then used as the dependent variable in a regression equation.

The purpose of the regression was to estimate the relationship between the bank scores and the observed probabilities. This relationship was assumed to be a continuous function, approaching 0 for large positive scores and approaching 1 for large negative scores. Furthermore, the function was assumed to be monotonic, that is, for any two banks the one with the lower score (meaning that it is more vulnerable) should have a higher probability of receiving a low supervisory rating subsequent to the base year.

A conveniently available trigonometric function having the required properties is

$$P_1 = 0.5 + \frac{1}{\pi} \arctan (a_0 + a_1 S_1)$$

where P_1 is the probability that each bank will receive a low supervisory rat-

---

[7] The interval was one bank score unit on either side of each bank's score.

Table 3   Regression Coefficients Estimating Probabilities of Deterioration

Base Year	Estimation period	a_0	a_1	$\bar{R}^2$
1969	1970–1972	−2.7	−0.62	0.94
1971	1972–1974	−1.9	−0.60	0.91

ing, a_0 and a_1 are the coefficients to be estimated from the regression, and S_1 is each bank's score. A simple transformation yields an equation which can be estimated using linear regression techniques:

$$\tan\left[\pi\left(P_1 - 0.5\right)\right] = a_0 + a_1 S_1$$

Changes in the value of a_0 shift the curve to the left or right, without changing the function's shape, while a larger absolute value of a_1 increases the steepness of the curve (Figure 1)[8]

The estimated coefficients of the arctangent regressions for the base year 1969 (estimating probabilities of deterioration in 1970–1972) and the base year 1971 (estimating probabilities of deterioration in 1972–1974) are shown in Table 3.

The fit is good in both periods, as indicated by values of $\bar{R}^2$ in excess of .90. While the a_1 coefficients, which relate changes in bank scores to changes in probability, are not significantly different, the constant terms a_0 differ significantly between the two base years. The shift appears to reflect overall changes in banking practices as well as differences in the external economic environment during these years. The lower negative value of a_0 in the latter period suggests that banks faced a higher risk of deterioration or failure for any given level of bank score as a result of the generally more difficult economic and financial conditions at the time. Figure 1 illustrates the relationship between bank scores and the probability of receiving a low supervisory rating, given the bank scores in base years 1969 and 1971 and the supervisory ratings assigned to these banks over the subsequent 3 years.

---

[8] The choice of the arctangent function is arbitrary and was heavily influenced by convenience for programing the regressions. Other estimating procedures are being explored and will be reported on in subsequent papers. Of particular interest is logit analysis, a technique that treats the actual occurrence or nonoccurrence of an event as a dependent variable, without the construction of observed probabilities. It also dispenses with the intermediate step of combining the independent variables into a single bank score; the relative weights of the variables in the estimated probability function are computed within the regression itself. The technique is described by Strother H. Walker and David Duncan, "Estimation of the Probability of an Event as a Function of Several Independent Variables," *Biometrika* (1967), and is applied to credit analysis in *The Journal of Commercial Bank Lending* (August 1974) by Delton L. Chesser.

The probability function can be related to the earlier efficiency measurement in which banks were designated either resistant or vulnerable and supervisory resources were allocated primarily to the vulnerable group. Essentially what was done was to classify as vulnerable all banks whose probability of receiving a low supervisory rating was greater than a given cutoff probability level. If the optimal cutoff points developed earlier are translated into the probability of a bank receiving a low supervisory rating subsequent to the base year, then all banks with a probability of about 15 percent or greater will be considered vulnerable. As shown in Table 4, the efficiency of other specific probability levels can be determined. For example, the first line in the table indicates that, if banks with a 10 percent or higher probability of receiving a low supervisory rating had been examined, the gain in efficiency relative to annual examinations would have been 34 percent in the 1970–1972 period and 14 percent in 1972–1974.

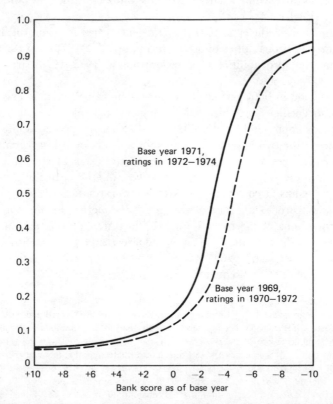

Figure 1 Relationship between bank scores in the base year and the probability of subsequently receiving a low supervisory rating. Probability of receiving a low supervisory rating subsequent to the base year.

Table 4   Analysis of Gains in Efficiency from Classification of Banks into Resistant and Vulnerable Groups on the Basis of Various Probability Levels

Cutoff Probability Level, %	1970–1972 Percent of Banks Having Low Supervisory Ratings Correctly Identified	1970–1972 Gain in Efficiency (%)	1972–1974 Percent of Banks Having Low Supervisory Ratings Correctly Identified	1972–1974 Gain in Efficiency (%)
10	94.7	34.3	96.4	14.1
Optimal[a]	86.8	47.2	92.9	42.2
20	55.3	34.7	75.0	25.6
30	39.5	19.5	58.9	6.6
40	21.1	3.4	41.1	−41.1
50	15.8	3.2	26.8	−74.8
60	13.2	−1.5	21.4	−89.6
70	5.3	−13.9	16.1	b
80	2.6	−15.9	10.7	b
90	0	−15.6	3.6	b

[a] 13 percent for 1970–1972; 16 percent for 1972–1974.
[b] Large loss.

FORECASTING SUPERVISORY RATINGS

A good test of the forecasting ability of the early warning function would be to calculate probabilities of receiving low ratings beyond the period used to estimate the function. This test is not yet possible for the function estimated over the 1972–1974 period, since the data for a comparable 3-year period are not yet available. Nonetheless, we conducted preliminary tests, assuming economic conditions similar to those of 1972–1974, and the results are encouraging (see Table 5). By use of the function computed over the period 1971–1974, the estimated probability of a bank receiving a low supervisory rating in 1975–1977 was obtained for each Second Federal Reserve District member bank, based on 1974 financial reports. The banks were classified into five ranges of probabilities. We expected that the proportion of banks that actually received low supervisory ratings in 1975 would increase as the range of estimated probability increased to higher levels. Table 5 shows that this is in general what happened, although 1975 represented only one-third of the forecast period. Only 2.2 percent of the banks with probability estimates of 20 percent or less received low ratings in 1975, but 41.5 percent of the banks with probability estimates of 80 percent or more had low ratings.

Since this test included some banks that had low supervisory ratings not only in 1975 but also in earlier years for which the function was originally estimated, a further test was conducted. In this test, low-rated banks in each probability range were included only if they had received low supervisory rat-

Table 5 Performance of an Early Warning Function in Predicting Banks Likely to Receive a Low Supervisory Rating in 1975

Estimated Probability of Receiving a Low Rating (as of 1974) (%)[a]	Percentage of Banks in Various Probability Ranges as of 1974 that	
	Had a Low Supervisory Rating in 1975[b]	Received a Low Rating for the First Time in 1975[c]
0 to 20	2.2	0.7
20 to 40	10.2	1.5
40 to 60	17.3	6.9
60 to 80	16.1	6.5
80 to 100	41.5	19.5

[a] Assumes an economic environment similar to that of 1971–1974. Probability estimates are derived from 1974 financial statements of Second Federal Reserve District member banks.
[b] All banks with low supervisory ratings in 1975, regardless of previous ratings.
[c] Banks with low supervisory ratings in 1975 which did not have low ratings in 1974.

ings for the first time in 1975. These were banks that, on the basis of a naive decision rule employed in 1974, might have been expected to continue to receive high or intermediate supervisory ratings in 1975. The third column in Table 5 shows that only 0.7 percent of the banks in the probability range of 20 percent or less received low supervisory ratings for the first time in 1975, compared with 19.5 percent for those with probabilities of over 80 percent. More than half the banks that received low supervisory ratings for the first time in 1975 were in the highest probability range in 1974. This test, while rough and based on the relatively small number of banks that received low supervisory ratings in 1975, suggests that the early warning function has a significant capability for identifying vulnerable banks in years subsequent to the estimation period.

CONCLUDING REMARKS

The probability approach shows considerable promise as a useful guide to the degree and intensity of supervision appropriate for banks within an overall group designated vulnerable in any base year. Banks with relatively high probabilities of deterioration could be considered candidates for the most immediate and intensive supervisory attention. However, to achieve substantial overall gains in efficiency, supervisory resources must also be allocated to banks with relatively low probabilities of deterioration subsequent to the base period. While the precision and efficiency of the forecasts can be expected to improve with more sensitive measures to detect financial weakness at an early stage, some uncertainty is bound to remain in view of the probabilistic nature of financial early warning systems.

New approaches are in process of development. For example, we are exploring methods to estimate the probabilities of failure or of a low supervisory rating directly from the early warning variables involved without the intermediate step of the bank score. This change involves a specific weighting of variables and may lead to improvements in the sensitivity of the probability functions. A great deal more must be done to sharpen the measures employed as early warning indicators, thus ensuring that future areas of weakness do not escape notice.

There is also a need in early warning research for a far more thorough analysis of the structure of bank loan portfolios than has been available thus far. In particular, the consequences of industry or geographic concentrations of loans and investments during a period of adverse economic or financial developments are areas that deserve careful study. The balance sheet and income data banks are now providing in greater detail and frequency should prove valuable in future early warning research. We are optimistic, however, that the approaches outlined here can do much to assist bank supervisors in spotting potentially vulnerable banks before the problems of these institutions threaten their viability.

2.
Problem and Failed Banks, Bank Examinations, and Early Warning Systems: A Summary

JOSEPH F. SINKEY, JR.

The purpose of this paper is to summarize my research and views on problem and failed banks, bank examinations, and early warning systems.[1] Although the focus is on early warning systems, some fundamental questions related to problem and failed banks and the bank examination process need to be considered. For example, What is a problem bank? Can bank failures be predicted? How do bank examiners identify problem and failing banks? This paper begins with a discussion of these questions. The main focus of the paper, an early warning system for identifying problem commercial banks, follows these remarks. The paper ends with a section entitled, "If I Were the Banking Czar."

[1] Formerly Senior Financial Economist, Economic Research Unit, Federal Deposit Insurance Corporation; Now Associate Professor of Banking, University of Georgia. The views expressed in this paper are my own and not necessarily those of the FDIC. The articles I have written on these subjects are listed at the end of this paper. The number of persons who have contributed to my research efforts are too numerous to mention, but I would be remiss if I did not mention Robert A. Eisenbeis, Edward J. Kane, and Edward I. Altman.

PROBLEM AND FAILED BANKS

What is a Problem Bank?

Banking agencies have interpreted their "safety-and-soundness" mandate as one of failure prevention.[2] By identifying banks with the highest failure risks, so-called problem banks, the banking agencies hope to achieve this goal. The FDIC's Division of Bank Supervision identifies three classes of problem banks, which are separated according to examiners' perceptions of failure (or insolvency) risks. Banks perceived as having at least a 50 percent chance of requiring FDIC financial assistance in the near future are classified as *potential payoffs* (PPOs). Banks that appear to be headed for PPO status unless drastic changes occur are referred to as *serious problems* (SPs). And finally, banks that have significant weaknesses, but a lesser degree of vulnerability than PPO or SP banks, are called *other problems* (OPs).

In a recent letter from former FDIC Chairman Frank Wille to Senator Proxmire, the FDIC's general guidelines for identifying SP and OP banks were described:[3]

SERIOUS PROBLEM. This category usually includes banks in which the nature and volume of weaknesses and the trends are such that correction is urgently needed. The net capital and reserves position of such banks (i.e., their book capital and reserves less supervisory adjustments for *all* adverse asset classifications, nonbook liabilities and shortages) is likely to be substantially negative. In addition, management is usually rated Unsatisfactory or Poor. Representing the greatest area of financial exposure to the Corporation, "Serious Problem" nonmember banks necessarily receive the most concentrated FDIC attention and supervision.

OTHER PROBLEM. Generally, a bank may be designated an "Other Problem" bank if net capital and reserves are nominal or a negative figure. However, the adequacy of net capital is not the only criterion for the Other Problem designation. There will be some banks whose net capital and reserves are positive figures but which, nevertheless, belong in this problem bank category because of excessive loan delinquencies, a rapid rate of asset deterioration, significant violations of law or regulations, and unusually low "adjusted" capital position (i.e., book capital and reserves less all assets classified Loss and 50 percent of all assets classified Doubtful), an undesirable liquidity posture, pronounced management deficiencies or other adverse factors. Generally speaking, management has been rated Unsatisfactory, with a rating of Fair or Satisfactory the exception.

---

[2] Congressional oversight and recent hearings on problem and failed banks have reinforced this interpretation.

[3] This letter was dated February 5, 1976 (copies are available from FDIC's information office). Regarding PPO banks (ones that could fail in the near future), the letter stated that no specific guidelines are used.

The FDIC's December 31, 1975 Problem Bank List

This list, which is maintained with the cooperation of the Comptroller of the Currency and the Board of Governors of the Federal Reserve System, consisted of 347 commercial banks with total deposits of $20.4 billion. The insured deposits of these 347 banks were estimated to be $9.9 billion, or 48.5 percent of their total deposits.[4] Sixty-nine of the 347 banks (19.9 percent) were members of the Federal Reserve system (52 of the 69 were national banks). These 69 banks, however, accounted for 65 percent of the total problem bank deposits and for 45 percent of the estimated insured problem bank deposits.

According to degree of problem status, the list consisted of 27 PPO banks (7.7 percent), 88 SP banks (25.4 percent), and 232 OP banks (66.9 percent). The average OP bank had total deposits of $65 million, with $28 million (43.1 percent) estimated to be insured. The average SP bank had total deposits of $54 million, with $33 million (61.1 percent) estimated to be insured. And finally, the average PPO bank had total deposits of $20 million, with $15 million (75 percent) estimated to be insured.

Since the holding company form of organization now dominates the commercial banking industry, it is important and interesting to look at the holding company affiliations of problem banks. (As of year end 1974, bank holding companies controlled 3462 commercial banks with $509 billion in deposits, accounting for 68.1 percent of all commercial bank deposits.)[5] Only 53 of the 347 problem banks (15.3 percent) were affiliated with multibank holding companies.[6] Sixteen of the 53 affiliated banks were lead banks of multibank holding companies, while 37 banks simply were affiliates of multibank holding companies. Lead banks accounted for 9.8 percent ($2 billion) of the total problem bank deposits and 14.2 percent ($1.4 billion) of the estimated insured problem bank deposits; the corresponding figures for affiliated nonlead banks were 7.6 percent ($1.6 billion) and 12.3 percent ($1.2 billion). The average lead problem bank had total deposits of $450 million (the median deposit size was only $84 million and the average, with one multibillion dollar outlier excluded, was $134 million). Estimated insured deposits at the average lead problem bank were $87 million (the median was $57 million). The average affiliated nonlead

[4] As of June 30, 1975, the FDIC's deposit insurance fund contained $6.4 billion. Recent adverse publicity about problem and failed banks has caused some unwarranted concern about the size of the FDIC's insurance fund relative to its risk exposure. This should not cause undue concern because (1) the FDIC has special drawing rights with the U.S. Treasury in the case of an emergency; (2) not all of a failing bank's assets are "bad"; and (3) the prevention of widespread depression failures is the province of monetary and fiscal policy.

[5] Robert C. Holland, "Bank Holding Companies and Financial Stability," *Journal of Financial and Quantitative Analysis,* November 1975, pp. 577–587.

[6] One-bank holding companies are not included in these figures.

problem bank had total deposits of $42 million and estimated insured deposits of $33 million. The average independent (or one-bank holding company) problem bank had total deposits of $57 million and estimated insured deposits of $25 million.

Can Bank Failures Be Predicted?

On March 25, 1809, *The Providence Gazette* reported the failure of the Farmers Exchange Bank, Glocester, Rhode Island.[7] Farmers was the first American bank ever to fail. The *Gazette* stated that the directors and managers of the bank ". . . practiced a system of fraud beyond which the ingenuity and dishonesty of man cannot go." The Rhode Island legislative report of 1809 indicated that business at the Farmers Exchange was conducted ". . . as the perplexed and confused state of the books sufficiently evinces, negligently and unskillfully."

For over 167 years, the major cause of bank failures, dishonest bank managers, basically has remained the same. The form of dishonesty (e.g., insider transactions, embezzlement, manipulation, etc.) has varied, but the driving force has not changed. For example, of the 84 banks that failed between 1960 and April 30, 1976, 45 of the failures were due to improper loans to officers, drectors, or owners, or loans to out-of-territory borrowers (there was misuse of brokered funds in 22 of these cases); 25 of the cases could be traced to embezzlement or manipulation; and finally, 14 of the failures were due to managerial weaknesses in loan portfolio administration.[8] To summarize, nothing essentially is new in the causes of bank failures.

Something that is new in bank failures is the recent phenomenon of the large-bank failure.[9] Since the FDIC was established in 1934, 9 of the 10 largest U.S. bank failures have occurred since 1970 (see Table 1). Why have larger banks suddenly become failure-prone? I do not pretend to know the precise answer to this question. However, for the most part, the causes of these large-bank failures have not been much different from those of small-bank failure. For example, the failures of United States National, Northern Ohio, and Sharpstown State can be traced mainly to some form of dishonest managerial practice;[10] the collapses of Franklin National, Birmingham-Bloomfield, and

---

[7] Bray Hammond, *Banks and Politics in America* (Princeton, N.J.: Princeton University Press), 1957, pp. 172–177.

[8] George W. Hill, *Why 67 Insured Banks Failed—1960–1974* (Washington, D.C.: Federal Deposit Insurance Corporation), 1975. Updated through 1976 using FDIC Division of Liquidation reports.

[9] Paul M. Horvitz, "Failures of Large Banks: Implications for Banking Supervision and Deposit Insurance," *Journal of Financial and Quantitative Analysis,* November, 1975, pp. 589–601.

[10] C. Arnholt Smith's alleged manipulations with his California Westgate Corporation in the United States National case are the most notorious.

Table 1   Ten Largest U.S. Bank Failures

Bank	Year Closed	Total Deposits (million $)
1. Franklin National Bank, New York, N.Y.	1974	1445
2. United States National Bank, San Diego, Calif.	1973	932
3. Hamilton National Bank of Chattanooga, Tenn.	1976	870
4. American City Bank & Trust, Milwaukee, Wis.	1975	145
5. American Bank & Trust, Orangeburg, S.C.	1974	113
6. Northern Ohio Bank, Cleveland, Ohio	1975	95
7. Public Bank, Detroit, Mich.	1966	93
8. Sharpstown State Bank, Sharpstown, Texas[a]	1971	67
9. State Bank of Clearing, Chicago, Ill.	1975	61
10. Birmingham-Bloomfield Bank, Birmingham, Mich.	1971	58

Source: Annual Report, FDIC (various issues).
[a] Indicates a deposit payoff; others are deposit assumptions.

Public were caused mainly by incompetent management rather than dishonest management; and finally, the failures of Hamilton National, American City, American, and State Bank of Clearing were associated with overextended real estate loan portfolios that were caught in the real estate and construction slump of the past few years. Generalizing from these causal factors, it appears that the failure of larger banks can be traced more to incompetent management (and/or increased economic uncertainty) rather than to the dishonesty factor that has been so prevalent in the closing of smaller banks. Except for failures due to severe economic depression (such as those that occurred during the 1930s) or local economic problems, a bank's viability ultimately rests with the honesty and ability of its managers and board of directors. Managers who cannot or will not manage and directors who cannot or will not direct are the causes of bank failures. Can such managers and directors be identified through balance sheet and income expense data? In other words, can bank failures be predicted?

Meyer and Pifer concluded that ". . . even when failure frequently results from embezzlement and other financial irregularities, financial measures can evaluate the relative strengths of firms."[11] The firms in this case were 39 commercial banks that failed between 1948 and 1965. The fact that Meyer and

[11] Paul A. Meyer and Howard W. Pifer, "Prediction of Bank Failures," *Journal of Finance,* September, 1970, pp. 853–868.

Pifer's model was never implemented by the FDIC (where it was developed) could be interpreted as a lack of confidence in it. However, since changes in bank supervision or examination are difficult to implement, this may be an unfair criticism.

Given some of the difficulties encountered with problem prediction models (discussed below) and the lack of failure prediction studies in banking (except for Meyer and Pifer's), I have undertaken to reexamine the failure prediction question. Thirty-seven banks that failed between 1970 and 1975 will be analyzed in this forthcoming study.

THE BANK-EXAMINATION PROCESS

Bank Capital, Loan Evaluations, and Problem Banks

The banking agencies interpret their "safety-and-soundness" mandate as one of preventing bank failures. By identifying banks with the highest failure risks, so-called problem banks, banking authorities hope to achieve this goal. The problem bank identification procedure is rooted in the bank examination process. The purposes of a bank examination are:[12]

1. To determine asset quality
2. To determine the nature of liabilities
3. To ascertain compliance with laws and regulations
4. To evaluate controls, procedures, accounting practices, and insurance
5. To evaluate management and its policies
6. To determine capital adequacy.

It is shown later in this paper that the multidimensionality of this process can be reduced to a single ratio which combines the asset quality and capital adequacy factors, the FDIC's net capital ratio.

Although the banking agencies' manuals refer to benchmark measures of capital adequacy and the incorporation of other factors, in practice, the most important indicator (to banking authorities) of a bank's "safety and soundness" flows from the loan evaluation process, that is, the ratio that relates a bank's adversely classified assets to its capital and reserves. Regarding loan evaluations, the FDIC's *Manual of Examination Policies* states:

> One of the most important aspects of the examination process is the evaluation of loans, for, in large measure, it is the quality of a bank's loans which determines the

[12] Bank Examiners' Orientation Course, mimeographed notes, (FDIC, 1973). For additional information concerning bank examinations see George J. Benston, "Bank Examination," *The Bulletin,* Nos. 89–90, (May, 1973), NYU Graduate School of Business.

risk to depositors. To a great extent, conclusions regarding the condition of the bank, the quality of its management, and its service to the community are weighted heavily by the examination's findings with regard to loans. (Section H, p. 1.)

Adversely classified assets (mainly low-quality loans) are listed as "loss," "doubtful," or "substandard" based upon an examiner's estimation of probable default. The classification of assets is an art and not a science; that is, an examiner's judgment is the primary determining factor.[13] According to the FDIC manual, the primary measure of a loan's riskiness is ". . . the willingness and ability of a debtor to perform as agreed . . ." (Section H, p. 1). The manual interprets this to mean that the borrower has the financial resources to meet his or her interest and principal payments as contracted.[14]

ALTERNATIVE WEIGHTED CAPITAL RATIOS

The FDIC's Form 96 provides a statistical summary of a bank examiner's report. The information on this form is further condensed into a ratings vector consisting of two capital adequacy ratios, an earnings ratio, and a managerial rating.

The FDIC's Adjusted Capital Ratio

The adjusted capital ratio (ACR) is defined as:

$$ACR \equiv [K + R + N - L - 0.5D]/A, \tag{1}$$

where K = total capital accounts
    R = valuation reserves
    N = nonbook sound banking values
    L = "loss" classifications
    D = "doubtful" classifications
    A = quarterly average of gross assets for the calendar year, where gross assets are defined as total balance sheet assets including reserves but excluding expense accounts and cash shortage accounts.

---

[13] The FDIC manual states: "Loan evaluation is not an exact science. The broad scope of the lending function and changing patterns in banking preclude the use of a single formula in the appraisal of loans. Much depends on the Examiner's knowledge, judgment, perception, analytical technique, and the ability to reach sound conclusions; attributes which are developed through training and experience." (Section H, p. 1.)
[14] The manual adds, "[This] does not mean, however, that borrowers must at all times be in position to liquidate their loans for that would defeat the original purpose of extending credit." (*Ibid.*)

Equation (1) compares a bank's "loss" and 50 percent of its "doubtful" classifications to its capital and reserves (N is relatively small and can be ignored in this discussion). Equation (1) assigns a weight of 0 to the "substandard" classification.

The FDIC's Net Capital Ratio

The net capital ratio (NCR) is defined:

$$NCR \equiv [K + R + N - L - D - S]/A, \tag{2}$$

where S = "substandard" classifications. In Eq. (2), all three adverse classification categories are assigned a weight of 1, that is, Eq. (2) relates a bank's total classified assets to its capital and reserves. Ignoring N, Eq. (2) can be written:

$$NCR \equiv [K + R - C]/A, \tag{2'}$$

where $C = L + D + S$

The FDIC's justification for its conservative treatment of the "substandard" category is contained in its manual: ". . . it is the function of the Substandard classification to indicate those loans which are unduly risky and which may be a future hazard to the bank's solvency. No bank can safely hold a large amount of low quality loans, even though they are not presently subject to either a Doubtful or Loss classification" (Section H, p. 5).

It is shown below that NCR is the most important discriminator between problem and nonproblem banks. That is, a bank's volume of "substandard" assets relative to its capital and reserves is the most important factor in identifying a problem situation.

A Probability-Weighted Capital Ratio

Because of inappropriate and arbitrary weighting schemes, Eqs. (1) and (2) either understate or overstate, respectively, a bank's risk exposure to adversely classified assets. These two formulas should be discarded in favor of the following probability-weighted capital ratio (WCR):

$$WCR \equiv [K + R + N - \gamma_L L - \gamma_D D - \gamma_S S]/A, \tag{3}$$

where the γ coefficients are "prospective probabilities" ($1 \geq \gamma_L > \gamma_D > \gamma_S \geq 0$). One way to estimate these prospective probabilities is to examine historical charge-off rates for each of the classified asset categories. That is,

$$\hat{\gamma}_L = \frac{L^*}{L}$$

and

$$\hat{\gamma}_D = \frac{D^*}{D} \qquad (4)$$

$$\hat{\gamma}_S = \frac{S^*}{S}$$

The variables with asterisks indicate the dollar amount of the particular classified asset category that was actually written off against bank capital; they are *ex post* measures. In contrast, the variables without asterisks are examiners' *ex ante* measures of loan quality. To estimate the γ coefficients would involve an extensive and detailed follow-up on individual classified assets. Moreover, since the coefficients may differ for different size banks and for different stages of the business cycle, these factors (and other ones deemed relevant) should be controlled for when estimating the γ coefficients. Given the resources available to the banking agencies and the need for a more relevant measure of a bank's risk exposure, such a study should be undertaken immediately.[15]

EMPIRICAL FINDINGS

The discriminant analysis tests presented in this section show that the NCR is the most important variable separating problem banks from nonproblem banks. These tests are descriptive and not predictive. That is, examiner-determined problem and nonproblem banks are being reclassified statistically to clarify how examiners distinguish between such banks.

The problem banks analyzed were the 143 commercial banks on the FDIC's March 31, 1974 problem bank list.[16] These banks were compared with a random sample of 163 nonproblem banks, drawn from the 9060 banks (about 65 percent of the population) with examination reports for the year 1973 on file with the FDIC as of December 31, 1973. If a bank had more than one report on file for the year, the latest one was used. Although no deliberate pair-

---

[15] I have recommended that the FDIC develop such a project. The banking agencies should develop a coordinated effort in this regard.

[16] The list consisted of 113 insured nonmember banks, 11 state member banks, and 19 national banks. The typical problem bank was a unit bank with total deposits of $9.4 million. Five of the problem banks had total deposits greater than $100 million but less than $1 billion. Originally, 175 banks were selected for the nonproblem group, however, 12 banks were eliminated because of incomplete data.

ing was made, there were no statistically significant differences between the two groups in terms of average size or average number of banking offices.

The purposes of discriminant analysis are to test for group mean and dispersion matrix differences, to describe the overlap between groups, and to construct rules to classify observations into appropriate groups.[17] Based on 1973 examination data, these tests are reported in Table 2. A total of 21 examination variables was tested. The results for 6 of these variables and a bivariate combination are presented in Table 2. The 6 variables are the components of the ratings vector, except for the managerial rating which is a qualitative measure, and three ratios of classified loans (assets) to total loans (assets).[18]

The tests of equality of group means and equality of group dispersion matrices were rejected for all six variables, including a bivariate test of NCR and NIA [net income (after taxes and securities gains and losses) as a percentage of total assets].[19] The most significant variable and the most important discriminator between the groups (on either a univariate or multivariate basis) was the net capital ratio [NCR, see Eq. (2)]. The NCR for the average problem bank was −2.3 (5.2) compared to 7.6 (3.0) for the average nonproblem bank. (Figures in parentheses are standard deviations.) The NCR F statistics were 428.8 for the group means (significant at the 0.29282 E-12 percent level) and 42.6 for the dispersion matrices (significant at the 0.67734 E-8 percent level). With use of the Lachenbruch "holdout" classification technique, 95.4 percent of the 306 banks were reclassified correctly.[20] The type I error was 4.9 percent (7 banks), while the type II error was 4.3 percent (7 banks). The classification rule used for reclassifying the 306 banks was:[21] Classify as a problem bank if $NCR \leq 2.74$ percent.

To summarize, the NCR is the most important variable for distinguishing between problem and nonproblem banks. Recalling the construction of ACR and NCR [see Eqs. (1) and (2)], it is clear that a bank's volume of "substan-

---

[17] The foundations of discriminant analysis are described in Eisenbeis and Avery, *Discriminant Analysis and Classifications Procedures* (Lexington, Mass.: Lexington Books), 1972.

[18] The FDIC managerial ratings are good, satisfactory, fair, unsatisfactory, and poor. The most common rating for the problem-bank group was unsatisfactory (65 percent of the banks), while for the nonproblem bank group it was satisfactory (71 percent).

[19] The test of dispersion matrix equality is important because, if this hypothesis is rejected, a quadratic classification equation rather than a linear one should be used. See Eisenbeis and Avery (1972), especially pp. 37–52.

[20] The Lachenbruch technique withholds the observation to be classified and computes the classification equation using $N − 1$ observations. The withheld observation then is classified. This procedure is repeated until all observations have been classified.

[21] This rule was derived from the following quadratic equation: $1.8195(NCR) − 0.071387(NCR)2 − 4.4503 \leq 0$. If the value of the left-hand side of this equation is equal to or less than zero, the bank is classified as a problem bank.

Table 2 Discriminant-Analysis Tests: 143 Problem Versus 163 Nonproblem Banks Using 1973 Examination Data

Test Number	Variables	Mean (%) (Standard Deviation) Problem	Nonproblem	Test of Equality of Group Means	Test of Dispersion Matrix Equality between Groups	Misclassification[a] Rate (%) (306)	Type I Error (%) 143	Type II Error (%) 163
1	ACR	6.4 (2.6)	8.8 (2.5)	Reject ($F = 68.6$)	Reject ($F = 55.2$)	26.8	35.0	19 6
2	NCR	−2.3 (5.2)	7.6 (3.0)	Reject ($F = 428.8$)	Reject ($F = 42.6$)	4.6	4.9	4.3
3	NIA[b]	0.16 (1.21)	0.85 (0.53)	Reject ($F = 43.0$)	Reject ($F = 97.8$)	34.3	66.4	6.1
4	NCR NIA	(see above)		Reject ($F = 233.6$)	Reject ($F = 47.8$)	5.5	7.0	4.3
5	SUB[b]	11.6 (7.2)	1.9 (2.2)	Reject ($F = 268.9$)	Reject ($F = 182.1$)	12.4	19.6	6.1
6	TCL[b]	14.6 (8.2)	2.3 (2.5)	Reject ($F = 331.9$)	Reject ($F = 182.1$)	11.1	16.1	6.7
7	TCA[b]	10.1 (5.5)	1.4 (1.5)	Reject ($F = 370.4$)	Reject ($F = 218.5$)	9.8	14.0	6.1

[a] Classifications were made using (1) the Eisenbeis and Avery (1972) computer program MULDIS, (2) a quadratic discriminant function, since the null hypothesis of dispersion matrix equality between groups was rejected, (3) the Lachenbruch "holdout" classification technique, and (4) the sample proportions as *a priori* probabilities of group membership.

[b] NIA = Net income (after taxes and securities gains or losses) as a percentage of total assets; SUB = substandard loans as a percentage of total loans; TCL = total classified loans (i.e., substandard plus doubtful plus loss) as a percentage of total loans; TCA = total classified assets (loans and securities) as a percentage of total assets. ACR and NCR, components of the ratings vector, are defined in the text.

[c] Additional multivariate tests, not reported here, could not improve upon the classification accuracy of NCR, even when NCR was included in the set.

34

dard" loans relative to its capital and reserves is the kicker in the NCR formula. However, because of the conservative weight attached to the "substandard" category, banking agencies tend to overstate a bank's true risk exposure.[22]

AN EARLY WARNING SYSTEM FOR IDENTIFYING PROBLEM COMMERCIAL BANKS

A Realistic Objective and Potential Advantages

The proposed early warning system is not designed to be a substitute for existing bank examination procedures and personnel, nor is it intended to be a replacement for the human skills and judgments needed in solving problems of bank supervision. The realistic and limited objective of the system is to act as an aid in scheduling bank examinations. That is, potential problem banks would be examined more frequently and more intensely than nonproblem banks.

The major potential advantages of an effective early warning system are:

1. *Prevention of bank failures.* The safety-and-soundness mandate of bank regulation has focused upon the prevention of bank failure. Early identification of problem banks may result in fewer bank failures and smaller losses for the FDIC's deposit insurance fund. Moreover, large losses, such as the $150 million loss the FDIC incurred in United States National's failure, reduce the percentage rebate of the net insurance assessment income by the FDIC to insured banks. Clearly, an effective early warning system could have monetary benefits for bankers.

2. *More efficient allocation of banking agencies' resources.* Advance information regarding the condition of a bank should be an important factor in determining the order, scope, intensity, and frequency of a bank's examination. Such information should enable banking agencies to allocate resources more efficiently among problem and nonproblem banks.

3. *Increasing the usefulness of balance sheet and income data.* All three federal banking agencies regularly collect these data from the banks they supervise. These data are the primary inputs to the early warning system. The value of these preexamination data would be enhanced greatly by an effective problem bank detection mechanism.

---

[22] Regarding the usefulness of substandard loan data, Benston and Marlin concluded that ". . . the value of the loan-criticism function is not demonstrated and, thus, is questionable" (p. 42). "Bank Examiners' Evaluation of Credit," *Journal of Money, Credit and Banking,* February 1974, pp. 23–44.

4. *Making the identification of problem banks more objective.* Relative to a bank's capital position, "substandard" loans are perhaps the most important variable separating problem from nonproblem banks. Regulatory authorities admit that the procedure for uncovering these risky loans is an art and not a science. A more objective appraisal of a bank's potential riskiness would strengthen bank examination procedures.

5. *Supplying banking agencies with data to evaluate their examination and supervisory performances and the effectiveness of the early warning system.* Given a prediction of a bank's "safety and soundness," the agencies would be able to evaluate bank examiners' ratings and vice versa. Moreover, an early warning system should be an important pedagogical device for bank examiners and banking schools.

The Information Content of Balance Sheet and Income Expense Data

The basic concept (or null hypothesis) of any early warning system focuses upon the information content of the data being analyzed. In this particular case, the null hypothesis concerns the information content of balance sheet and income expense data relevant for identifying future problem banks. Having analyzed these data for about 3 years, there is no doubt in my mind that the information content is there. This means that information relevant for scheduling bank examinations and even for excluding certain banks from the traditional bank examination process is available. It does not mean that on-the-spot bank inspections would be eliminated entirely or that 100 percent accuracy in identifying problem banks would be achieved.

With regard to implementation of an early warning system, two critical problems remain. First, the information must be extracted in a timely and efficient manner. And second, supervisory and examination personnel must be convinced that the information is useful. The first problem can be resolved by having on-the-spot examinations begin after the data have been analyzed. For example, what is so sacred about starting examinations in January of each year? Why not start on-site examinations *after* year-end data have been analyzed? Based upon past experience, such examinations (for the entire population of insured banks) could begin in early May. In addition, since large banks present the greatest potential risk exposure to the FDIC insurance fund and the economy, they could be analyzed separately and therefore with increased timeliness. Moreover, with income expense data now being collected quarterly for the largest banks and semiannually for other banks, additional information for monitoring banks on a year-round basis will be available.

A Statistical Model

The basic statistical technique being used in the proposed early warning system is multiple discriminant analysis. The critical feature of this procedure is that it permits simultaneous consideration of several factors reflecting problem bank status. The specific model being used is a seven-variable one. It was developed to distinguish between, and reclassify, groups of examiner-determined problem and nonproblem banks. The seven variables used in the model are:

1. LRI = interest and fees on loans as a percentage of total operating income (measures revenue concentration)
2. $OEOI$ = total operating expense as a percentage of total operating income (measures operating efficiency)
3. USA = U.S. government securities as a percentage of total assets (measures liquidity and asset composition)
4. SLA = state and local securities as a percentage of total assets (measures asset composition)
5. LA = total loans as a percentage of total assets (measures loan volume)
6. NFA = net federal funds (sales minus purchases) as a percentage of total assets (measures federal funds activity and aggressiveness of liability management)
7. KRA = capital and reserves for bad debt losses on loans as a percentage of total assets (measures capital adequacy).

It should be emphasized that there is nothing magical about these *particular* seven variables. If certain dimensionalities are captured, the form that the individual variables take is relatively unimportant. Moreover, using only the loan revenue (LRI) and operating efficiency ($OEOI$) variables, the classification results were quite comparable to those using all seven variables. However, statistically speaking, we have more confidence in the seven-variable model. Using the seven-variable model, about 75 percent of the previously identified problem-nonproblem situations can be reclassified correctly.

Year-end 1975 data for these seven variables, stratified according to (1) problem (group 1) and nonproblem (group 2) status, and (2) total deposits greater than or equal to $100 million or less than $100 million, are presented in Tables 3 and 4. These data are for all banks that have passed data editing checks. The number of banks in each group is listed in Table 5.

Comparison of the means and standard deviations in Tables 3 and 4 (and of the variance-covariance matrices) indicate that there is substantial overlap between the problem and nonproblem groups. (Lack of separation between groups tends to reduce classification accuracy.) Not surprisingly, identification

Table 3   Problem-Nonproblem Data—Total
Deposits ≥ $100 Million (December 31, 1975)

Variable	Mean	Standard Deviation
Group 1		
1	69.1586914	9.6096869
2	102.7339020	17.4362183
3	9.9596987	5.3950968
4	9.1377068	5.7388134
5	57.8825989	7.8070116
6	−0.4411117	4.6645279
7	7.6206331	1.7653618
Group 2		
1	64.4605865	9.5528612
2	87.1609802	7.3002062
3	12.8995619	7.8169279
4	12.9021988	5.1964607
5	51.6375580	9.3493404
6	0.1067407	6.2188101
7	8.1263905	1.5832119

of banks with characteristics more similar to those of problem banks than those of nonproblem banks produces classification errors. This implies that there is no substitute for the judgment and analysis of the examination staff, particularly with respect to "close" cases. Thus the real usefulness of such early warning systems will not be as a substitute for bank examination, but rather as a means to direct examination talents to those areas where judgment and further analysis will result in the highest payoff.

An additional feature of the early warning system is the computation of three statistics indicating how similar each predicted problem bank is to all insured commercial banks in (1) the United States, (2) the bank's FDIC region, and (3) the bank's state. This feature indicates how similar a bank is to all other banks in its nation, region, and state.[23]

An Alternative Approach: The Outlier Technique

Because of the high degree of overlap between examiner-determined problem and nonproblem banks (on the basis of balance sheet and income expense com-

---

[23] The present computer early warning system is quite flexible. For example, it can handle different sets of variables and alternative comparisons across different classes of banks. In addition, the print routine enables flagged banks to be printed out by state or by FDIC region.

Table 4 Problem-Nonproblem Data—Total Deposits < $100 Million (December 31, 1975)

Variable	Mean	Standard Deviation
Group 1		
1	70.9135437	9.6027336
2	106.0741577	28.8503418
3	13.8828249	9.2217979
4	7.4121246	6.6670637
5	57.8737030	10.5903721
6	3.2493048	6.0943060
7	8.0725117	2.2649603
Group 2		
1	60.0428162	12.7342634
2	83.8326569	10.7402124
3	19.5872803	11.8564816
4	12.3208561	7.1627436
5	49.6287231	11.8667755
6	4.3126907	6.0482178
7	8.8678141	2.3825607

parisons), an early warning system based upon examiners' definitions and groups may not provide an appropriate foundation. An alternative approach is to abandon examiner-determined groups and work with peer groups (e.g., all banks with deposits greater than $100 million). In this peer group or outlier analysis, each bank in the group (which may include both problem and non-problem banks) is compared with the average performance of the group. The Eisenbeis and Avery multiple discriminant analysis program (MULDIS) has been adapted to handle this one-group outlier technique. A chi-square score, which serves as a measure of resemblance between a particular bank and the

Table 5 Problem-Nonproblem Data—Number of Banks in Deposit Size Classes

Deposit Class	Group 1, Problem	Group 2, Nonproblem	Total
≥ $100 million	27	837	864
< $100 million	302	12,430	12,732
Total	329	13,267	13,596

group average, provides an approximation of the percentage of the population of peer group banks that can be expected to lie farther from the peer group's center (in either direction from the mean vector) than a particular bank.

Experiments with the proposed outlier technique in the cases of the failure of Franklin National and United States National and the emergency merger of the Security National Bank of Long Island have been conducted. (A sample of these results is presented in Appendix B.) In addition, outlier tests using alternative peer groups have been performed. A simple but effective outlier (or ranking) variable is a bottom line or operating efficiency measure (such as *OEOI* described above). For example, Keefe Management Service of New York City attempted to evaluate the riskiness of the FDIC's largest banks. They came up with a 35-variable measure of riskiness and ranked the banks on this basis. The rank correlation coefficient between their 35-variable ranking and a 1-variable ranking [net operating income (before taxes and securities gains or losses) as a percentage of total assets] was 89.1 percent. After all, the bottom line is really what it is all about.

IF I WERE BANKING CZAR

If I were banking czar, I would issue the following guidelines to my Department of Supervision and Examination *and* to the public:

1.   Problem and failed banks have existed for a long time and will continue to exist in the future. Our job is to keep such institutions, especially failed ones, at a level consistent with maintaining confidence in the banking system. Accordingly, the actual number of failures or problems during any period of time is not important, as long as the confidence factor is maintained. (We should anticipate inquiries from Congress and other interested parties regarding how we intend to measure the confidence factor and its critical level. In this regard, we should explore such potential measures as customer confidence surveys; monitoring of bank stock prices, deposit flows, large certificate of deposit rates and flows, federal funds flows and rates, etc.).

2.   Supervision and examination procedures will be directed toward preventing, monitoring, and eliminating the dishonest, incompetent, and inequitable elements in banking. Our supervision-and-examination arsenal will consist of two main weapons: (1) computerized early warning mechanisms and (2) on-site bank inspections. Alternative early warning models will be employed as screening devices to schedule on-the-spot bank inspections. With regard to the traditional bank examination and its focus on loan evaluations, the basic

premise will be that such examinations for every bank in every year are not necessary. On-site bank inspections will not be eliminated. On the contrary, every bank will be inspected *at least* once a year to check for violations of laws and regulations, unfair lending practices (e.g., "redlining" and other forms of discrimination), and other irregular and anticompetitive banking practices. These mandatory inspections will of course require much less time and money than the traditional bank examination. Known problem banks and banks that have been flagged as being in need of special supervision or potentially in need of special supervision will be given more detailed and thorough bank inspections. These inspections will be designed to pinpoint problems and potential remedies. Peer group analyses (hence peer group pressure) will be used in explaining actual and potential problem areas. In some cases, even traditional loan evaluations will be made. However, loan evaluations and criticisms should be handled delicately so as not to encourage discriminatory lending practices. Although our inspection system will have a bottom line focus (banks are given monopoly power, in varying degrees of course depending upon their particular market, hence they should be able to generate a reasonable profit), we will not be myopic in this regard. For example, if a bank has low earnings because it is providing full service to *all* its customers, this will be given appropriate weight. In contrast, if a bank has low earnings because of self-serving and/or incompetent managers and/or directors, this will be given appropriate weight also, but with a negative sign. Moreover, in cases where banks have appeared to abuse their monopoly power, we will encourage greater competition. Clearly, our inspection system will require substantial human input and analysis; it will not be a machine-sans-human system. The major changes will include (1) increased computer analysis as a filtering mechanism for identifying banks with financial difficulties, and (2) reallocation of human resources (*a*) away from detailed loan evaluations and toward more productive areas and (*b*) away from safe-and-soundness banks and toward problem banks.

APPENDIX A: 1975 BANK EXAMINATION CAPITAL RATIOS

The data in this appendix update the bank examination capital ratios (*ACR* and *NCR*) presented in Table 2 of the text. Note that (1) for the 1973 nonproblem bank group a random sample of nonproblem banks was used and all other figures were for existing *populations,* and (2) because of the 1974–1975 recession, lower capital ratio (i.e., larger volumes of classified assets) were excepted in 1975. The 1975 data are shown in Table 6.

Table 6   1975 Bank Examination Capital Ratios (Means and Standard Deviations)

Ratio	Problem (%)[a]	Nonproblem (%)[b]
ACR	6.14	9.38
	(2.95)	(4.48)
NCR	−3.77	7.94
	(6.44)	(3.25)

[a] 347 banks.
[b] 14,524 banks.

APPENDIX B: OUTLIER TESTS—FRANKLIN NATIONAL BANK OF NEW YORK AND SECURITY NATIONAL BANK OF LONG ISLAND

A two-variable outlier test for Franklin and Security is presented in Table 7 and Figure 1. The two variables used in the test were:

1. NOA = net operating income (before taxes and securities gains or losses) as a percentage of total assets, a return measure
2. $NLLL$ = net loan losses as a percentage of total loans, a measure of loan quality or risk.

Franklin's risk-return data indicate that in 1971, 1972, and 1973 it was an outlier compared to the control group. The results for Security indicate that it was an outlier in 1973 and 1974. During these years, both Franklin and Security were characterized as low-return high-risk banking institutions. In contrast, Morgan Guaranty Trust Co. also was an outlier in 1971, 1972, and 1973. However, it was a safe-and-sound outlier, characterized by high return and low risk. It is interesting to note that Morgan (then Franklin's major correspondent bank) stopped selling federal funds to Franklin in the fall of 1973.

The risk-return grid in Figure 1 was constructed using the grand means for the control group listed at the bottom of Table 7. Over the years 1969–1974, the average control bank earned, before taxes and security gains or losses, $1.07 per $100 of assets and charged off only 26 cents per $100 of loans. (The averages for the 1969–1973 period were 1.09 and 0.24). The extreme lower right-hand area of Figure 1 (i.e., the very-high-risk and very-low-return area) is the "red-flag" section. By year end 1970, both Franklin and Security appeared in the above-average risk and below-average return quadrant. At this time, however, they were not significantly different from banks at the center of

Table 7 Risk-Return Data and Outlier Tests, 1969–1974

Bank and Year	*NOA*	*NLLL*	Chi-Square Score	Significance Level (%)
Franklin				
1969	0.98	0.02	2.70	25.89
1970	0.81	0.40	1.84	39.80
1971	0.48	0.83	6.50	3.87
1972	0.30	0.48	7.65	2.18
1973	0.30	0.71	8.86	1.19
Security				
1969	1.14	0.14	0.19	90.83
1970	1.03	0.56	2.51	28.44
1971	0.85	0.30	0.51	77.45
1972	0.70	0.31	0.98	61.13
1973	0.51	0.94	16.71	0.02
1974	−2.65	3.73	155.58	0.00[a]
Morgan				
1969	1.55	0.04	2.12	34.53
1970	1.71	0.35	2.45	29.41
1971	1.75	0.07	6.74	3.44
1972	1.68	0.08	8.11	1.73
1973	1.69	0.03	6.26	4.38
1974	1.61	0.27	3.07	21.48
FNC				
1969	1.14	0.11	0.22	89.36
1970	1.24	0.52	1.53	46.39
1971	1.21	0.41	0.61	73.46
1972	1.41	0.29	2.99	22.44
1973	1.45	0.47	3.40	18.22
1974	1.58	0.45	3.66	16.02
Average control bank[b]				
1969	1.28	0.12	—	—
1970	1.24	0.30	—	—
1971	1.04	0.33	—	—
1972	0.93	0.21	—	—
1973	0.98	0.22	—	—
1974	0.95	0.38	—	—
Average	1.07	0.26		

Source: Reports of Income and Condition, December 31, 1969–1974, FDIC.

[a] Indicates a very small positive number.

[b] The control group consisted of the 50 largest banks (as of December 31, 1973). *NOA* = net operating income (before taxes and security gains and losses) as a percentage of total assets, and *NLLL* = net loan losses as a percentage of total loans.

the control group. By year end 1971, Franklin was a significant outlier and, by year end 1973, Security was a significant outlier. Both Franklin and Security failed to return to the center of the control group once they had gone astray.

It is interesting to contrast and compare the movements of Franklin, Security, and First National City Bank in Figure 1. As of year end 1969, these three banks were bunched relatively close together, both to each other and to the center of the control group. However, from 1970 to 1974, Franklin and Security moved southeast, while FNC moved northeast. A northeasterly movement indicates that higher loan losses were being compensated for by higher operating income, the so-called risk-return trade-off. In contrast, Franklin and

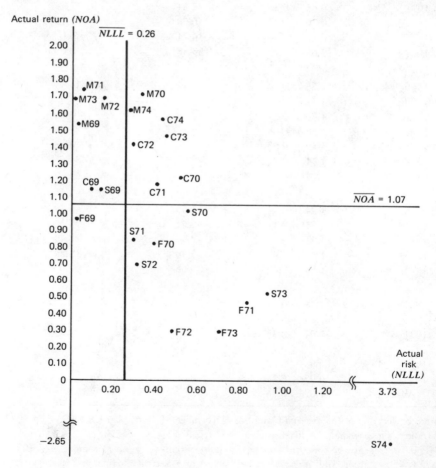

Figure 1   Risk-return diagram, 1969–1974. F, Franklin; S, Security; M, Morgan; C, FNC.

Security were not compensated for their increased riskiness. They incurred both higher loan losses *and* lower operating income over the years 1970–1974.

Finally, let us examine the risk-return performance of four additional low-level outliers. Since one of these banks currently is considered a problem bank and two of the other three banks have been receiving adverse publicity because of their poor performances, the power of the risk-return analysis tends to be enhanced by these findings. The four banks are referred to as outliers 1, 2, 3, and 4. The average NOA and average $NLLL$ for these four banks for the 1969–1974 period were:

Bank	$\overline{NOA}$	$\overline{NLLL}$
Outlier 1	0.67	0.44
Outlier 2	0.76	0.58
Outlier 3	1.19	0.80
Outlier 4	0.43	0.37

Outlier 1 is the current problem bank. Outlier 3 has shown the most rapid and serious deterioration as exhibited by the following data:

Year	NOA	$NLLL$
1972	1.52	0.48
1973	0.91	0.83
1974	−0.09	1.18
Average	0.78	0.83

Finally, note that for the year 1973 a simple univariate ranking of outlier 3 based upon NOA would not have been as meaningful as the combined [NOA, $NLLL$] analysis.

In Table 8 bank stock prices for Security National, and Moody's averages over the period 1971–1974, are presented. At one time, Security was considered "a glamour stock among investors and analysts."[24] During January 1971, Security's stock was selling for about $40 per share; on January 13, 1975, 6 days before its emergency merger with Chemical National Bank, Security traded (over the counter) at $4 per share. In less than 4 years, its price had declined 90 percent. On balance, this decline was a steady one and not a sudden drop-off. For example, during January 1972, Security sold for about $34 per share; during January 1973, its price was $30 per share; and during January 1974, the price was $14 per share.

The data in Table 8 indicate that for the period January 1971–January 1974

---

[24] *The Wall Street Journal*, January 13, 1975.

Table 8   Bank Stock Prices: Security National Bank of Long Island and Moody's Averages

Date	Security		Moody's Averages		
	Low	High	New York City	Outside NYC	Combined
January 1971	39.50	40.25	171.84	107.24	135.52
July 1971	37.50	38.25	163.27	105.09	130.49
January 1972	34.25	35.00	188.39	112.86	146.02
July 1972	30.75	31.25	222.61	142.32	177.54
January 1973	30.12	30.62	240.95	140.47	184.83
July 1973	17.12	17.62	259.44	142.53	194.11
January 1974	17.50	18.00	244.59	145.21	189.23
July 1974	12.25	12.75	182.75	89.10	130.75
December 1974	4.75	5.50	170.86	82.95	121.85
Change: Jan. 1971–Dec. 1974	−34.75	−34.75	−0.98	−24.29	−13.67
Percent	−87.98	−86.34	−0.57	−22.65	−10.09
Change: Jan. 1971–Jan. 1974	−22.00	−22.00	72.75	37.97	53.71
Percent	−55.70	−54.66	42.34	35.41	39.63
Change: Jan. 1974–Dec. 1974	−12.75	−12.75	−73.73	−62.26	−67.38
Percent	−72.86	−70.83	−30.14	−42.88	−35.61

Sources: Bank and Quotation Record and Moody's Bank and Finance Manual.

Security's stock price *declined* by about 55 percent, while Moody's three averages *increased* in the 35–42 percent range. During 1974, with the impact of the United States National and Franklin National failures and the REIT crisis providing significant adverse publicity for the banking industry, Security's stock price and Moody's averages declined by 71 percent and 30 to 43 percent, respectively. The largest decline in the price of Security's stock occurred over the 6-month period January 1973–July 1973, when it dropped 13 points (43.2 percent) from 30 to 17. In contrast, for the same period, Moody's averages increased by 2 to 19 points. On balance, for most of the period 1971–1974, Security's stock price was declining, while Moody's averages were increasing. Analysis of bank stock prices, especially for the nation's largest banks, should provide useful information regarding investors' expectations about the viability of these banks.

REFERENCES

Sinkey, Joseph F., Jr., *Problem and Failed Institutions in the Commercial Banking Industry* (Greenwich, Conn.: Johnson Associates Inc.), forthcoming 1977.

Sinkey, Joseph F., Jr., "The Bank-Examination Process and Major Issues in Banking: A Survey," *The Bankers Magazine,* forthcoming.

Sinkey, Joseph F., Jr., "Can Bank Failures Be Predicted?" Research-in-progress.

Sinkey, Joseph F., Jr., "Security National Bank of Long Island: A Balance-Sheet and Income-Expense Analysis of Our Largest Emergency Merger," Research-in-progress.

Sinkey, Joseph F., Jr., "Bank Capital, Loan Evaluations, and "Problem" Banks," FDIC Working Paper No. 76-2.

Sinkey, Joseph F., Jr., "Franklin National Bank of New York: A Portfolio and Performance Analysis of Our Largest Bank Failure," FDIC Working Paper No. 75-10. This paper has been revised slightly and is forthcoming in two parts: one in the *Journal of Financial and Quantitative Analysis* and the other in the *Journal of Bank Research.*

Sinkey, Joseph F., Jr., "Early-Warning System: Some Preliminary Predictions of Problem Commercial Banks," *Proceedings of a Conference on Bank Structure and Competition,* May, 1975, pp. 85–91.

Sinkey, Joseph F., Jr., "A Multivariate Statistical Analysis of the Characteristics of Problem Banks," *Journal of Finance,* March 1975, pp. 21–36.

Sinkey, Joseph F., Jr., "Adverse Publicity and Bank Deposit Flows: The Cases of Franklin National Bank of New York and United States National Bank of San Diego," *Journal of Bank Research,* Summer 1975, pp. 109–112.

Sinkey, Joseph F., Jr., "The Failure of United States National Bank of San Diego: A Portfolio and Performance Analysis," *Journal of Bank Research,* Spring 1975, pp. 8–24.

Sinkey, Joseph F., Jr., "The Way Problem Banks Perform," *The Bankers Magazine,* Autumn 1974, pp. 40–51.

Sinkey, Joseph F., Jr., and Robert D. Kurtz, "Bank Disclosure Policy and Procedures, Adverse Publicity, and Bank Deposit Flows," *Journal of Bank Research,* Autumn 1973, pp. 177–184.

Sinkey, Joseph F., Jr., and David A. Walker, "Problem Banks: Identification and Characteristics," *Journal of Bank Research,* Winter, 1975, pp. 208–217.

3.
The National Bank Surveillance System

ROBERT A. MULLIN

In this nation's dual banking system of state and nationally chartered banks, only one federal agency, the Comptroller of the Currency, issues bank charters. From the beginning of this dual banking system (1863) to date, national banks have been supervised primarily through personal visits to each national bank by national bank examiners.

In this 113th year, a new system of national bank supervision is being implemented. One part of this system is known as the National Bank Surveillance System (NBSS). The story of its development is not simply a report on the statistical testing of certain ratios and theories which might be used in bank supervision. It is a summary of the events, attitudes, traditions, and methods that must be utilized or avoided to implement successfully a logical system of bank supervision which utilizes various statistical ratios and theories. This system will not only change bank supervision, it will also change the performance of the national banking system.

A CLIMATE FOR CHANGE

Traumatic changes in bank supervision are usually a result of bank failures. These changes can result in substantial improvements or damage to the

48

nation's banking system, depending upon the strength and character of the leadership involved at the time. The attitude of the person in charge and the attitude then assumed by the staff involved is absolutely essential to the ultimate success of any project.

On October 18, 1973, about 3 months after James E. Smith became the Comptroller of the Currency, he declared the United States National Bank of San Diego to be insolvent. This was the first of a series of traumatic happenings thrust upon this new comptroller by the past procedures of his office.

United States National had about $90 million in outstanding standby letters of credit in the hands of foreign bankers, and the receiver, the FDIC, would not pay such credits until their character was determined. The foreign bankers promptly met as a group with the senior officials of the three federal banking agencies in Washington, D.C. One of the complaints they presented to the then new comptroller was that the letters of credit they held were not reflected on the official statements of national banks. The comptroller asked the deputy controller *what* was being done in that respect, and was informed that the financial statements of U.S. banks, unlike those of foreign banks, do not reflect the outstanding amounts of standby letters of credit. He then turned to the foreign bankers and told them that the amounts of the standby letters of credit of all national banks *would be* shown on the official reports of condition of all national banks commencing with the next reporting date.

That inquiring and responsive *attitude* of the person in charge in the fall of 1973 established the first of the essential elements of the evolving NBSS. The other essential elements of the NBSS developed over the course of the next two years as a consequence of an outside review of "what we are doing" and an inside evaluation, culminating in the directive of September 2, 1975.

THE INTERIM MEASURES

During the two intervening years, several temporary measures for improving bank supervision were implemented. Following 4 months of heavy foreign exchange losses by the Franklin National Bank of New York it was apparent that annual examinations of a bank's foreign exchange activities were inadequate. The acquisition and review of weekly and monthly foreign exchange reports was implemented as an early warning measure against the recurrence of such disasters.

Following closure of the ill-fated Franklin National in the fall of 1974, not because of a net worth insolvency but an insolvency caused by a warranted lack of confidence, the comptroller initiated a new procedure for dealing with problem banks. Because no time was available and because the traditional examination reports were the best supervisory tools then available, he activated an immediate program known then as "Victor." This program simply accelerated communication between examiners in newly discovered problem banks and a special staff in the Washington office. This program provides special attention for well-known cases. It deals with after-the-fact problems, real recovery matters, and was not intended as an early warning or preventative care system. Even with the necessary establishment of this system, the need for the development of a completely new system of detecting possible future problems was recognized.

CREATION OF THE NBSS

On September 2, 1975, the Office of the Comptroller was reorganized from geographic, regional lines to functional lines. The NBSS was one of the newly designated functions of the office.

The NBSS was to be developed by a small staff of experienced examiners assisted by specialists in the office and others from the staff of an outside firm, Haskins and Sells. The NBSS was a first-priority project for the use of computer time, programmers, statistical staffs, and so on. Its successful implementation was deemed to be essential as a part of the reorganization.

About 2000 national bank examiners are one of the principal proven resources of the comptroller's office. Their ability to analyze financial statements is tested many times daily during discussions with the best lending officers in our banking system. However, by tradition, they had devoted at least 80 percent of their time to the analysis of the financial statements of borrowers, not banks. The comptroller's office needed bank examiners, not borrower examiners. The NBSS had to redirect the examiners' skills and provide them with bank financial data in an analytical form.

THE GATHERING OF DATA

The initial search for good bank data was directed toward those regularly gathered and processed jointly by the three federal banking regulators. While the Office of the Comptroller required each national bank to submit financial reports on a quarterly basis, these data were used only for historical and statistical purposes. Because these data were processed for about 14,000 banks for the combined monetary, insurance, and statistical purposes of the three agencies, processing and editing time was excessive. Fast and accurate data were needed only from the 4700 national banks and then only for supervisory purposes.

To establish a data base for prior years, data that had been captured and recorded on tape by the interagency process for the years 1968 through 1974 were transferred to an outside computer service. These were not complete data. Reports of condition for some periods had never been recorded, and some report schedules had never been captured.

RESULTS OF TESTING DATA

The data base through 1974 was tested primarily in the months of October and November of 1975 for NBSS purposes. This procedure could lead to a programming error, a key punch error, or a reporting error. Some such errors could be clearly identified and corrected, and the number of errors detected was substantial.

A peer group of banks with resources of $100 million to $500 million was used as a testing base. This peer group was relatively clean, not having the sharp seasonal swings of smaller banks or of the foreign activities of larger banks.

The computer was programed to run many traditional ratios, and histograms were run on these many ratios. If the maximum, the minimum, or the mean of these ratios appeared abnormal, the original source documents were checked.

Also, a statistical sampling was made of all the condition and income reports filed by 62 banks over a 5-year period. Again, many types of errors were found, and correction costs were prohibitive.

METHODS OF CORRECTING DATA

In relating net earnings to average assets to produce a ratio on the return on average assets, we disclosed a series of data base problems requiring some form of correction.

The provision for possible loan losses is an expense item which is a leading indicator of possible future problems. The manner in which this expense item is utilized can cause significant changes in a bank's reported net profits and its return on assets. The accuracy of this expense item was tested by computing the valuation portion of the reserve for bad debts from 1968 through 1974 for each of 4700 banks.

This portion of the reserve was found to have a negative balance in several banks. This was a clear indication that their profits had been overstated in prior periods. We attempted to obtain corrected figures by mailing forms and instructions to all national banks. The results of that survey indicated that the majority of the banks were computing their valuation reserves incorrecctly or had made corrections of prior period amounts without a restatement.

Under the interagency system, restatements were not accepted in the data base. The instructions and forms utilized through December 31, 1975, unintentionally permitted banks to understate or overstate earnings and then reconcile capital accounts with a one-line, seldom-identified entry. Consequently, our data base included some banks showing good earnings and also showing a declining net worth.

Achieving complete correction of all the major errors and omissions in the prior years' data base was an impossibility. However, a portion of the NBSS staff was detailed to revise completely the forms and instructions for reports of condition and income. These revisions became effective on March 31, 1976, and they involved more than 30 significant changes. The avenues for improperly reporting earnings were closed, and restatements were required for subsequently discovered errors. The three portions of the reserve for bad debts were required to be disclosed, and the valuation portion, the reserve for possible loan losses, was required to be shown as a deduction from total loans.

On March 31, 1976, income reports from all banks of $300 million or more were required for the first time on a quarterly basis. They were also fully consolidated, including foreign operations. For smaller banks such information will be required semiannually.

It was also necessary to establish an editing procedure for the new reports. Interagency editing procedures were tight to the extent of checking changes in account totals between periods, and they even included daily changing accounts such as Federal Reserve funds. However, they did not check errors in basic accounts such as capital structure. An inspection of 1580 statistically selected reports showed a surprising number of banks reporting a capital structure on their income report that was significantly different from that shown on their condition report as of the same date.

Faced with a reporting error rate of nearly 50 percent, the comptroller issued a mailgram and a letter on this matter to the chief executive officer of each national bank. The response from national banks has been excellent in the form of fast, accurate reports.

NBSS SPECIALISTS

While computers are used in the compiling, editing, and calculating process, the NBSS is not a mechanical system. The analysis process must involve the expert judgment of experienced examiners on a case-by-case basis. A core of such NBSS specialists has been trained for the Washington office, and at least one such specialist has been or is being trained for each of the 14 regional offices.

These specialists are trained for one primary purpose. To convert the computerized product into a series of questions which will cause bank management to make decisions and take early corrective action. They deal with the diverse set of personalities found among 14 regional administrators, 2200 examiners, and 4700 bankers. Their observations and questions for investigation and response must involve the proper psychological approach in each case. This element is not supplied by the computer, but with this element, the NBSS *will* work.

RATIOS AND PERCENTAGES

One computerized portion of the NBSS currently produces a 15-page performance report on each national bank. The report program is flexible and is improved and expanded frequently. The ratios, percentages, and dollar figures shown on this report cover all of the items found in a bank's financial reports during the past 5 years.

The banks have also been sorted into 14 peer groups. While the present sort involves asset size, number of branches, and locations within or outside an Standard Metropolitan Statistical Area (SMSA), the system permits many additional sorts. For example, during recent years, many country bankers found the business of taking deposits and selling them as Federal Reserve funds to city banks at 11 percent easier and more profitable than making local loans. But, last winter, with Federal Reserve funds selling at 4½ percent, the bankers were losing money. They were also in a box. They would have had to invest in maturities of more than 1 year to even earn 6 percent, and they could not do that with a crop loan demand due within 6 months. In a matter of minutes, a peer group of banks that had been net sellers of Federal Reserve funds during the last 2 years was examined.

Each ratio and percentage shown in the 15-page performance report for each bank has a comparable peer group ratio or percentage conveniently displayed in the same report. Each of the most significant ratios or percentages has a percentile ranking of its relative position within the peer group.

All these ratios and percentages are tested daily in the work of the NBSS specialists. These specialists meet daily to review case studies, as would a committee of bank lending officers. When it is noted that certain computerized ratios are defective or are not of value, these ratios are corrected or eliminated from the program. Conversely, if the specialist is found to be computing his or her own ratios and they are valid, they are added to the computerized program.

The specialists are trained to look for high- or low-percentile rankings, for short-term changes and long-term trends. They must look for leading indicators, not lagging indicators, and they should avoid using the words "good" and "bad."

When a bank's management decides to increase the growth rate, or move into municipal bonds or make more real estate loans, the first leading indicators of these or other management decisions appear in the data for the current or following quarter.

An NBSS specialist, is not expected to render a judgment as to the good or bad effects of, for example, a high growth rate in real estate loans. He or she must simply report the observation of that factual happening and request an immediate inquiry as to the propriety of the change.

NBSS ANOMALY SEVERITY RANKING REPORT

Most of the NBSS specialists will be located at the 14 regional offices, close to the banks and the examiners. All 4700 banks will be subjected to some degree of review quarterly. But which banks should be selected for a priority review when the data are updated with each quarterly report? This basic question is answered by a second type of computerized report on each peer group and for all national banks.

Ratios or percentages from the bank performance report that have been designated key leading indicators are ranked for each bank in relation to those of its peers. There are three conditions of interest involved in each indicator: current position, short-term change, and long-term trend. This system, for example, gives a top priority review ranking to a bank that has either the highest or the lowest return on assets. This ranking score, when combined with 26 other ranking scores for the bank, give it a total score comparable with those of its peers.

Why should a bank with the highest return on assets be designated for priority review? Such a performance should be considered good. NBSS specialists avoid thinking in terms of "good" or "bad." They look for leading indicators and, if the highest return on assets was produced by high-yielding, high-risk loans, and without adequate management, adequate loan loss provisions, and adequate capital, that initially high return on assets can lead to a problem situation in the future. Possible problems are to be detected and future problems are to be prevented.

The anomaly severity ranking system has been tested repeatedly, and it works as intended.

THE NBSS ACTION CONTROL SYSTEM

This is the third type of computerized system in the NBSS. To date, it has been programed, but does not become effective until the next quarter's data are processed. Its use is absolutely essential for the operation of the combined new programs.

The action control system serves to record and monitor the *results* of all segments of the NBSS. All entries to this system are made by regional or Washington specialists. The system issues frequent reports on the number, type, and current status of conditions detected for investigation and correction.

After each quarterly updating of the performance data and the rendering of the anomaly severity report, only banks designated for priority review are placed in the action control data base. Only their aggregate number and their names and locations are initially entered in this data base.

Each time a bank's performance report is analyzed by a specialist, the findings are entered in code in the action control system. There are action codes, condition codes, and response codes for the system. All condition codes require a response within a number of days. This number can be selected by the regional administrator but cannot exceed 30 and, if no date is entered, the program sets a 10-day response date.

Status reports are issued at 10-day intervals, and each regional administrator sees in summary the current status of the exact conditions that require clearance at each bank. How those conditions are cleared will continue to be a judgmental factor to be determined by the banker and the regional administrator. However, the NBSS keeps these factual conditions locked in a computer until a satisfactory response is received.

Summary reports on conditions in the banking system and how they are being handled are rendered to the comptroller at least quarterly. These reports are utilized for the basic policy, operations, and planning functions of the office.

SUMMARY

By using the best combinations of people, equipment, and attitudes, the NBSS has been successful in its initial applications. It is also being expanded both as to its data base and its use by the various functional divisions of the Office of the Comptroller. The data base is intended to be made available in a quarterly summary form to bankers.

The system must remain flexible to cope with rapid changes in the banking system. It must also maintain proper balance between its machine-operated segments and those involving good human judgment. With these ingredients, the final product will be an improved national banking system.

Discussion

Jack M. Guttentag

The reports on early warning systems indicate that important and useful work is going on in the regulatory agencies, which will improve their ability to identify problem institutions at an early stage. Yet this work has some important methodological shortcomings which deserve emphasis and attention.

The first shortcoming is that the methodologies developed are designed (implicitly to be sure) to catch *small* problem banks. This is ironical, since concern over the potential failure of large banks has motivated the work on early warning systems. Sinkey's bibliography, which must comprise at least two-thirds of the citable items on early warning systems, postdates the first large bank failure (United States National Bank of San Diego).

The second shortcoming is that most of the work on early warning systems has aimed to replicate or forecast bank examination ratings. Yet the principal causes of bank failure in the past have been fraudulent and other unsound banking practices associated with conflicts of interest, which bank examiners have not been very successful in uncovering.

I return to each of these problems in the course of reviewing the several statistical methodologies that can be used to construct an early warning system.

The most direct and obvious approach to the early warning problem is to identify statistical predictors of bank failure. The questions posed are "Were banks that failed significantly different, in terms of objective measurable characteristics 2 or 3 years before failure, from banks that did not fail? What are the statistical discriminators?"

This approach has not been much used because the statistical basis is very thin; there have not been enough failures. If one views very large banks as belonging in a separate category, furthermore, which is appropriate, this approach resolves itself into case studies of United States National, the Franklin National Bank of New York, and the Security National Bank of Long Island. Sinkey has given us some case history material on these banks that is suggestive, but that is all.

A second approach, referred to both by Sinkey and by Korobow et al., is to attempt to explain statistically bank examiner ratings. Do banks rated as problems by examiners have objective characteristics significantly different from those of other banks? What are the best statistical discriminators?

A weakness of this approach, as indicated earlier, is the assumption that bank examination ratings accurately reflect the probabilities of bank failure. I suspect that the reason for the uncritical acceptance of this assumption is that both the FDIC and the Federal Reserve Bank of New York view the purpose of early warning systems as that of complementing and assisting the bank supervisory function. Given this premise, it is reasonable to begin by trying to replicate by computer the judgment of the examiner. Even so, I would expect these efforts to be accompanied by a hard look at how good bank examination classifications are. So far I have not seen any such efforts.

The ability to replicate statistically examiner judgments on a contemporaneous basis strikes me as being almost useless, because to a very substantial degree it must be tautological. Examiners in making their determinations must look at the same factors that enter the discriminant functions or factors that are closely related.

The ability to *forecast* examiner judgments 1 or 2 years ahead would be quite useful I am sure. It is not obvious to me from reading the Sinkey and the Korobow et al. papers, however, that they can really do this in any useful way. A useful forecast in 1976 of bank examination classifications for 1978 would be one that contains more information than bank examination classifications for 1976. After all, over a time span of only a few years there must be very strong autocorrelation in bank examination ratings. I would be interested in seeing an explicit test of the Korobow et al. model using this criteria.

The third approach to early warning systems is the statistical outlier method. Sinkey has done some interesting retrospective outlier testing for Franklin National, United States National, and Security National. The Office of the Comptroller of the Currency (OCC) has based its early warning system entirely on the outlier approach, evidently without any testing at all.

The statistical outlier approach attempts to identify banks that are atypical, relative to members of the banks' peer group, with respect to a variety of indicators considered relevant to bank soundness. Under the comptroller's procedure these atypical banks (those with a high "anomaly severity ranking") are singled out for attention by specialists.

An interesting feature of the comptroller's system is that surveillance, control, and remedial action are integrated into one system. Banks determined by the computer to have a high "anomaly severity ranking" are fed back into the computer which then subsequently asks the regional administrator what actions he plans to take or has taken to "clear" the reported anomalies. Thus only OCC is attempting to deal with a basic problem that has always bedeviled bank supervision, namely, that discovering bank problems is one thing, and getting a regulator to take prompt and effective action is something else.

The statistical outlier approach has several major weaknesses. First, the statistical indicators used are chosen on the basis of informed judgment but have not been tested empirically.

Second, all indicators are measured relative to a peer group, so that the approach provides little insight into the changing vulnerability of the banking system as a whole.

Third, the outlier approach is ill-suited for dealing with the very largest banks, say the top 25 with deposits of $4 billion or more. Yet this is true also of the other two approaches. None of the approaches discussed above are capable of dealing effectively with very large banks. Early warning systems for large banks involve special problems that demand special treatment.

One relevant characteristic of large banks is the great diversity of their activities. Because of this diversity, statistical comparisons covering specific activities have little value (compared to its peers every large bank is bound to be an outlier in some respect or other). Because of this only basic bottom line comparisons are likely to be meaningful.

In addition, the social costs associated with the failure of a large bank are exceptionally steep. Because they have relatively large amounts of uninsured liabilities large banks in trouble are subject to "runs," which can spill over to other large banks. Failure of a large bank can also cause a serious short-run depletion of the deposit insurance reserve fund, which could undermine confidence in the deposit insurance system.

The high social costs of large-bank failure and the weakness of statistical approaches to monitoring large banks call for a fundamentally different approach to early warning systems. What is needed is to develop a hand-tailored model for each large bank. The model would be used to simulate changes in the bank's balance sheet—especially its net worth position—under a variety of assumed economic scenarios. The bank's soundness rating would be based on the least favorable set of conditions it could survive. The ratings of each large bank would be independent of those of other banks but, when the ratings were aggregated, they would provide a meaningful indicator of the vulnerability of large banks as a group.

George J. Benston

It seems evident that some form of bank surveillance by government is a permanent feature of our financial system. The FDIC, which must repay most depositors should a bank with insufficient assets fail, clearly has an interest in developing better systems to reduce the incidence of failures and to mitigate the amount of loss. The other regulatory agencies also have reason to be concerned with bank failures, since they often are criticized by Congress and the press when one of "their" banks goes under. Of course economists and even regulators and even some members of Congress realize that the cost of some failures may be an amount well worth paying for innovative behavior by bankers, which occasionally turns out badly, and for the salutary effect that the possibility of failure has on efficiency. Several writers have pointed out and recent experience has shown that the failure of a bank results in few problems for the general public—certainly fewer than the failure of most other similarly sized enterprises. Nevertheless, though the number of bank failures in recent years is very small relative to pre-World War II experience and relative to the number of active banks, they have been sufficient to raise public cries for reform. The articles presented in this book bear witness to the efforts of bank regulators to reform and improve methods of bank supervision.

The three papers describe computer-based methods of identifying banks that are more likely than others to be in financial difficulty. All the papers recognize that on-site examination, upon which regulatory supervision has been based at least since the mid-1800s, is a costly and often insufficient method. However, none of the supervisory agencies intend to eliminate on-site examinations. Rather, they view early warning systems as a means of complementing and supporting the bank examiner's job.

The papers differ somewhat in emphasis. The procedures described by Korobow, Stuhr, and Martin, developed for the New York Federal Reserve Bank (FRB) of New York and by Sinkey of the FDIC essentially are based on discriminant analysis of examiners' evaluations. They used discriminant analysis to associate quantitative data available from banks' balance sheets and income statements with examiners' classifications of banks as problem or no-problem. The purpose of the exercise is to determine which set of available data can best predict whether a bank will or will not be considered a problem in advance of the examiner's on-site evaluation. Mullin described a somewhat different system used by the Comptroller of the Currency (CC). The CC's system, developed by Haskins and Sells with the aid of a multimillion dollar contract, consists essentially of a computer analysis of various ratios constructed from a bank's balance sheet and income statement data. The ratios for a given bank are compared with ratios derived from a "comparable peer group." When the ratios appear to be out of line in amount or trend, the bank is considered a candidate for further investigation.

The three early warning systems described, though similar in their use of computer-stored and -accessed financial data, are dissimilar in several important respects. First, the FRB of New York and FDIC systems are based on research that statistically associates financial data with bank examiner's judgments, while the CC's system is designed to give examiners readier access to data that has not been subjected to formal analysis. Second, the FRB of New York and FDIC systems are preliminary in the sense that they have not as yet been integrated into the agencies' bank supervision system. The CC's system, on the other hand, is designed to be actively used for bank supervision. The reasons for this difference in application are interesting and are best left to other authors with more experience than I in the politics of regulatory agencies.

I do wish to comment, though, on a similarity of the three systems—their explicit or implicit reliance on the validity of examiners' evaluations. The FRB of New York and FDIC early warning models are based on replicating the examiners' designations of banks as problem or no-problem. The CC bank surveillance system depends on examiners' judgments, since it uses no model to determine whether an unusual ratio is "good" or "bad." My concern here is not that the examiners' judgments are necessarily unreliable, rather that we have little reason to believe that they are reliable. Indeed, the few studies that have been published are not flattering to the examiners. In particular, in a study I completed for the Presidential Commission on Financial Structure and Regulation, I found that 59 percent of the 56 banks that failed over the period January 1959 through April 1971 were rated "no problem" in the examination prior to failure.[1] A paper I published with John Marlin, which analyzed the factors related to examiners' determination of "substandard loans," concluded that the magnitude and change in these numbers could be explained only by differences among examiners and supervisory agencies and not by factors related to bank management, monetary changes, or economic conditions.[2] I know of only one study that found that the examiners do, in fact, meaningfully classify substandard loans. And this paper, by H. K. Wu, has serious shortcomings, primarily as a consequence of the limited amount of data involved.[3]

[1] George J. Benston, "Bank Examination," New York University, Graduate School of Business Administration, Institute of Finance, *The Bulletin*, Nos. 89–90, May 1973, p. 43.
[2] George J. Benston and John Tepper Marlin, "Bank Examiners' Evaluation of Credit: An Analysis of the Usefulness of Substandard Loan Data," *Journal of Money, Credit and Banking*, Vol. 6, (February 1974), 24–44.
[3] Hsiu-Kwang Wu, "Bank Examiner Criticisms, Bank Loan Defaults, and Bank Loan Quality," *The Journal of Finance*, Vol. 24 (1969), 697–705. (See the papers cited above for a critical analysis of Wu's study.)

Nevertheless, as Sinkey found, the level of a bank's substandard loans is the most important factor in its classification as a problem bank. Thus the FRB of New York and the FDIC early warning systems are based on a criterion whose validity is questionable.

The CC system, however, does not appear to be based on any research that seeks to determine which ratios and what ratio magnitudes or changes are predictive of financial distress. Perhaps some research will be undertaken now that the national banks' financial data have been checked for accuracy (or at least consistency) and fed into computer memories. However, it would have been preferable for some theorizing and testing of hypotheses to have preceded the rather expensive system the comptroller purchased.

I do not wish to seem negative in these comments. Perhaps because I (among others, such as Ernest Bloch) have suggested that computer-based early warning systems be developed that would direct field examinations more effectively and relieve most banks and regulatory agencies of the cost of unnecessary examinations, I applaud the preliminary work reported in the papers. I strongly suggest, though, that some basic research be undertaken by the regulatory agencies (and others). For example, the actual and potential causes of bank failures should be studied carefully. (My study—"Bank Examination"— revealed that fraud and irregularities accounted for 66 percent of the failures between January 1959 and April 1971. Since the financial statements of a fraudulently managed bank or one subjected to undiscovered embezzlement are likely to be advertently or inadvertently misstated, the early warning systems discussed in the papers cannot be useful.) The methods used by examiners also should be subjected to critical analysis. (Despite the fact that fraud is a very important cause of bank failures, examiners do not appear to consider it a major concern of a field examination.) The possibilities of using enforcable capital requirements and mandated diversification as a means of reducing the probability of failure also should be researched.

To reemphasize an earlier comment, I realize that the systems described are preliminary and are not claimed to be completed systems of bank supervision. However, unless the procedures described are based on theory and basic research, they probably will become no more than exercises of limited value rather than the beginnings of a greatly improved system of bank supervision.

Robert A. Eisenbeis

As evidenced by the general topic of this section and the content of the papers, significant resources are being devoted by both the government and private sectors to sophisticated quantitative research which attempts to rank (or classify) firms according to their current and/or projected risk characteristics. In assessing this work, it is important to recognize that it is still in its infancy. We have only begun to scratch the surface, both in terms of the application of the models and their results to the day-to-day decision-making and supervisory process. What I propose to do is to highlight briefly the status of the implementation of the more sophisticated quantitative early warning systems such as have been presented, and then indicate the directions I see this work taking in the next few years.

CURRENT STATUS OF EARLY WARNING SYSTEMS

In addition to the systems described in this section from the Federal Reserve Bank of New York and the FDIC, efforts are currently underway at the federal level at the Home Loan Bank Board and informally at the Federal Reserve Board to develop quantitative discriminant analysis-type scoring models for use in early warning systems to identify depository institutions most likely to experience financial difficulties.[1] The State of California Department of Savings and Loans was of course the pioneer in sponsoring the development and use of statistical scoring models to evaluate the financial conditions of depository institutions.[2] I am sure that other states by now have plans for their own systems.[3] But aside from the California State Department of Savings and Loans, I know of no regulator—either state or federal—who *up to now* has a statistical scoring model in place and functioning as an *integral* part of its line operations or who relies to any significant extent on the predictions from such a system in day-to-day supervisory activities.[4] Several agencies are close, but it is fair to represent the existing work as still being in the design and testing phases.

I do not know about the rest of the agencies, but part of the reason we have not made better progress at the FDIC in the implementation of such work has

[1] The Home Loan Bank Board is currently in the process of installing a model developed by Altman (1975) to supplement its existing financial evaluation system, an exception-type system similar to that being developed at the Office of the Comptroller of the Currency. In addition, I understand that the State of Illinois Banking Department has continued the work on its system which is the prototype of the system being developed at the Office of the Comptroller of the Currency.

[2] This early work is described in Price Waterhouse (1967).

[3] We have had inquiries from both the Michigan and California Banking Departments. The FDIC has made predictions from its systems available to state bank supervisors attending conferences at the FDIC, and its model is generally available to the public. Finally, there are several instances in state regulation of the insurance industry where statistical scoring models are being used to identify weak insurance companies.

[4] The National Association of Security Dealers (NASD) developed a model to screen broker-dealer firms. This work is described in Altman and Lorris (1976). But it does not appear that the model has been maintained or integrated into the supervisory process.

been our noticeable lack of success at breaking through the barrier of human resistance to new techniques that pose a potential threat to older, more established supervisory methods. This is particularly true when the new methods have been developed outside the line examination function and report to replicate what examiners are doing in the field. This barrier is so strong that I now doubt that there is a significant chance for further development of this type of system at the FDIC. This raises an important consideration that must be recognized by any group wishing to put such work into operation. Our experience is probably not too different from that of operations research groups who have sought to introduce new ways of performing existing line functions in banks and business and suggests that such work will only be adopted if substantial "selling" and educational effort is made to the potential user and/ or if there is such an overriding commitment from top management to adopt and use the models that resistance at lower levels can be broken down. In neither case, however, will full confidence exist until people in the line operations have adopted or accepted the system as their own.

DIRECTIONS OF FUTURE WORK

The ultimate usefulness and generality of the results from early warning systems hinge upon how well they capture and reflect meaningful concepts of risk. This is the Achilles' heel in the work to date and where the greatest emphasis in future work must be. As we are finding out, the conceptualization and quantification of risk in order to make inferences about the relative riskiness of firms is particularly difficult and elusive. In the final analysis, we are not yet sure how risk should be defined for supervisory purposes or how it should be measured. Faced with this dilemma it is interesting, but not surprising, to note that both the FDIC and the Federal Reserve Bank of New York research started at essentially the same point, by first looking at risk as it is currently perceived by bank examiners.[5] After all, examiners have been in the business of defining and subjectively evaluating risk for a long time. It seems logical to first investigate the substance and empirical content of what they are currently doing rather than striking out on our own.

This initial work at both the FDIC and the Federal Reserve Bank of New York confirms what is stated in the examination manuals. That is, in the examiner's view asset quality as measured by the volume of classified relative to nonclassified assets is the chief determinant of bank risk. Empirically, this is

[5] The work at the Office of the Comptroller of the Currency and at the Illinois Banking Department also started here. The work by Altman (1975) for the Home Loan Bank Board used more objective criteria to form their risk classes of Savings and loan associations: those that (1) failed, (2) required financial assistance from the Home Loan Bank System, and (3) all other associations.

verified by the role that loan classifications play in separating the problem and nonproblem banks identified by the examiners.[6]

Objectively, examiner classifications are only as good as the loan review process and become more or less meaningful depending upon the relationship between the classifications and loan quality. Recent work by Graham and Humphrey (1976), and Wu (1969), and Benston and Marlin (1974) suggest that there may not be a very strong relationship between examiner classifications and bank loan loss experience. These results have important implications for both the examination process and the examiner's risk index.

I think from reading Korobow's (1976) paper, as well as from my knowledge of the work at the FDIC, that none of us are particularly comfortable with the risk concepts currently used by examiners.[7] This is not because the examiners are viewed as being wrong, but rather because our review of the data on failures and recent events suggests that their approach is probably incomplete. Asset quality, while important, is but one of many factors determining risk. For example, the recent emphasis on liability management suggests that the liability side of the balance sheet and its interactions with the asset portfolio are both very important factors affecting risk. The failure of the Birmingham-Bloomfield Bank drove this point home quite plainly.[8] This bank relied on interest-sensitive, short-term sources of funds to finance an asset portfolio dominated by low-quality, high-yielding, municipal securities and other long-term assets. If interest rates fell, the bank was in great shape. The cost of funds would fall, the asset portfolio would appreciate, and its return on assets would be high. The problem was that rates rose.

Korobow is correct in noting that recent bank failures have been due more to financial and economic factors than to fraud and defalcations. The latter have accounted for more than two-thirds of all failures since 1934 and well over two-thirds of all the FDIC's losses. However, I am not sure that the recent phenomenon represents a significant trend or factor for the long run. It is true that the nature of bank risk taking has changed over time. Structural changes such as the rise of bank holding companies and their expansion into nonbanking activities, the growth of Real Estate Investment Trusts (REITs), and the expansion of foreign operations; the introduction of new instruments such as certificates of deposit and federal funds; and the development of new management concepts such as liability management; have broadened the extent of bank risk exposure. These, coupled with the extreme recession we have experienced

[6] For example, Sinkey (1976) shows that, using only the net capital ratio, it is possible to correctly classify over 95 percent of both problem and nonproblem banks.

[7] This work has been done by Joseph F. Sinkey, Jr., and a complete listing is included under his name in the references.

[8] The $58 million Birmingham-Bloomfield Bank failed in 1971 and was one of the banks in the Parson's Group.

undoubtedly put pressure on weaker institutions. But I am not sure that this implies that fraud and defalcation will decline in overall importance in the long run. Nevertheless, all of the above factors have important implications for risk measurement for the development of early warning systems and suggest that there are three important dimensions that need to be address in future work to make it even more meaningful.

First, any method that ignores fraud, defalacation, and self-dealing overlooks what have proved to be the most important causes of failures, and hence represent significant determinants of risk in banking.[9] This is not to suggest that one should attempt to develop statistical screening models to detect fraud and defalcation. I would be rather sketpical of the prospects for this line of attack since one would expect the perpretrator to attempt to keep such activity from appearing on, or affecting the balance sheet and income statements. It is for this reason that many such as Benston (1973) have argued that bank examination should focus less on asset quality and become more of an audit. He also suggests that the outside audits should be required on a regular basis.

Second, the dynamic nature of banking implies that our conception of risk must be an adaptive one. That is, to the extent that the determinants of risk change over time with the development of new methods and new services, this means that we must continually reestimate and revise our models. This of course also suggests that the models focusing on the prediction and identification of banks likely to experience problems sometime in the future will be subject to greater error than models used for the identification of banks experiencing current difficulties. Today's models focusing on today's problems may not capture tomorrow's problems very well.

Finally, what has heretofore been an overlooked point is that economic and other factors, exogenous to the firm, may have an important impact on our assessment of relative bank risk. Monetary policy, inflation, the level of and changes in interest rates, and the general state of the economy are all factors beyond an individual bank or savings and loan association's control, which can impact different portfolios differently and can affect our assessment of risk. For example, our view of the current relative riskiness of a bank heavily involved in REIT loans depends, upon other things, on the state of the housing industry and on our expectations about future housing conditions. In a healthy environment, such risks look quite different than in a down economy. Three or four years ago, how many heard anyone talking about the riskiness of REIT loans? It was only after things began to sour that the risks became more apparent. This is not to say that we should not have done a better job in looking at the REIT situation. Certain activities are inherently more risky than others, and we will have to do a better job in ferreting them out. Rather, the point is that,

[9] See Slocum (1973) and Barnett (1972)

given the REIT situation, the fact that it appeared as the more immediate problem rather than foreign banking activities, for example, was largely dictated by forces beyond the banks' control.

What does all this imply for bank examination and methods of assessing risk? First, it suggests that new supervisory procedures should be introduced to deal with the problems of fraud, defalcation, and insider dealings. A move toward greater emphasis on audit-type activities and/or requiring outside audits appears warranted by the experience to date. Similarly, rules and record keeping, such as those recently promulgated by the FDIC to deal with insider transactions, go a long way toward making such transactions explicit and placing a greater burden of responsibility on a bank's board of directors. To deal with the changing nature of banking and the influence of exogenous forces, it seems that, as suggested in the Haskins and Sells report (1975), more attention should be given to evaluating the entirety of a bank's performance and less to asset quality problems alone. There should be greater emphasis on financial analysis as the base of the examination process. Additionally, I am sure that Guttentag (1975) would argue that the agencies should attempt, via simulation methods, to determine the ability of certain types of portfolio compositions to sustain various types of shocks.[10] The wider the safety margins, the less risky an institution is. This is in essence the direction Korobow and his colleagues have begun to pursue in their work. Conceptually, the approach has great appeal, given the complexity of the problem, especially in evaluating large banks. It also promises to be a fruitful way of developing a feel for the risk implications of new activities and management policies.

It should be clear by now that this early work on financial early warning systems has in fact generated more problems and questions than it has answered. What started out as a fairly straightfoward empirical and descriptive classification problem has brought us face to face with the extremely complex task of defining and quantifying risk. The extent to which the future research is successful in meeting this challenge will have important implications for a broad range of policy questions affecting the supervision and regulation of financial institutions.

REFERENCES

Altman, Edward I. "Predicting Performance in the Savings and Loan Association Industry," Salomon Brothers Center for the Study of Financial Institutions, Working Paper No. 70, New York University, 1975, *Journal of Monetary Economics,* in press.

Altman, Edward and T. Lorris, "A Financial Early Warning System for Over-the-Counter Broker Dealers," *Journal of Finance,* September 1976.

[10] By portfolio I mean the entirety of a bank's balance sheet.

Barnett, Robert E., "Anatomy of a Bank Failure," *The Magazine of Bank Administration,* April 1972.

Benston, George J. and John Tepper Marlin, "Bank Examiner's Evaluation of Credit: An Analysis of the Usefulness of Substandard Loan Data," *Journal of Money, Credit, and Banking,* Vol. 1 (February 1974).

Gilbert, R. Alton, "Bank Failures and Public Policy," Federal Reserve Bank of St. Louis *Monthly Review* November 1975.

Graham, David and David Humphrey, "Predicting Net Loan Losses Using Disclosed and Undisclosed Bank Data: A Comparison," paper presented at the Conference on Bank Structure and Regulation, Federal Reserve Bank of Chicago, 1976.

Guttentag, Jack M., "Reflections on Bank Regulatory Structure and Large Bank Failures," Proceedings of a Conference on Bank Structure and Competition," Federal Reserve Bank of Chicago, 1975.

Haskins and Sells, *Haskins and Sells Study 1974–1975* (Washington, D.C.: Office of the Comptroller of the Currency), 1975.

Korobow, Leon, David P. Stuhr, and Daniel Martin, "A Probabilistic Approach to Early Warning of Changes in Bank Financial Conditions," Chapter I above.

Price Waterhouse, Inc. *A Proposed Analytical System to Provide an Objective Basis for Supervision,* Price Waterhouse, Inc., Dec. 21, 1967 (prepared for the State of California Division of Savings and Loan).

Sinkey, Joseph F., Jr., "Can Bank Failures Be Predicted?" FDIC Working Paper1, in press.

Sinkey, Joseph F., Jr., "Security National Bank of Long Island: A Balance-Sheet and Income-Expense Analysis of Our largest Emergency Merger," FDIC Working Paper, in press.

Sinkey, Joseph F., Jr., "Bank Capital, Loan Evaluations, and 'Problem' Banks," FDIC Working Paper No. 76-2.

Sinkey, Joseph F., Jr., "Franklin National Bank of New York: A Portfolio and Performance Analysis of Our Largest Bank Failure," FDIC Working Paper No. 75-10.

Sinkey, Joseph F., Jr., "Early-Warning System: Some Preliminary Predictions of Problem Commercial Banks," *Proceedings of a Conference on Bank Structure and Competition,* May, 1975, pp. 85–91.

Sinkey, Joseph F., Jr., "A Multivariate Statistical Analysis of the Characteristics of Problem Banks," *Journal of Finance,* March 1975, pp. 21–36.

Sinkey, Joseph F., Jr., "Adverse Publicity and Bank Deposit Flows: The Cases of Franklin National Bank of New York and United States National Bank of San Diego," *Journal of Bank Research,* Summer 1975, pp. 109–112.

Sinkey, Joseph F., Jr., "The Failure of United States National Bank of San Diego: A Portfolio and Performance Analysis," *Journal of Bank Research,* Spring 1975, pp. 8–24.

Sinkey, Joseph F., Jr., "The Way Problem Banks Perform," *The Bankers Magazine,* Autumn 1974, pp. 40–51.

Sinkey, Joseph F., Jr., and David A. Walker, "Problem Banks: Identification and Characteristics," *Journal of Bank Research,* Winter 1975, pp. 208–217.

Slocum, John, "Why 57 Insured Banks Did Not Make It—1960 to 1972," *Journal of Commercial Bank Lending,* August 1973.

Wu, Hsui-Kwang, "Bank Examiner Criticisms, Bank Loan Defaults and Bank Loan Quality," *Journal of Finance,* September 1969.

Failure Models for Nonfinancial Institutions

ERNEST BLOCH

Business failure is costly to society, and its prediction is therefore beneficial. Indeed, investigation of the problem through discriminant analysis has led to a better understanding of tendencies in the direction of failure for nonfinancial units—and this process of course may be considered an analog to the early warning systems developed for financial institutions discussed elsewhere in this volume.

Taking this point a step further, one may argue that forecasts concerning the fail*ing* (rather than the fail*ed*) company should be assessed more carefully. This is so because even moderately effective management can benefit from models that predict or at least support the typically unpleasant decisions required by new pejorative information. One may even wonder whether it is difficult to predict failure very far ahead because some managements react with a degree of appropriateness to bad news, thereby preventing (or at least staving off) the ultimate unpleasantness.

To be sure, the use of prophylactic models would, if successful, prevent the emergence of absolute empirical evidence, such as bankruptcy, but none of the authors would, I am sure, object to the "successful" use of their work in that sense.

The papers below fall into two general categories: Altman and Deakin offer state-of-the-art reviews of failure prediction models, while McWilliams and

Blum apply available failure prediction models to investment management and to antitrust law, respectively.

Altman's paper views the work done by himself and others since the publication of his original linear discriminant analysis (LDA) Z-score model (1968). He finds that the results have stood the test of time and indeed that subsequent experiments with a quadratic version (QDA) did not significantly improve results; nevertheless, he argues that both versions (LDA and QDA) are worth trying. Another section of the paper considers the raw material of discriminant analysis, namely, the structure of financial and accounting statements and their data components. Lease capitalization policy, in particular, is given attention, since bankrupt firms were found to be using leases far more frequently than healthy firms (Elam, 1975).

Deakin's paper points to a statistical problem faced by all failure prediction models, namely, that failure involves a minuscule number of any sample of firms—the number of failed firms in the Compustat 1800 Company file comes to less than 1 percent, and under a less stringent definition (Beaver, 1967), to about 3 percent. A naive model predicting zero failures thus would, at worst, be correct 97 percent of the time. The point subsequently made argues that, while the identification of failure is difficult, the *cost* of *not* identifying failure is unacceptably high. Both Deakin and Altman agree on the following cost asymmetry: Misclassification of a company as failing that does *not* in fact fail is much lower than *non*identification of failure for a firm that is destined to fail.

Moreover, Deakin argues that as early as possible diagnosis should be made by auditors using annual data, rather than quarterly data which may be more subject to manipulation. Since most failure models work best with a one-period lag, a two-period prediction requires auditors to qualify or disclaim their opinions two annual reports prior to the expected failure point. Deakin found that quadratic (rather than a linear) discriminant analysis permits him to predict companies as fail*ing*, rather than as having reached the irreversible situation of the fail*ed*. Of course, the problem of *ex-post* identification then becomes difficult—perhaps Deakin's model could be viewed as an analog to the process of credit-rating companies faced with making changes in the *lowest* classifications of credit quality. To that extent, his results differ from replication of the perhaps less graded responses of the opinions of auditors.

McWilliams' application of failure models is to investment management. His paper uses a variety of approaches, including discriminant analysis, in the evaluation of a change in the quality of a firm's financial performance. The methods used include bank loan supervisory and credit-scoring techniques which employ traditional ratio analysis, including those used in Beaver's (1967) study. McWilliams finds these techniques useful as evaluators of financial quality change but supplements them with other techniques because ratios alone do not offer a single-value estimator of performance or failure as, for example, the Z-score model does. Indeed, he finds that in using Altman's model it is adaptable to a diagnosis of declining quality even when the firm being examined is obviously not a candidate for failure.

McWilliams paper illustrates the use of Beaver's ratio codes, Z scores, and Wilcox's work (which sets probabilities of ultimate failure) to evaluate and monitor the performance of firms that may or *may not* be in trouble. McWilliams shows that each of the methods can track an increase in a company's difficulties (including a prediction of failure), as well as *recovery* from a negative evaluation. McWilliams concludes that this type of analysis can more readily identify a potential price drop in the company's shares than its opposite, a potential rise.

Blum's work applies failure analysis in a peculiarly apposite area of law. This involves the failing company doctrine which permits an otherwise illegel business combination under the antitrust laws because the failing company is merged with a healthy one. Blum distinguishes between two types of applica tion to failing companies: those in regulated industries (say, banking) where a merger of a weak and a strong bank continues to provide a public service which could decline in quality with the disappearance of the weak. In *non*regulated industries, the decision problem for the Justice Department may arise as follows: Should a proposed merger *not* be contested because one of the parties could be shown, by a failure prediction model, to be in danger? Blum points out that in the regulated industry case the administrative agency concerned with supervising the industry may be more persuaded by the forecasted cost of misclassifying a potential failure (i.e., a loss of service) than the Justice Department may be for nonregulated industries. Clearly, the research work done in costing out failure misclassifications is tilling fertile soil.

But perhaps Blum's most interesting point is the proposition that court evaluations of, or suits concerning investment or loan decisions by, fiduciaries may be evaluated for "reasonableness" by submitting decisions *ex-post* to tests of failure model predictions. As a defensive device for decision makers, Blum suggests the routine use of failure models to support the prudence of actions taken by the fiduciaries. This suggests increased use of work by those trained in finance; but, in conclusion, Blum indicates that lawyers will not be slighted in this game: The *evaluation* of the quality of decision making remains in the courts of law.

4. Business Failure Prediction: An Empirical Analysis

EDWARD B. DEAKIN

The failure of a business organization often has significant economic effects for its owners, creditors, and employees. In addition, such failures can result in costs to the auditors of the company as a result of lawsuits, legal fees, and loss of revenues. Governmental bodies may suffer loss of tax revenues and loss of part of the economic base of a community. The accountant has a special interest in the prediction of failure, since external financial reports are generally prepared on a going concern basis. If the company is unlikely to continue as a going concern, there should be some reporting of this to the several parties interested in the firm. Such a reporting may arise either through an explicit statement by the auditor, or from an analysis of financial data.

BACKGROUND

Various attempts have been made to predict the failure of companies. Beaver (1966, 1967) considered the predictive ability of individual financial ratios for this purpose. Altman (1968) used discriminant analysis to combine several predictors into a model which was more successful in predicting failure than models using only individual financial ratios. Deakin (1972) used a similar model based on financial ratios and obtained improved predictability up to 2 years prior to the date of failure. Libby (1975) factor-analyzed the 14 ratios used in the Beaver and Deakin studies and presented a reduced model which had predictability similar to that of the Deakin model, but which required the use of only 5 financial ratios.

Other authors have presented models for predicting small-business failure (Edmister, 1972) and for considering the effect of lease data on the predictive ability of discriminant-based bankruptcy models (Elam, 1975). In addition, Blum (1974) presented a model that considered the use of failure-predicting models in the decision of whether to allow a merger to meet the requirements of the failing company doctrine in antitrust regulations.

Several shortcomings are apparent in all these studies, which need to be addressed before further research on failure prediction can proceed. As pointed out by Altman (1976), there have been several developments in the use of discriminant-based classification techniques, which may prove useful in accounting-related applications. The most significant of these was proposed by Eisenbeis and Avery (1972). They suggest that, when inequality in dispersion matrices between classification groups is present, linear classification rules may not be appropriate. In such a circumstance, a quadratic classification rule may be indicated.

A second drawback to the present research has been failure to consider the frequency of errors likely to obtain in a real world use of the model. All the cited studies were based on individual group sizes that were equal or approximately equal. Under such circumstances, the stated error rates may not reflect the extent of each type of error. The most serious effect would be a tendency to understate the misclassification of nonfailing companies into the failing group. Figure 1a demonstrates the approximate area for classification errors that would be observed in an experimental setting with equal failing and nonfailing group sizes. However, the actual environment is more likely to appear as in Figure 1b. Under such circumstances, a large number of nonfailing companies are likely to be classified as failing, even though they ultimately do not fail.

The extent of this error can be appreciated in relation to the number of failed firms in any given year. The *Wall Street Journal Index* classification "Bankruptcies" listed 34 new bankruptcies in 1972 and 41 in 1973. While this listing refers only to companies that have actually filed bankruptcy petitions, efforts to locate companies that have failed under somewhat less stringent conditions also yield few observations. Beaver (1966) included companies that had defaulted on loan agreements or had omitted preferred dividends as failed companies. However, attempts to compile a list of such companies seems to be a hit-or-miss proposition.

Another approach to determining the extent of failure would be to refer to a data base such as the Compustat 1800 Company file. Of the approximately 1780 companies in the 1973 version of this file, none went bankrupt in 1973, and 8 filed bankruptcy petitions in 1974. An additional six were found to have filed bankruptcy as of August 31, 1975. From this source, then, the frequency of bankruptcy is 0.79 percent. As we report later, the number of companies that would have been included under Beaver's less stringent definition of failure would have been 54 companies, or 3.03 percent of the file. A rule that classifies all companies as nonfailing would then be accurate at least 96.97 percent of the time.

Using a statistical model such as Deakin's model for 2 years prior to failure (1972, Table 8), one would expect a total of 10 percent of the nonfailing companies to be erroneously classified as failing, and 9 percent of the failing companies to be erroneously classified as nonfailing. This would result in expected classifications for failing and nonfailing companies as presented in Table 1. The total correct classifications would be comprised of 1602 companies (the 1553 in column 2 and the 49 in column 3). This would indicate correct classification only 90.00 percent of the time. Thus one concludes that the statistical model performs less satisfactorily than a naive model which eliminates the possibility of failure.

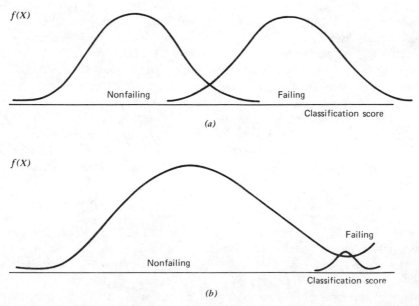

Figure 1 Indicated error frequencies. (a) Relative errors—experimental data. (b) Relative errors—environmental data.

Table 1   Expected Classifications With a Statistical Model

	Classification		
Actual	Nonfailing	Failing	Total
Nonfailing	1553	173	1726
Failing	5	49	54
Total	1558	222	1780

Of course, these error rates have not considered the costs that might be associated with each error type. Depending upon the relationship of the classifier to the company classified, the cost differences for each type of error may be substantial. A new lender to the company would find the relative cost of failure to identify a failing company far greater than the cost of failure to identify a nonfailing company. Other classifiers may have different error preferences.

Another shortcoming of many of the proposed models is that they tend to be accurate only for the year before failure. Thus, for example, a model can indicate that a company will fail during the year following the close of the fiscal year for which the annual report was prepared. However, in many cases that report is delayed for failing companies and may not be available until after the failure event. Altman, Dervan, and Lorris (1974) proposed the use of quarterly data in order to help alleviate this problem, although there have been some questions about the usefulness of quarterly data because of the manipulations of the data and because of the general paucity of extensive quarterly data for many companies.[1] A good feature of a model, then, would be an ability to predict the bankruptcy or other failure event on the basis of annual data from at least 2 years prior to the event.

Finally, the cited research has not considered the predictive ability of alternate models which may be used in the environment. Since the event of failure often has a material effect on the financial statements of a company, one may expect that the auditors for the company would use some model to assess the probability of failure. If the company were predicted to fail, then the auditors would be expected to disclose such a prediction in their opinion. Indeed, Statement on Auditing Standards (SAS) #1, ¶547 indicates that in the presence of material uncertainties about future events, the auditor may be required to qualify or disclaim an opinion. Similar standards were also required under Statement on Auditing Procedures (SAP) #33. Thus we consider the results of

[1] Recent recommended changes to SEC 10-Q filings may serve to eliminate this problem

the auditors' ability to predict failure as indicative of the outcomes from their failure model(s).[2]

In this paper, the five-financial-ratio model developed from data 2 years prior to the event of bankruptcy is used to classify all companies in the 1973 Compustat 1800 Company file based on financial information available for fiscal years ending in 1971. This is the same model as that used by Deakin and modified by Libby. This part of the research is designed to provide an indication of the frequency and nature of misclassification of nonfailing companies likely to arise from use of the model. Since most failed companies are eliminated from the file, this part of the study is not likely to provide much indication of the results of misclassification of failing companies.

In order to assess the impact and frequency of misclassification of failing companies, the model was used to classify all new bankruptcies listed in the *Wall Street Journal Index* for 1972, 1973, and 1974. The list of bankrupt companies found in the index was further limited to those for which the necessary data were available for fiscal years ending in 1971. A total of 48 companies was included in this data set.

An assessment of the auditors' prediction model was carried out by reviewing the auditors' opinions on the 48 failed companies as well as on a sample of 116 nonfailing companies chosen at random from the Compustat 1800 Company file data base referred to above. The auditors' opinions on the 48 failed companies were used to assess ability to predict failure, while the opinions on the nonfailed sample were used to assess ability to predict nonfailure.

THE MODEL

The bankruptcy prediction model for this study was based on the original model proposed by Deakin (1972), which incorporated the 14 financial ratios used in the Beaver (1966, 1967) studies. These variables were factor-analyzed by Libby (1975), resulting in a set of 5 ratios which contained virtually all the predictive ability of the original set of 14 variables.

The five variables chosen by Libby to represent the identified factors were: (1) net income/total assets, (2) current assets/total assets, (3) cash/total assets, (4) current assets/current liabilities, and (5) sales/current assets. While the set of variables used is not expected to be totally uncorrelated, it does provide a minimum of multicollinearity problems. In addition, it requires a minimum of input data.

---

[2] This approach is similar to the argument used by Altman and McGough (1974). However, our classification method is somewhat different, and this paper presents the results of applying the model to all firms on a given data file in one specific year, rather than just to companies found to have failed or to have received qualified audit opinions.

A sample of 63 bankrupt companies was used to comprise the classification "failing" for development of the model. Data for these companies were taken from financial reports for 2 years prior to the filing of bankruptcy petitions. Most of these firms were the same as those used in the Deakin study. In addition, the companies that failed in 1970 and 1971 as listed by Altman (1971) were also included in the failing company data base. The companies failed between 1966 and 1971, and the financial data were obtained for fiscal years ending from 1964 to 1969.

A sample of 80 nonfailing companies was selected from Moody's *Industrial Manual* for the same period of time in order to provide a data base for "nonfailing" companies for model development. No attempt was made to match nonfailing companies with failing companies by industry, asset size, or other criteria. Industry matching had been used in other studies (e.g., Blum, 1974) but was rejected for this study on the grounds that industry factors could confound the results. In fact, the industry mix of failing companies in 1964 was found to be somewhat different from that in 1970–1971, and both of these were different from the mix of failing companies in 1973–1975.

These data were then entered into the Eisenbeis and Avery computer program (1972) in order to find a set of classification equations that would allow maximum discrimination between the two groups. In accordance with a suggestion by Altman (1976), a test was made of the equality of dispersion matrices for the failing and nonfailing groups. The relevant F ratio is referred to in Eisenbeis and Avery (1972, Appendix A). For this test, the F ratio took on a value of 102.6 with 15 and 70,993 degrees of freedom for the numerator and denominator, respectively. The hypothesis of dispersion matrix equality was thus rejected at the .001 level or less.

From this, it appeared that the linear classification rule might not be completely satisfactory. Accordingly, analysis of the classification rules was carried out using both the quadratic and linear methods. The relevant correlation matrices for each group are presented in Table 2. (This matrix form is presented instead of the dispersion matrix, because it presents the same information in standardized form.) The correlation matrix for the total sample is also presented in Table 2.

The discriminant model resulted in the discriminant function presented in Table 3. In addition, the vector of scaled scores for each of the five variables is also presented in Table 3. Because of the multicollinearity evident in the correlation matrices, it is difficult to attribute discriminating power to each of the predictor variables. The group means on each variable are also presented in Table 3. Wilk's Λ for the hypothesis of equality of group means had a value of 10.4 with 5 and 137 degrees of freedom. This was significant at less than the .001 level.

The reduced space centroid of the nonfailing group was .0479, while the

Table 2   Correlation Matrices

	NI/TA	CA/TA	C/TA	CA/CL	S/CA
Failing group matrix					
NI/TA	1.				
CA/TA	−.013	1.			
C/TA	.059	.359	1.		
CA/CL	.173	−.079	−.001	1.	
S/CA	−.172	−.250	.012	−.312	1.
Nonfailing group matrix					
NI/TA	1.				
CA/TA	.232	1.			
C/TA	.033	.314	1.		
CA/CL	.113	.391	.400	1.	
S/CA	−.158	−.379	−.110	−.301	1.
Total correlation matrix					
NI/TA	1.				
CA/TA	.070	1.			
C/TA	.078	.338	1.		
CA/CL	.298	.158	.207	1.	
S/CA	−.134	−.302	−.039	−.284	1.

reduced space centroid of the failing group was .0444. The dispersion for the nonfailing group in reduced space was .0036, and for the failing group .0061. Because of the potential overlap of groups resulting from the use of reduced space classification techniques, the classification was carried out in full (test) space. The expected overlap in classification could not be accurately determined since, as observed by Deakin (1976), the assumptions of multivariate normality are unlikely to hold for financial ratios.

Table 3   Discriminant Function Data

Variable	Coefficient	Scaled Vector	Group Means	
			Failing	Nonfailing
NI/TA	.0400	.0523	−.0666	.0500
CA/TA	.0028	.0094	.5711	.5844
C/TA	.9992	1.0000	.0604	.0701
CA/CL	−.0088	−.2171	1.5806	2.8188
S/CA	−.0003	−.0101	3.1635	3.1964

Table 4   Classification Equations

Linear

Variable	Coefficient
IN/TA	13.855
CA/TA	.060
C/TA	−.601
CA/CL	.396
S/CA	.194
Constant	−1.369

Quadratic

Variable	Linear Terms	Variables				
		IN/TA	CA/TA	C/TA	CA/CL	S/CA
IN/TA	−8.242	−70.06				
CA/TA	−31.57	−5.65	−22.06			
C/TA	12.93	20.49	50.82	−204.7		
CA/CL	−5.79	.68	−2.06	1.0	−.88	
S/CA	−.42	−.57	−1.46	2.5	−.34	.17
Constant	1.78					

The linear and quadratic classification equations are given in Table 4. However, since the initial prior probability of membership in the failing group was considered very small, and since the assumption of multivariate normality is unlikely to hold, classification rules were based on the relative distance of an observation mean vector from the centroids of the failing and nonfailing groups. Thus an observation was classified as belonging to the failing group if its mean vector was closer to the failing group centroid than to that of the nonfailing group.[3]

In testing the model on the data used to generate the model, the Lachenbruch holdout method was used (Eisenbeis and Avery, 1972, p. 21). With this method, a classification model is developed using all the observations in the sample except the one to be classified. The observation held out of the development of the model is then classified by the computed model. This process is repeated for all the items in the sample. The results of the use of the technique

---

[3] The distance is measured in terms of Mahalanobis distance, which is still somewhat subject to normality assumptions. As can be seen, though, the method appears to be fairly robust with respect to these assumptions.

Table 5   Classification Errors in Sample Data

| | Classification | | |
Actual	Failing	Nonfailing	Total
Quadratic rule			
Failing	62	1	63
Nonfailing	22	58	80
Total	84	59	143
Linear rule			
Failing	56	7	63
Nonfailing	1	79	80
Total	57	86	143

on classifying the 143 observations used to develop the model are shown in Table 5. As can be noted from the table, the quadratic rule classified far more companies as failing than actually were in the failing category. However, the linear model failed to classify several failing firms properly. Since we were unable to resolve the trade-off between the costs of the two types of error, and since the number of nonfailing companies in the environment is likely to be large, the following decision rule was adopted for use in the study:

Classify as failing if both rules classify as failing.
Classify as nonfailing if both rules classify as nonfailing.
Investigate further if the rules are in conflict.

With this type of decision process, one can expect to minimize the overall misclassification rate, although the size of the investigate further group is uncontrolled and may be excessively large.

RESULTS

Interpretation of the results of the classifications must be considered in light of the nature of the process a company follows prior to failure. Clearly, it would not be productive to classify companies as bankrupts, since that is a judicial determination. By classifying companies at some time prior to the bankruptcy event, one is then making a classification of fail*ing* companies, rather than of companies that have already fail*ed*. The problem with this type of classification scheme is that there is little information available to help one decide upon criteria to identify a prefailure firm. Indeed, if the failure process is a dynamic process, then a company may be able to enter the failing state, yet avoid entering the final failed state. Because of the possibility of avoidance of the final, identifiable state, identification of erroneous classifications becomes extremely difficult.

When the adopted classification rule was applied to the 1780 companies' data in the Compustat 1800 Company file for fiscal years ending in 1971, 290 companies were classified as failing. An additional 173 companies were not classified on account of conflicting classification outcomes. The remaining 1317 companies were classified as nonfailing. As expected, the number of organizations classified as failing far exceeded the number that would actually fail within the immediate future. In order to determine the number of companies that did fail, the financial histories of the 290 companies identified as failing were reviewed for the next 3½ years. Thus the history of each of these firms was traced for the years 1972–1975 through June 30. Standard and Poor's *Corporation Records* and *Moody's Industrial Manual, Bank and Finance Manual*, and *Transportation Manual* provided the major source of data on company histories. In addition, the annual reports of several of the companies were reviewed when the data in the manuals were insufficient.

This review indicated that companies classified as failing tended to cut or omit common dividends and to make major dispositions of assets. In addition, several of these companies omitted preferred dividends or were in technical default on loan agreements. These technical defaults were generally a result of failure to maintain adequate working capital or retained earnings according to the terms of loan agreements. Of the 290 companies, 18 had undergone bankruptcy, recapitalization, or reorganization by arrangement with creditors, or were liquidated in the 3½ years following classification as failing. However, 66 of the companies classified as failing experienced no such obvious difficulties.[4] The results of this survey are shown in Table 6.

A sample of 100 nonfailing companies was selected in order to make a comparative study of company histories. Of the 100 companies, 15 omitted common dividends and 20 made major dispositions of assets during the 3½ years following classification. None of these companies had omitted preferred dividends or experienced liquidation or reorganization as observed for the other group. The observations on this sample are also summarized in Table 6.

When these comparative data are entered into a chi-square contingency

---

[4] The summary tables present data on specific events, in a dichotomous classification scheme only. Thus, certain events remain hidden. For example, of the 66 companies, virtually all of them continued to have low profit performances in subsequent years and were required to pay substantially high interest rates on loans. Of the dividend cuts reported for the failing group, most were substantial and few were restored in subsequent years. With respect to the nonfailing sample reported later, many of the companies remained highly profitable, and many increased dividends. Of the dividend cuts reported, few remained permanent and were restored within 1 or 2 years.

Table 6   Summary of Company Histories

(1) Group	(2) Number	(3) Merged	(4) No Pre- fail Events	(5) Dividend Cut or Omitted	(6) Major Disposal of Assets	(7) Default, Preferred Dividend Omitted	(8) Bankruptcy, Liquidation, or Reorganization
Failing	290	7	66	124	123	46	18
Nonfailing	100	2	68	15	20	0	0
Binomial probability of equal population proportions for event			.000	.000	.000	.000	.002
Value of χ^2 for contingency table constructed of prefail events (cols. 4–8)					141.5		
Probability of χ^2 with 4 degrees of freedom					.000		

82

table, a chi-square value of 141.5 is obtained. The value is significant at less than .001, thus indicating that the frequency of events in columns 4 to 8 of Table 6 were significantly different for the failing group than for the nonfailing group. Of course, aggregating all the events into one contingency table could eliminate certain nonsignificant differences in individual events between groups. For this reason, binomial probabilities were computed for each of the events in columns 4 to 8 to test the hypothesis that the proportion of one group that experienced the event in the column heading was no different from the proportion of the second group under that heading. In all cases, the null hypothesis was rejected at very small probabilities (less than .002 for the largest of the five computed probabilities). We did not compute the differences in merged companies between groups because it was not considered an event of interest.

Under a strict definition of failure, which allows a failing company to be considered classified correctly if and only if such failure (in the form of bankruptcy, reorganization, or liquidation) occurred within the observed time period, only 18 of the companies (or 6.4 percent) were properly classified. If the definition were expanded to include Beaver's consideration of omission of preferred dividends and loan defaults, both the column-7 and column-8 observations would be considered correctly classified. Omitting the overlap in the two groups results in a total of 58 companies experiencing one or both of these bankruptcy events. This improves the correct classification rate to 20.5 percent.

However, since the classification procedure was for failing companies, and if we extend that group to include all companies classified as failing that have experienced at least one of the events in columns 4 to 8 in Table 6, 224 of the companies were correctly classified—a correct classification rate of 224/283 or 79.2 percent. Merged companies have been omitted, because the outcome of their classification is ascertainable.

Because of the inability to define a failing company precisely, we conclude that the correct classification of failing companies ranges between 20.5 and 79.2 percent of the group classified as failing. The user of the model has to assess the correct classification proportion on the basis of the definition of failing that best meets his or her needs.

Since the number of companies listed in the Compustat 1800 Company file that eventually fail is very small, another approach had to be used in order to assess the likelihood that the proposed classification rule would properly classify a failing company. In order to accomplish this, the *Wall Street Journal Index* was scanned for "Bankruptcies" in the years 1972 to 1974. The initial list of companies obtained was then used to construct a data base for failing companies similar to the data base used in the first part of the test. Financial ratios were obtained using the Leasco microfiche files of annual reports and the Moody's manuals. Data were obtained for 47 companies.

Table 7   Classification of Failing Companies

	Failing in:			
Classification	1972	1973	1974	Overall
Failing	7	24	8	39
Nonfailing	0	1	0	1
Not classified	2	3	2	7
Overall	9	28	10	47

Of these companies, 40 were classified by the decision rule above, and 7 were not classified. The model was better able to predict companies failing 2 years from the date of the close of the fiscal year than companies failing within 1 year or during the third year from the date of the report; 83.0 percent of the 47 companies were correctly classified as failing. These results are presented in Table 7. Of the 8 companies classified as not failing or not classified, 5 had January 31 fiscal year closings, indicating that the data were somewhat older than that for other failing companies. By ignoring the potential model improvement with the elimination of these observations, the classification for this set of companies was significantly different than for the Compustat 1800 Company file. Using a contingency table approach, a chi-square value of 161.3 was obtained. With 2 degrees of freedom, this value is significant beyond the .001 level.

Computation of binomial probabilities for equality of group assignments between the Compustat 1800 Company file and this data set resulted in rejection of the hypothesis of equal assignments to the failing and nonfailing groups at very small alpha levels. However, the frequency of companies not classified appeared to be similar between groups with an alpha significance of .08.

From this, it appears that the model is fairly accurate in its ability to classify a failing company as failing, with 83 percent of the companies correctly classified, 2 percent incorrectly classified, and 15 percent not classified.

COMPARISON WITH THE AUDITORS' MODELS

Inasmuch as the failure of a company is likely to have a major economic impact on its financial statements, one expects that the independent auditor is likely to make some assessment regarding continuation of the business entity as a going concern [see Altman and McGough, 1974 for further discussion of this]. However, an auditor's cost considerations may cause him or her to limit classification of failing companies in order to minimize the potential misclassification of nonfailing companies. Altman and McGough found that auditors did not perform as well as their model in classifying a company as failing. They also found that auditors' classifications of companies as failing did not necessarily mean that the company would fail. These results of their study are summarized in Table 8.

Since auditors did not appear to do well in either classification, one should consider the overall error rates for auditors' opinions with regard to the frequency of bankruptcy and the frequency of qualified opinions for going concern reasons. In order to assess these probabilities, we read the auditors' opinions for the 47 bankrupt companies in our data base for the 1971 fiscal year annual report. In addition, the auditors' reports were read for a sample of 116 companies from the Compustat 1800 Company file for 1971 data. The results of these observations are summarized in Table 9. An auditor is considered to have classified a company as failing if he or she has issued a major subject to opinion that refers to ability to continue profitable operations or to meet existing debts as they come due or to a going concern exception, or has disclaimed an opinion for going concern–related reasons. "Clean" opinions are considered to include not only unqualified opinions, but also those that are qualified on account of specific contingencies which do not effect the ultimate failure of a company or which relate to changes in accounting principles.

As can be seen in Table 9, the frequency of issuance of qualified opinions is expected to take on an overall probability of .009 for nonfailing companies, and of .149 for failing companies. This difference is significant at the .001 level using binomial probabilities. However, as can be seen from the table, the auditor is not particularly successful at predicting the failure of companies as long as 2 years prior to the failure event. However, it appears that an auditor is unlikely to issue a qualification to a nonfailing company.

Of course, there are two possible explanations for the small number of quali-

Table 8 Auditors' Error Rates

	Classified as		
Actual	Failing	Nonfailing	Total
Failing	7 (20.6%)	27 (79.4%)	34

	Actual		
Classified as	Failing	Nonfailing	Total
Failing	6 (28.6%)	15 (71.4%)	21

Source: Altman and McGough (1974).

Table 9   Auditors' Error Rates (This Study)

	Actual Classification	
Type of Opinion	Failing	Nonfailing
Qualified	7 (14.9%)	1 (0.9%)
"Clean"	40 (85.1%)	115 (99.1%)

fications in the auditors' opinions. In the first place, since so few firms actually fail, the auditor places a small prior probability on the failure event. If the auditor acts in a Bayesian decision sense, the process of probability revision will require a substantial amount of evidence for failure before the probability of failure exceeds the probability of nonfailure. The auditor can then minimize the overall error rate by minimizing classifications of companies as failing.

Second, the relative costs of classification errors for the auditor should also be considered. To the auditor, the classification of a nonfailing company as failing can result in loss of the client and can also cause the company to fail. (However, evidence for this suggestion has not been borne out by a review of the companies in the Altman-McGough study.) The auditor may then be using an optinal classification rule when cost factors are considered and when the prior probabilities of failure are incorporated into the model.

LIMITATIONS

Although the ability to predict the failure of a company may be of interest, the appropriate classification model may be significantly different from the one used here. As noted, classification rules should also consider the relative costs of misclassifications. In addition, if discriminant analysis techniques are found to be robust with respect to violations of the multivariate normality assumption, it may be possible to assign probabilities of group membership. Such assignments may permit a better cost assessment procedure.

The data used in this study were drawn from fiscal years ending in 1971, and histories were traced up to June 1975. If substantial changes take place in the structure of failing and nonfailing companies, the model may no longer be appropriate. Any assessment of such change must wait until sufficient time has elapsed to permit a study of the history of each classified company.

Finally, the ability of the statistical model has been compared with only one other prediction model. No attempt has been made to compare the model's predictions with those of other models such as the capital asset pricing model. Until such efforts are reported, it is not possible to assess the economic significance of use of the model.

CONCLUSIONS

As a result of these observations, it appears that discriminant-based classification models based on financial accounting ratios can predict the failure of a company with a high degree of accuracy. It appears, however, that the number of companies classified as failing will greatly exceed the number that ultimately do fail. Such a rate of misclassification can serve to limit use of the model to situations in which misclassification of nonfailing companies is not a costly matter.

In comparison with the auditors' evident decision model for classifying failing companies, the statistical model results in fewer classification errors for failing companies. However, the auditors' models apparently result in fewer misclassifications of nonfailing companies. These results may be explainable in terms of the auditors' prior assessments of group membership probabilities, as well as cost considerations.

REFERENCES

Altman, E. I., "Financial Ratios, Discriminant Analysis and the Prediction of Corporate Bankruptcy," *Journal of Finance,* September, 1968, pp. 589–609.

Altman, E. I., *Corporate Bankruptcy in America* (Lexington, Mass.: D. C. Heath), 1971.

Altman, E. I. and T. P. McGough, "Evaluation of a Company as a Going Concern," *The Journal of Accountancy,* December 1974, pp. 50–57.

Altman, E. I., E. J. Dervan, and B. Lorris, "A Financial Early-Warning System for Over-the-Counter Broker-Dealers," N.Y.U., Salomon Brothers Center for the Study of Financial Institutions, Working Pater No. 25, 1974, and *Journal of Finance,* September 1976.

Altman, E. I., "The Effect of Lease Data on the Predictive Ability of Financial Ratios: A Comment," *The Accounting Review,* April 1976.

Beaver, W. H., "Financial Ratios as Predictors of Failure," *Empirical Research in Accounting: Selected Studies, 1966,* supplement to Vol. 5, *Journal of Accounting Research,* pp. 71–102.

Beaver, W. H., "Alternative Financial Ratios as Predictors of Failure," *The Accounting Review,* January 1968, pp. 71–111.

Blum, M., "Failing Company Discriminant Analysis," *Journal of Accounting Research,* Vol. 12 (Spring 1974), pp. 1–25.

Deakin, E., "A Discriminant Analysis of Predictors of Business Failure," *Journal of Accounting Research,* Spring 1972, pp. 167–179.

Deakin, E., "On the Nature of the Distribution of Financial Accounting Ratios: Some Empirical Evidence," *The Accounting Review,* January 1976, pp. 90–96.

Edmister, R., "An Empirical Test of Financial Ratio Analysis for Small Business Failure Prediction," *Journal of Financial and Quantitative Analysis,* March 1972, pp. 1477–1494.

Eisenbeis, R. A., "Comparison of Linear and Quadratic Classification Procedures with Unequal Sample Dispersions," FDIC Working Paper, No. 71-16, 1971.

Eisenbeis, R. A., and R. B. Avery, *Discriminant Analysis and Classification Procedures: Theory and Practice* (Lexington, Mass.: D. C. Heath), 1972.

Elam, R., "The Effect of Lease Data on the Predictive Ability of Financial Ratios," *The Accounting Review,* January 1975, pp. 25–43.

Lachenbruch, P. A. and M. R. Mickey, "Estimation of Error Rates in Discriminant Analysis," *Technometrics,* February 1968, pp. 1–11.

Libby, Robert, "The Use of Simulated Decision Makers in Information Evaluation," *The Accounting Review,* July 1975, pp. 475–489.

Marks, S., and O. J. Dunn, "Discriminant Functions When Covariance Matrices are Unequal," *Journal of the American Statistical Association,* June 1974, pp. 555–559.

Moody's Industrial Manual, 1972–1974.

Moody's Bank and Finance Manuals, 1972–1974.

Moody's Transportation Manuals, 1972–1974.

Standard and Poor's Corporation Records, 1975.

5.

The Z-Score
Bankruptcy Model:
Past, Present,
and Future

EDWARD I. ALTMAN

The reaction on the part of academicians and practitioners to my initial bankruptcy prediction model (Altman 1968, 1971) has been encouraging, stimulating, and challenging. Over the past 9 years, many readers have commented (not always favorably) on various facets and uses of the model and have made suggestions and inquiries about its extensions. In addition, I have expanded the scope and refined the interpretation of the model to incorporate new statistical developments and to test it on recent bankruptcies. More than anything else, however, I believe that the continued interest in this model and in several others, for example, Edmister (1970), Wilcox (1971, 1974), Deakin (1972, 1976), Blum (1974), and Sinkey (1975), among others, is due to the dramatic increase in recent years in the number of large corporate bankruptcies and in aggregate failure liabilities and in their consequent importance to various sectors of the economy. This is particularly true for the nation's financial institutions which have provided capital for failing enterprises.

The purpose of this paper is to present a retrospective and prospective analysis of the original Z-score model and planned extensions of it for the future. The first sections briefly review the contents and results of the original model to provide a background for those not familiar with it. In addition, the results from two subsequent tests are discussed. Next, the results of some current research are presented, which assess the efficiency of the Z-score model for bankruptcy prediction compared to two other prediction strategies, and also the use of the model to determine the stock market's efficiency with respect to the price behavior of securities that have a ratio profile similar to bankruptcies. In the next section I discuss some present plans for recalibrating and extending the model to consider such factors as a more up-to-date sample of bankruptcies, introducing new variables and/or modifying existing ones to reflect recent changes in reporting standards for financial statements and to incorporate a more efficient structure into the discriminant analysis statistical procedure. The final section presents a summary of conclusions.

THE Z-SCORE MODEL: REVIEW OF PAST RESULTS

The original Z-score model (Altman, 1968) utilizes a profile of five financial ratios within a statistical procedure known as linear discriminant analysis (LDA). This multivariate approach was built upon the foundations laid by traditional financial ratio analysis which is basically a univariate, one-ratio-at-a-time approach to firm analysis. The purpose of the model was to discriminate between a sample of bankrupt *manufacturing* firms and a matched (by industry and asset size) sample of healthy firms. The sample was derived from bankrupts over the period 1946–1965, and the asset size ranged from $1 million to $25 million.[1] A model was developed in which five ratios were combined and objectively weighted so as to achieve maximum classification accuracy for the original two samples. Each firm is assigned a Z-score based on the five measures:

$$Z = 1.2X_1 + 1.4X_2 + 3.3X_3 + .6X_4 + 1.0X_5$$

where Z = overall score[2]
   X_1 = working capital/total assets
   X_2 = retained earnings/total assets
   X_3 = earnings before interest and taxes/total assets
   X_4 = market value of equity and preferred/total liabilities
   X_5 = sales/total assets.

[1] One of the characteristics of the prospective new model is to construct it based on larger firms and to expand the industry coverage to include at least retailers in addition to manufacturers.
[2] Note that the coefficients cited here are not identical to those found in the 1968 article. All we have done is move the decimal point two places to the right for variables X_1 to X_4 to conform with the more typical expression of ratios as decimals rather than absolutes. For example, an X_1 of 42 percent will read .42 and not 42.0 as in the original representation. Ratio X_5 is unchanged.

This Z score is the basis for classification into the bankrupt or nonbankrupt group; firms with scores below 1.81 are classified as bankrupt, and those with scores above 2.99 are classified as healthy. The overlap range (see Figure 1) represents an area where misclassifications are observed. A score of 2.675 was determined as the most efficient cutoff value for bankrupt-nonbankrupt assignment.

The accuracy of the model for the original sample was over 95 percent based on data from one financial statement prior to bankruptcy, with the type I error (that of classifying a firm as healthy when in fact it went bankrupt) approximately 6 percent and the type II error (that of classifying a firm as a bankrupt when it remained healthy) 4 percent. Several validation tests confirmed the accuracy of the model based on one statement prior results. In fact, an independent sample of bankrupts yielded a type I error of 4 percent (24 out of 25 correct). The accuracy of the model deteriorated as the data became more remote from the bankruptcy date, with 72 percent accuracy two statements prior and unimpressive results earlier.

SUBSEQUENT TESTS

One of the important tests of any model is to assess its accuracy for observations made after the parameters have been determined. This not only assesses the practical effectiveness of the results but also the stability and consistency of the model over time. Results from a study by Altman and McGough (1974), based on a sample of 34 bankrupts during the period 1970–1973, showed that the Z-score model classified 28 (82 percent) of the observations correctly when the data were from one statement prior to failure.[3] The type I error for samples of firms taken several years after the model was developed increased but was still impressively low. We discuss the costs of this error type in the next section and compare this model with alternative classification strategies.

One other purpose of this study was to examine accounting auditors' opinions on bankrupt firms just prior to bankruptcy and, surprisingly, we found that in 15 of the 34 cases (44 percent) the auditors expressed a qualified opinion as to the going concern value of the company. This percentage, although much lower than the Z-score model's accuracy, was higher than expected. Auditors are not really in the bankruptcy prediction business, and their questionable "arms-length" profile in certain instances led us to assume that qualified opinions as to going concern problems would not be observed too frequently.

---

[3] In several cases, the last statement was well over 1 year prior to failure. This test utilized the 2.675 cutoff score. A large number (15) of the observations had scores between 1.81 and 2.99.

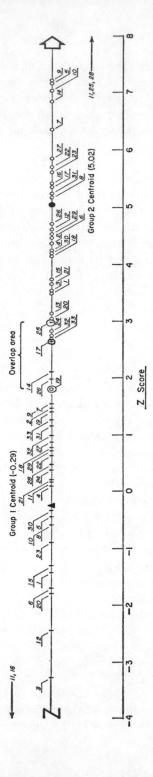

$(Z = .012 X_1 + .014 X_2 + .033 X_3 + .006 X_4 + .999 X_5)$

Z Score

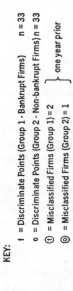

KEY:

†	= Discriminate Points (Group 1 - Bankrupt Firms) n = 33
o	= Discriminate Points (Group 2 - Non-bankrupt Firms) n = 33
①	= Misclassified Firms (Group 1) = 2
⊚	= Misclassified Firms (Group 2) = 1

one year prior

Figure 1 Individual firm discriminant scores and group centroids—1 year prior to bankruptcy $(Z = .012X_1 + .014X_2 + .033X_3 + .006X_4 + .999X_5)$.

92

Another current study (Altman and Brenner, 1976) looks at the type II error more closely. From a sample of approximately 1800 firms listed on Compustat data tapes, all firms whose Z score fell below 2.675 for the years ending 1960–1963 were isolated for subsequent stock market performance analysis. We observe 92 instances where this occurred and, since none of the firms listed by Compustat were bankrupts, each instance is a type II error. The error rate 92/1800 (5.1 percent) is only a crude approximation of the type II error, since it is based on 4 years of observations instead of the traditional individual year assessment; it does not include firms that had Z scores below 2.675 in 1959 and is based on a population of firms that are not representative of all firms, particularly because it does not include smaller publicly held firms. Still, the 5 percent error rate is probably much closer to the true type II error than the 21 percent error rate assumed by Joy and Tollefson (1975) in their discussion on model efficiency (see the section that follows).[4]

TESTS OF MODEL EFFICIENCY

Almost all the prior empirical studies concerning bankruptcy prediction with the use of discriminant analysis reported results in terms of predictive accuracy where the objective was to minimize misclassifications. Little, if any, discussion was devoted to minimization of the *expected total cost* of misclassification, except in a conceptual sense. Works by Eisenbeis and Avery (1972), Eisenbeis (1975), and Joy and Tollefson (1975) have emphasized the conceptual importance of introducing appropriate prior probability of group membership estimates and expected cost estimates of the various types of prediction errors. The last-mentioned study is particularly explicit about the importance of these considerations and provides a helpful framework for evaluating the overall efficiency of various bankruptcy prediction strategies. One of these strategies is the original Altman Z-score model, and we discuss this model's efficiency within the framework specified by Joy and Tollefson.

Joy and Tollefson assert that, where the objective is to minimize the expected total cost of misclassification, a critical Z value should be employed. We have altered their formula to correct ambiguities:

$$Z = \ln \frac{q_1 C_{12}}{q_2 C_{21}}$$

---

[4] Joy and Tollefson (1975) assessed the type II error from classification accuracy results on a sample of nonbankrupt firms that suffered at least 1 year of negative earnings (Altman, 1968, p. 602). The 21% error cannot be used as an unbiased estimate, since obviously the sample was not randomly selected from the population.

where Z = critical or cutoff score

q_1 = prior probability of classifying an observation as bankrupt

q_2 = prior probability of classifying an observation as nonbankrupt

C_{12} = cost of classifying an observation as healthy when it is a bankrupt

C_{21} = cost of classifying an observation as bankrupt when it is healthy

Most prior studies have either assumed that $q_1 = q_2$ or that the two prior probabilities were equal to the observed representation of q_1 and q_2 in the sample of firms used to construct the discriminant model.[5] Altman and Lorris (1976) attempt to assess the exact representation of failed broker-dealer over-the-counter firms as a percentage of the total broker-dealer population in their classification scheme. Usually, exact specification of population prior estimates will be difficult if the underlying population parameters are unknown. Even more difficult is to estimate accurately the costs of the various errors of misclassification.

Since both prior probability and expected error cost estimates are necessary to evaluate unambiguously the efficiency of various models, we now attempt to assess the efficiency of three bankruptcy prediction strategies. Utilizing the Joy and Tollefson conceptual framework and inserting what we believe are more realistic estimates of prior probabilities of group membership, we arrive at an estimate of the ratio of cost criteria C_{12}/C_{21} which can be used to determine which of the various strategies is more efficient.

The three strategies itemized by Joy and Tollefson and also examined here are the Altman LDA model, the proportional chance model, and the maximum chance model. The Altman model is the same as that discussed earlier; the proportional chance model randomly assigns entities to groups with probabilities equal to group frequencies; and the maximum chance model assigns all entities to the group with highest prior probability (obviously the nonbankrupt group in our analysis). The expected cost in a decision-making Bayesian context for each of the three models is:[6]

$$EC_{\text{LDA}} = q_1\left(\frac{n_{12}}{n_1}\right)C_{12} + q_2\left(\frac{n_{21}}{n_2}\right)C_{21}$$

$$EC_{\text{prop}} = q_1 q_2 C_{12} + q_1 q_2 C_{21}$$

$$EC_{\text{max}} = q_1 C_{12}$$

where q_1, q_2, C_{12}, and C_{21} are as before, n_{12}/n_1 = observed percentage of

---

[5] Of course, discriminant analysis is not limited to two groups, and the observed representation of entities in each group will yield G prior probability estimates; for example, Altman and Katz (1976) utilized four different bond quality ratings in a quadratic bond analysis study, and the priors were a function of the samples' frequencies.

[6] Joy and Tollefson (1975, pp. 736–737).

bankrupts misclassified (type I), and n_{21}/n_2 = observed percentage of nonbankrupts misclassified (type II).

The estimate probability that a randomly selected firm will be misclassified by the LDA model as a member of the bankrupt group is $q_2(n_{21}/n_2)$, and as a nonbankrupt is $q_1(n_{12}/n_1)$.

Joy and Tollefson conclude, based on the observed Altman "validation" results, that the LDA model would be superior to the proportional chance model if the type I error were 21.1 times greater than the type II error and that it would be superior to the maximum chance model if the type I error were 21.8 times greater than the type II error.

It is easy to show that, with the inappropriate type II error estimate (see footnote 4), the Joy and Tollefson relative cost ratios of 21.1 and 21.8 times are grossly overstated (see the following section). In addition, we show in a later section just what may be the ratio of error costs C_{12}/C_{21} from the standpoint of one of the most interested potential users of bankruptcy prediction models—the commercial bank loan officer.

MODEL EFFICIENCY COMPARISONS: ESTIMATION PROCEDURE

Assuming the LDA model's type I bankruptcy classification error is identical to the one observed by Altman and utilized by Joy and Tollefson, that is, n_{12}/n_1 = .04, and a type II error n_{21}/n_2 in the .05 to .10 range and q_1 = .01, q_2 = .99[7], we can express the expected cost functions for each of the three alternative prediction strategies in the Bayesian context:

$$EC_{LDA} = .01(.04)C_{12} + .99(.05)C_{21} \text{ or } .99(.10)C_{21}$$

$$EC_{prop} = (.01)(.99)C_{12} + (.01)(.99)C_{21}$$

$$EC_{max} = .01C_{12}$$

Multiplying and solving for the consequent C_{12}/C_{21} ratio now shows that Altman's LDA model will be superior to the proportional chance model if

---

[7] The q_1 = .01, q_2 = .99 estimate is typically used by analysts to express the likelihood of an entity failing and is presumably based on failure rates among American companies in any one calendar year (Dun and Bradstreet's *Failure Record*). There is nothing magical, however, about the calendar year as the basis for failure estimation. Yet we sometimes find that observers, particular academicians, compare bankruptcy prediction models against the so-called no-bankruptcy strategy whereby something like a 1 percent error can be expected if all entities are assumed not to fail. In fact, the optimal cut-off score will change as both the priors and the costs are altered. In our case, the cut-off score falls slightly and there is no change in the observed error.

$C_{12} > 4.2C_{21}$, and superior to the maximum chance (no bankruptcy) model if $C_{12} > 5.2C_{21}$.[8] That is, if the cost of misclassifying a bankrupt is greater than 5.2 times the cost of misclassifying a healthy firm, the LDA bankruptcy prediction model will be superior to either of the other two alternative strategies. We now turn to an estimation of the error costs C_{12} and C_{21}.

ERROR COST ESTIMATION: COMMERCIAL LOAN REFERENCE

It is difficult to estimate precisely the relative cost differential between type I and type II errors, but we are convinced that the type I cost far exceeds the other. For example, a commercial loan officer runs the risk of losing all or a portion of a loan should the applicant default and a portion of the loan is recovered. But the loss commensurate with a loan not being made when it should have been is probably extremely small when measured in terms of opportunity costs. That is, although the interest income (present and future) is forfeited on the particular loan in question, the loan officer is usually able to utilize the funds elsewhere either in a risk-free investment or an alternative loan.

We have attempted to measure the explicit costs involved with type I and type II errors for the commercial loan officer. Aggregate data on commercial loan losses and recoveries are not reported, so we have utilized a sample of individual banks that break down their loan loss experience in sufficient detail. The type I error involves, as noted above, loss of all or part of the loan (should there be recovery). We measure the cost of this error in percentage terms by[9]

$$C_{12} = 1 - \frac{LLR}{GLL}$$

[8] These calculations assume $n_{21}/n_2 = .05$. If a .10 estimate is used, the breakeven points will be 9.37 times and 10.31 times, respectively, for EC_{prop} and $EC_{\max}$. An example of these calculations is:

$$EC_{\mathrm{LDA}} = .01(.04)C_{12} + (.99)(.10)C_{21} = .0004C_{12} + .099C_{21}$$

$$EC_{\mathrm{prop}} = (.01)(.99)C_{12} + (.01)(.99)C_{21} = .0099C_{12} + .0099C_{21}$$

when

$$EC_{\mathrm{LDA}} = EC_{\mathrm{prop}} = .0004C_{12} + .099C_{21} = .0099C_{12} + .0099C_{21} = .0095C_{12} = .0890C_{21},$$

if $C_{21} = 1$, then $C_{12} = 9.37$ times.

[9] We are aware that other costs are involved, including legal, transaction, and loan charge-off officer time opportunity costs. Obviously, the type I error cost will increase if we include these non-reported but potentially important costs.

where LLR = loan loss recoveries

$\quad\quad GLL$ = gross loan losses (charged off loans)

The type II error cost percentage can be measured in terms of opportunity costs by the ratio,

$$C_{21} = r - i$$

where r = effective interest rate on the loan

$\quad\quad i$ = opportunity cost interest rate

We obtained the 1975 annual report of 25 of the nation's largest banks and scrutinized their reported loan loss and loss recovery performance statistics.[10] Only 4 of the 25 banks broke down their loan loss data by commercial and industrial versus all other (primarily consumer) loans. The aggregate loan loss ratio C_{12} for the period 1971–1975 was 83 percent (standard error, $s = 14$ percent) for the 25-bank sample and approximately 90 percent ($s = 5$ percent) for the 4 banks that reported commercial and industrial loans separately. When the loan losses were lagged by 1 year from the loss recoveries, the error cost C_{12} was 84 percent ($s = 16$ percent) for the 25-bank sample and 86.6 percent ($s = 5$ percent) for the 4-bank sample.[11] We conclude, based on our sample of commercial bank statistics, that the average type I error cost is in the 83 to 90 percent range of the loan.

The type II error cost can be conservatively estimated at 5 percent and probably more realistically at approximately 3 percent. The interest rate r on a risky loan is likely to be as much as 3 percent above the prime rate, which would be the differential rate in the numerator of C_{21} if the alternative to making the loan was to make another loan to a prime customer. If the alternative was to invest in a risk-free security of the same maturity, then our opportunity cost differential would be about 5 percent.

Based on the above estimates, we can measure C_{12}/C_{21} as somewhere in the broad range of $83/5 = 16.5$ times to $90/3 = 30$ times. The most likely comparison from the commercial banker's viewpoint is probably closer to 30 times but, whichever estimate is utilized, it will be far greater than the 4.2 to 5.2 times breakeven point estimated in the preceding section. The Altman LDA model is clearly superior to either the proportional chance or maximum chance strategy.

TESTS OF STOCK MARKET EFFICIENCY

Bankruptcy prediction models like the one described earlier seek to analyze publicly available information in order to assess the future solvency of enterprises. When the model first determines that a firm is indeed a potential

---

[10] Only 25 of the largest 40 banks reported the requisite data for making our calculations.

[11] One could argue that recoveries lag loss charge offs, so that to measure the two statistics on a concurrent basis biases the results.

failure, some new information may be provided to the investment community. The theory of efficient markets asserts that any new information available to the marketplace in general is instantaneously and efficiently reflected in the share prices of the relevant companies. If the new, relevant information, in our case the Z score of the firm, is not efficiently digested, then we will observe an ex-post stock market performance that is not expected. Clearly, we can expect, in fact we can observe (Beaver, 1968; Westerfield, 1971), a rather continuous deterioration in share prices among firms that eventually go bankrupt. The average price *decline* among firms that went bankrupt was 45% from the time the Z-score model first predicted failure until 1 month prior to the failure date (Altman, 1971, p. 143). But these firms continued to deteriorate and provided confirming evidence of imminent failure as it approached, and there is no evidence to show that the market was not efficient in its reaction.

If we concentrate instead on a sample of firms for which the Z-score model predicted bankruptcy but in fact the firms all survived (i.e., a sample of type II errors), we can assess if the market's reaction to the new information was efficient or not. In a current study by Altman and Brenner (1976), the ex-post residual behavior of a sample of firms that showed unambiguous signs of future deterioration was examined within the popularly accepted capital asset pricing model framework. If the new pessimistic information is not fully reflected in share prices prior to or on the date of publication of the financial data used to make the bankruptcy prediction, ex-post residual behavior should be significantly negative.

Significant negative residual behavior was found in the period after the information became available, indicating a slow but important market realization.[12] The results from this portfolio of type II errors are also compared directly to a control sample of firms selected in such a manner as to control for systematic (beta) risk. The results also indicate a distinct lag in the significant *negative* performance of stocks identified as potential bankrupts vis-à-vis the control sample.

The same firms noted in the second section as showing signs of failure for the first time at year end 1960, 1961, 1962, and 1963 were isolated for further analysis. That is, firms for which $Z \leq 2.675$ were analyzed, for a 20-month ex-post period after the data became available, within the following three market models,

$$\hat{e}_{jt} = R_{jt} - (\hat{\gamma}_{0t} + \hat{\gamma}_{1t}\hat{\beta}_{jt}) \tag{1}$$

$$\hat{e}_{jt} = R_{jt} - (R_{ft} + (R_{mt} - R_{ft})\hat{\beta}_{jt}) \tag{2}$$

$$\hat{e}_{jt} = R_{jt} - (\hat{\alpha}_j + \hat{\beta}_{jt}R_{mt}) \tag{3}$$

---

[12] These negative results manifest clearly for residuals based on two two-factor market models. Residuals from a third test using the single-factor market model, while mostly negative, are statistically insignificant.

where $\hat{e}_{jt}$ = residual rate of return from the $\gamma_0\gamma_1$ model [Eq. (1)], the capital
           asset pricing model (CAPM)[13] [Eq. (2)], and the single-factor
           market model [(Eq. (3)]
    R_{jt} = rate of return on security j in period t
    β_{jt} = systematic risk of security j in period t
  γ_{0t}, γ_{1t} = market factors which relate R_{jt} to β_{jt}
    R_{ft} = risk-free rate of return in period t
   R_{mt} = rate of return on the market (Fisher arithmetic index) in period t

Since annual report information is not available for several months after the year end, we calculate Z scores and scrutinize subsequent stock price performance starting a full 3 months after the year end. The first residual month therefore is April of the following year; for example, for 1960 data, the first residual month is April 1961, and so on. In order to assess the residual behavior for the bankrupt potential sample utilizing the three models specified above, we calculate the cumulative average residual CAR which is a useful statistic for testing the efficient market hypothesis EMH. The CAR accumulates the average residual over time and is given by

$$\overline{CAR}_T = \sum_{t=1}^{T} \bar{e}_t$$

where $\bar{e}_t = (1/N) \sum_{j=1}^{N} \hat{e}_{jt}$

and $\overline{CAR}_T$ is the average CAR for the entire portfolio of bankrupt potentials over the period $t, \ldots, T$. Our portfolio contains $N = 92$ firms and $t = 1, \ldots,$ 20.

The $\overline{CAR}$ based on the three models for our bankruptcy potential sample is given in Table 1. Also included are statistical significance tests t in parentheses, assessing whether or not the CAR is significantly different from zero.[14]

From Table 1, we observe that for the first two models there is a clear tendency for the CAR to decline in the postprediction period, but this decline does not start until month 5. After month 4, the decline is fairly steady,

---

[13] Equation (1) is probably the currently most accepted empirical specification that is consistent with the conceptual two-parameter CAPM; see Jensen (1972) and Fama and McBeth (1973).

[14] The simple significance test, assuming i.i.d. normally distributed residuals is given by

$$t_T = \frac{\overline{CAR}_T}{\widehat{CSD}_T}$$

where

$$\widehat{CSD}_T = \sqrt{\frac{\sum_{t-1}^{T} \sum_{i=1}^{N} (\hat{e}_{jt} - \bar{e}_t)^2}{n - 1}}$$

Table 1 Cumulative Average Residuals Using the Three Market Models, γ_0, R_f, and α, β

Month	$CAR(\gamma_0)$	$CAR(R_f)$	$CAR(\alpha,\beta)$	Month	$CAR(\gamma_0)$	$CAR(R_f)$	$CAR(\alpha,\beta)$
1	0.018	0.010	0.017	11	−0.153	−0.127	−0.056
	(1.59)	(0.95)	(1.58)		(−3.46)	(−2.99)	(−0.94)
2	0.004	0.001	0.023	12	−0.173	−0.135	−0.057
	(0.61)	(0.72)	(1.60)		(−3.63)	(−2.96)	(−0.81)
3	0.000	0.012	0.032	13	−0.173	−0.133	−0.049
	(0.04)	(0.35)	(1.43)		(−3.62)	(−2.91)	(−0.68)
4	0.001	0.007	0.033	14	−0.207	−0.146	−0.055
	(0.15)	(0.26)	(1.50)		(−4.02)	(−2.96)	(−0.64)
5	−0.065	−0.067	−0.034	15	−0.206	−0.133	−0.035
	(−2.03)	(−2.18)	(−0.78)		(−3.75)	(−2.49)	(−0.10)
6	−0.041	−0.041	−0.041	16	−0.191	−0.129	−0.025
	(−1.48)	(−1.53)	(−0.00)		(−3.40)	(−2.36)	(−0.10)
7	−0.055	−0.060	−0.014	17	−.202	−0.145	−0.035
	(−1.89)	(−2.07)	(−0.42)		(−3.51)	(−2.62)	(−0.07)
8	−0.097	−0.111	−0.058	18	−0.232	−0.156	−0.040
	(−2.90)	(−3.29)	(−1.53)		(−4.00)	(−2.82)	(−0.20)
9	−0.142	−0.145	−0.087	19	−0.228	−0.146	−0.018
	(−3.70)	(−3.84)	(−1.97)		(−3.91)	(−2.55)	(−0.14)
10	−0.111	−0.096	−0.030	20	−0.231	−0.155	−0.026
	(−2.58)	(−2.29)	(−0.33)		(−3.93)	(−2.78)	(−0 03)

[a] t-Value significance tests are given in parentheses.

although the average residuals are positive in several individual months. For the $\gamma_0 \gamma_1$ model, the CAR declines to a negative 23.2 percent by the eighteenth month and a negative 15.6 percent for the R_f model. Both two-factor models show clearly that the residual behavior is significantly negative starting from month 7, certainly by month 8, and continuing for the remainder of the post-bankruptcy prediction period.[15] The results, however, are not significant based on the single-factor market model indicating sensitivity of results to the specific residual model utilized.

Controlling for Systematic Risk

The 92 firm bankruptcy potential (BP) sample was comprised mostly of American Stock Exchange firms, and the prebankruptcy prediction average

---

[15] The results are virtually identical whether we utilize the prebankruptcy prediction beta throughout or one based on a moving average of beta where the last month in the beta estimation period is $T - 1$. The beta estimation period ranged from 24 to 60 months, depending upon data availability.

beta was quite high at 1.47. In order to assess the importance of this portfolio attribute, we selected a control sample (CS) of 276 firms, which was matched as closely as possible to our BP sample by beta. For each of the 92 firms, we selected 3 firms from the Center for Research in Security Prices (CRSP) tapes with similar betas. We then ran the identical residual tests on this control sample over the same time periods. We tested the *differences* in the *CAR*s for the two samples for each of the three market models. These results are illustrated in Table 2.

Note that by month 8 for the two two-factor market models, and month 9 for the single-factor market model, the difference in *CAR*s of the two samples is significant. These significant differences continue for the remainder of the residual period. This is clear evidence that the BP sample performed significantly worse than expected and, even more importantly, did worse than another sample with the same risk properties (Table 2). This conclusion does not change even when we observe residuals using the single-factor market model. The fact that these significant poor performances did not manifest until several months after data were available indicating (by the Z-score model) a potentially deteriorating picture for the firms is important evidence that the market was not efficient in its pricing.

It should be remembered that tests of market efficiency are weak in the sense that we are simultaneously testing for market efficiency and for the validity of the model we are using. If the results are not consistent with market efficiency, we will not be sure whether this observation indicates market inefficiency or whether the model is misspecified.

FUTURE Z-SCORE MODEL: VARIATION ON A THEME

The existing Z-score bankruptcy prediction model has performed well over the decade since its inception. We must recognize, however, that the economic environment has changed and relevant statistical techniques have been refined. Therefore one should consider a new model that takes the following into account:

1. The size of the average business failure has increased substantially, and any model should be constructed from as representative a sample as possible.

2. Refinements of computer software packages have made it possible to test the appropriateness of the typical linear discriminant structure, analyzing data by other structural forms if necessary.

3. New standards and guidelines for financial reporting will no doubt affect most of the popular financial ratios that reflect firm performance.

Table 2 Cumulative Average Residuals (CAR's) and Statistics Testing the Differences between CAR's on Samples of Equal Systematic Risk from Bankrupt Potential (BP) and Control Sample (CS) Firms—Estimates from Three Market Models

	$\gamma_0\gamma_1$ Model			R_f Model			α,β Model		
Month	BP Sample, $N=92$	CS Sample, $N=276$	t Test[a]	BP Sample, $N=92$	CS Sample, $N=276$	t Test[a]	BP Sample, $N=92$	CS Sample, $N=276$	t Test[a]
1	.018 (.032)	.001 (.006)	0.960	.010 (.032)	−.007 (.006)	0.908	.016 (.033)	−.001 (.007)	0.997
2	.004 (.063)	−.013 (.014)	0.693	.001 (.060)	−.009 (.014)	0.748	.023 (.064)	.001 (.015)	0.865
3	−.001 (.072)	−.012 (.017)	0.418	.012 (.069)	−.001 (.018)	0.491	.032 (.074)	.014 (.020)	0.672
4	.001 (.073)	−.007 (.021)	0.313	.007 (.073)	−.002 (.022)	0.355	.033 (.081)	.017 (.025)	0.585
5	−.065 (.088)	−.009 (.028)	−1.888	−.067 (.086)	−.013 (.029)	−1.873	−.035 (.097)	.011 (.032)	−1.473
6	−.041 (.135)	−.016 (0.33)	−0.678	−.041 (.128)	−.017 (.035)	−0.671	−.001 (.144)	.012 (.039)	−0.356
7	−.055 (.153)	−.015 (.040)	−1.015	−.060 (.143)	−.021 (.043)	1.024	−.014 (.162)	.012 (.048)	−0.654
8	−.097 (.155)	−.022 (.045)	−1.944	−.110 (.143)	−.037 (.047)	−1.972	−.058 (.169)	.001 (.051)	−1.465
9	−.142 (.177)	−.029 (.048)	−2.692	−.145 (.169)	−.036 (.050)	−2.682	−.087 (.200)	.007 (.055)	−2.099

10	−.111 (.174)	−.035 (.053)	−1.845	−.096 (.176)	−.024 (.051)	−1.708	−.030 (.221)	.023 (.062)	−1.149
11	−.153 (.191)	−.037 (.068)	−2.711	−.127 (.185)	−.019 (.066)	−2.582	−.056 (.232)	.034 (.081)	−1.896
12	−.173 (.195)	−.039 (.087)	−3.169	−.135 (.182)	−.010 (.079)	−3.042	−.057 (.241)	.046 (.098)	−2.187
13	−.173 (.201)	−.041 (.090)	−3.053	−.133 (.186)	−.010 (.081)	−2.971	−.049 (.259)	.052 (.105)	−2.040
14	−.207 (.230)	−.047 (.107)	−3.472	−.146 (.208)	.005 (.095)	−3.439	−.055 (.297)	.072 (.126)	−2.399
15	−.206 (.243)	−.038 (.115)	−3.554	−.133 (.223)	.026 (.103)	−3.501	−.035 (.318)	.097 (.141)	−2.439
16	−.191 (.267)	−.033 (.118)	−3.183	.129 (.244)	.021 (.106)	−3.155	−.025 (.360)	.097 (.148)	−2.107
17	−.202 (.273)	−.039 (.132)	−3.238	−.145 (.249)	.009 (.119)	−3.231	−.035 (.375)	.089 (.163)	−2.111
18	−.232 (.317)	−.048 (.142)	−3.403	−.156 (.287)	.018 (.127)	−3.377	−.040 (.432)	.103 (.182)	−2.250
19	−.226 (.325)	−.049 (.149)	−3.266	−.140 (.310)	.029 (.134)	−3.143	−.018 (.453)	.118 (.196)	−2.089
20	−.231 (.322)	−.060 (.144)	−3.129	−.155 (.313)	.008 (.132)	−3.007	−.026 (.488)	.102 (.194)	−1.885

[a] $t = \dfrac{CAR_{BP} - CAR_{CS}}{\sqrt{\dfrac{s^2}{N_{BP} - 1} + \dfrac{s^2}{N_{CS} - 1}}}$; variance is given in parentheses.

THE SIZE OF BUSINESS FAILURES

Recall that the original model utilized a sample of bankrupts over the period 1946–1965 with a *maximum* asset size of $25 million. It was extremely rare to find a larger U.S. firm succumbing to economic events, except in the case of fraudulent activities. Since the mid-1960s, and particularly the early 1970s, the number of relatively large firms that have failed in the United States has increased dramatically—even if one adjusts for inflation.[16] Since failure prediction is extremely important for the larger-firm population—witness the over $1 billion W. T. Grant failure in 1975—any new model should be representative of all sizes of firms that may go bankrupt in the future. In anticipation of a new model's development, we have compiled a sample of over 65 industrial firms that filed for bankruptcy in the period 1970–1975 and whose *minimum* asset size was $25 million. In addition to the manufacturing sector, this sample consists of a large number of retail establishments. Any new model(s) should consider including retailers either within a combined industrial model or, if sample size permits, within a separate industrial sector, similar to studies on railroads (Altman, 1973), commercial banks (Sinkey, 1975), and savings and loan associations (Altman, 1976).

DISCRIMINANT MODEL STRUCTURE

Until just recently (1975) every discriminant analysis failure prediction study utilized a linear structure. LDA assumes that the variance-covariance matrices of the G groups are identical and therefore pools all the data to construct the discriminant function. The original Z-score model was no exception. Yet, our subsequent experience has shown that only on rare occasions are the group dispersion matrices identical. Where the dispersions are not equal, a quadratic (QDA) structure is appropriate (Eisenbeis and Avery, 1972). An important advantage of QDA is that it can analyze within-group interaction as well as between-group characteristics.[17] We test for group dispersion similarity in the original two-group bankruptcy samples and, if they are different, observe results using QDA.

[16] In 1964, 1.1% of all firms that failed had short-term liabilities in excess of $1 billion. In 1974, this increased to 4.3% (*Failure Record*, 1974, p. 7.). Dun and Bradstreet statistics do not include long-term debt and certain industrial categories. Aggregate short-term liabilities in 1975 were $4.4 billion, whereas the amount averaged $1.2 billion for the period 1965–1969 and was $2.0 billion in 1972.

[17] The number of observations in *each* group, however, must be greater than the number of variables. The requirement for LDA is only that the *total* number of observations be greater than the number of variables.

Table 3   Linear and Quadratic Classification Results, Original Bankrupt and Nonbankrupt Firms[a,b]

	Predicted	
Actual	Bankrupt	Nonbankrupt
Bankrupt (linear)	31	2
	(94.0%)	(6.0%)
Bankrupt (quadratic)	31	2
	(94.0%)	(6.0%)
Nonbankrupt (linear)	1	32
	(3.0%)	(97.0%)
Nonbankrupt (quadratic)	0	33
	(0.0%)	(100.0%)

[a] Linear results from Altman (1968).
[b] Overall accuracy (linear) = 95.5%; overall accuracy (quadratic) = 97.0%.

In fact, we find that $H_1 = 12.1$ is significant at lower than the .001 level, indicating that the group dispersions are not identical. The classification accuracy for the original samples for LDA and QDA are listed in Table 3. The validation test results for LDA and QDA are listed in Table 4. Note that the accuracy of the two model structures is only slightly different. This is probably

Table 4   Linear and Quadratic Validation Test Results, Holdout Bankrupt and Nonbankrupt Firms

	Predicted	
Actual	Bankrupt	Nonbankrupt
Bankrupt (linear)	24	1
	(96.0%)	(4.0%)
Bankrupt (quadratic)	23	2
	(92.0%)	(8.0%)
Nonbankrupt (linear)	14	52
	(21.2%)	(78.8%)
Nonbankrupt (quadratic)	9	57
	(13.6%)	(86.4%)

[a] Linear results from Altman (1968).
[b] Overall accuracy (linear) = 83.4%; overall accuracy (quadratic) = 88.9%.

due to the fact that the five explanatory variables separated the two groups to such an extent that the statistical structure made little difference. The quadratic model was slightly more accurate in both the classification and validation tests. We find very little group overlap. In studies in which the overlap is substantial, QDA usually results in significantly higher classification accuracy.

The implication of the above is that any new bankruptcy model should involve quadratic as well as linear testing. While the former will no doubt provide more impressive results, the latter structure will be easier to implement and use.

FINANCIAL STATEMENT REPORTING CHANGES AND BANKRUPTCY PREDICTION

Another factor to consider is that in some instances financial statements in the future will look different than in the past, and any new model should attempt to include recent changes in reporting guidelines. Of particular interest to us is the more elaborate and informative reporting of lease capitalization and its consequent effect on financial ratios. Since 1973, certain financial leases have been capitalized in footnote reporting and, where the effect on reported earnings is material, revised earnings are noted. In a very short time, perhaps in 1977 annual reports, all leases that qualify will be capitalized and the firm's assets, liabilities, interest, and earnings will be affected directly on the financial statements.

The implications for bankruptcy prediction models are readily apparent. For one thing, the old Z-score model, if applied in the future, will show lower Z scores for all firms that lease. Lease capitalization will add to the book value of assets and liabilities. Since assets (X_1, X_2, X_3, and X_5) and liabilities (X_4) are in the denominator, all five ratios will deteriorate whenever leases are capitalized. This modification must be duly noted by analysts. In addition, in most cases reported earnings will fall, since the imputed interest plus depreciation of the new assets and liabilities will usually be greater than the lease payments formerly reported.

A relevant question recently asked and analyzed by Elam (1975), concerns the effect of lease data on the predictive ability of financial ratios. Elam used as an example bankruptcy predictability and assessed classification accuracy of discriminant models made up of financial ratios. One set of models used ratios that reflected lease capitalization, while the control models did not. Elam found that bankruptcy prediction accuracy was not significantly better with the capitalized lease data except in one isolated case (Elam, 1975, p. 38).

While Elam's study was interesting, and the lease adjustments carried out with considerable effort and creativity, one must be somewhat skeptical about the results. For one thing, Elam shows that bankrupt firms utilized leases far more than a control sample of healthy firms in the fifth through the third year prior to failure, and only slightly more frequently in the 2 years just prior to failure. Since it is easy to show that ratios deteriorate as capitalized leases increase, we would normally expect that, if the analyst adjusts for lease capitalization, discriminant results will *improve*, vis-à-vis unadjusted data, in those years in which there are substantial differences in lease utilization between the groups. Yet, Elam did not find better results with adjusted data, except in the third year prior to bankruptcy.

At this point, we suspect that lease capitalization will make a difference in a bankruptcy prediction model and intend to adjust recent lease data of our new sample firms carefully.[18]

Other areas of data modification may involve write-offs for intangible assets, unfunded pension liabilities, consolidation of captive finance company and international subsidiary operations, and several others. We do not pursue these details in this paper.

CONCLUDING COMMENTS

The purposes of this paper have been to review the primary characteristics of a bankruptcy prediction Z-score model, to present some recent evidence on the model's predictive efficiency and equity capital market reactions, and finally to speculate on the dimensions of a new model with the same objective. Evidence indicates that the old model has retained its validity and relevance over the last decade and efforts to update the procedure should be pressed.

REFERENCES

Altman, Edward, "Financial Ratios, Discriminant Analysis, and the Prediction of Corporate Bankruptcy," *Journal of Finance,* September 1968.

Altman, Edward, *Corporate Bankruptcy in America* (Lexington, Mass., D. C. Heath), 1971.

Altman, Edward, "Predicting Railroad Bankruptcies in America," *Bell Journal of Economics and Management Science,* Spring 1973.

Altman, Edward, "Predicting Performance in the Savings and Loan Association Industry," Salomon Brothers Center for the Study of Financial Institutions, *Working paper* No. 70, New York University, and *Journal of Monetary Economics,* July 1977.

Altman, Edward and Thomas McGough, "Evaluation of a Company as a Going Concern," *Journal of Accountancy,* December 1974.

Altman, Edward and Steven Katz, "Statistical Bond Rating Classification Using Financial and Accounting Data," M. Schiff and G. Sorter (eds.), in *Relevant Research in Accounting,* (New York: Ross Institute of Accounting Conference), 1976.

---

[18] See Altman, Haldeman and Narayanan, 1977.

Altman, Edward and M. Brenner, "Information Effects and Stock Market Response to Signs of Firm Deterioration," Salomon Brothers Center for the Study of Financial Institutions, Working Paper, No. 75, May 1976.

Altman, Edward And T. Lorris, "A Financial Early Warning System for Over-the-Counter Broker Dealers," *Journal of Finance*, September 1976).

Altman, Edward, Robert Haldeman, and P. Narayanan, "Zeta Analysis: A New Model to Identify Bankruptcy Risk of Corporations", *Journal of Banking & Finance*, June 1977.

Beaver, William, "Market Prices, Financial Ratios and the Prediction of Failure, *Journal of Accounting Research,* Autumn 1968.

Blum, Marc, "Failing Company Discriminant Analysis," *Journal of Accounting Research,* Spring 1974.

Deakin, Edward, "A Discriminant Analysis of Predictors of Failure," *Journal of Accounting Research,* Spring 1972.

Edmister, Robert, "An Empirical Test of Financial Ratio Analysis for Small Business Failure Prediction," *Journal of Financial and Quantitative Analysis,* March 1972.

Eisenbeis, Robert A., "Discriminant Analysis: Application, Potential and Pitfalls, *FDIC Working Paper* No. 75-2, and *Journal of Finance,* in press.

Eisenbeis, Robert and Robert Avery, *Discriminant Analysis and Classification Procedures* (Lexington, Mass.: D. C. Heath, 1972).

Elam, Rick, "Lease Capitalization Data and the Predictability of Ratios," *Accounting Review,* January 1975.

Failure Record Through 1974, Dun and Bradstreet, New York, New York.

Joy, O. M. and J. O. Tollefson, "On the Financial Applications of Discriminant Analysis," *Journal of Financial and Quantitative Analysis,* December 1975.

Sinkey, Joseph, "A Multivariate Statistical Analysis of the Characteristics of Problem Banks," *Journal of Finance,* March, 1975.

Westerfield, Randy, "Assessment of Bankruptcy Risk," Rodney L. White Center for Financial Research, Working Paper No. 71-1, University of Pennsylvania, February 1971.

Wilcox, Jarrod W., "A Gamblers Ruin Prediction of Business Failure," *Sloan Management Review,* Vol. 12, No. 3 (1971).

Wilcox, Jarrod W., "A Prediction of Business Failure Using Accounting Data," *Empirical Research in Accounting: Selected Studies, 1973,* Supplement to Vol. 2, *Journal of Accounting Research* (1974).

Discussion

James D. McWilliams

By considering themselves professionals, money managers and analysts hold themselves out to possess at least the skills of an ordinary person in investing monies and analyzing companies. At times they, and I consider myself in this category as well, have considered themselves nearer akin to gods than mere mortals, but that is probably a human enough failing. Be that as it may, the legal profession and irate clients on occasion bring us back to reality. Reese H. Harris, Jr., retired executive vice-president of Manufacturer's Hanover Trust Company, has some advice for at least those of us who work for trust departments, if not all of us, on this subject:

> There is in all of this a moral for professional investors; be sure to dot all the "i's" and cross all the "t's" as well as trying to behave prudently. If you do, the judges tend to be remarkably lenient; if you don't, they can be rough."

Most brokers, investors, and academicians have concerned themselves with the positive tail of the distribution of stock market returns. As proof, consider that most valuation models concentrate on growth in dividends or growth in earnings. When the growth rate is negative, many models tend to fall apart or go back to notions of book value. When you think about it, book value and liquidating value are really valuation models. Penn Central and W. T. Grant offer us recent object lessons on the shortcoming of just using book value and liquidating values, though, and this brings us to the subject at hand—failure models. The real power and attractiveness of failure models is that they, like betas, combine a lot of sophisticated financial analysis into one number and, on a subject (downside potential) that most people would rather not think about anyway. In short, they may offer us an attractive and easy-to-communicate early warning system.

TRADITIONAL DOWNSIDE PROTECTION

One of the interesting places to look for analytical methods of forecasting disaster is in commercial loan analysis. It, like common stock analysis, in an inexact science at best. Some general characterizations can be made concerning their differences though. Loan analysis is much more balance sheet–oriented and more ratio- and coverage-oriented; cash flow is emphasized; the analysis deals with loan covenants more than with residuals; and finally, growth is less of a fetish.

One thoughtful writer on the analysis of loans by traditional methods is K. D. Martin, Vice-President of the Bank of America in Los Angeles. In an 1973 article,[1] he tabulated 16 red flags to look for in monitoring a commercial loan. This tabulation is arranged in descending order of frequency, the most frequently occurring flags appearing first:

1. Slowness in submitting financial exhibits by the borrower
2. Declining deposit balances, overdrafts, and/or returned checks
3. Failure to perform on other obligations, including personal debt of the principals
4. Inventories become swollen
5. Loan payments become delinquent
6. Slowness in our ability to arrange plant visitations or meetings with principals
7. Borrower becomes a target of legal process or actions
8. Trade payables and/or accruals begin to build
9. Adverse information from competitors and customers
10. Receivables turn with increased slowness
11. Fixed assets increase substantially
12. Expansion occurs through acquisition or merger
13. Debt and debt-worth ratio begin to grow too quickly
14. Operations generate losses
15. Changes in management are evident
16. Lead or agent bank does not keep us fully informed of information necessary in the administration of the credit.

[1] K. D. Martin, "Problem Loan Signals and Follow-Up," *The Journal of Commercial Bank Lending,* September 1973.

Out of the 16 flags that Martin suggests, 8 can be fairly easily programed. There is a variety of problems associated with the approach Martin and the traditional credit analysts would have us use. One is that the tests are not unambiguous. For example, increasing inventories may not be bad if accompanied by increasing sales. Another problem with this approach is that the user has trouble ranking the relative importance of the tests and is not able to summarize them in one or two numbers.

Credit-scoring techniques offer one type of solution to this problem. Some years ago, Robert P. Abate, then Vice-President of the American National Bank and Trust Company of Chicago, suggested 11 criteria for scoring prospective loans.[2] They were:

1. Age of business
2. Years of present management
3. Successive years of increased profits
4. Number of days inventories
5. Number of days receivables
6. Quick ratio
7. Working capital ratio
8. If deficit quick ratio, percent of inventory to cover
9. Debt to net worth
10. Trade reports
11. Type of industry
12. Type and source of audit.

Eight of the first nine of these numbers or ratios are readily programable.

DECIDING WHICH RATIOS OR NUMBERS TO USE

Everyone making credit analyses eventually finds a set of favorite ratios. Using ratios and proving their efficacy are two entirely different matters. William H. Beaver, then an eager young assistant professor of accounting at the University of Chicago, addressed this problem in a 1966 article, "Financial Ratios as Predictors of Failure."[3]

Beaver studied 30 different financial ratios grouped into six categories: cash flow, net income, debt to total asset, liquid asset to total assets, liquid asset to current debt, and turnover ratios. The following list of ratios tested is from his study.

[2] Robert P. Abate, "Numerical Scoring Systems for Commercial Loans," *Banker's Monthly*, January 15, 1969.
[3] William H. Beaver, "Financial Ratios as Predictors of Failure" *Empirical Research in Accounting, Selected Studies*, 1966.

List of Ratios Tested

GROUP I   CASH FLOW RATIOS

1   Cash flow/sales
2   Cash flow/total assets
3   Cash flow/net worth
4   Cash flow/total debt

GROUP II   NET INCOME RATIOS

1   Net income/sales
2   Net income/total assets
3   Net income/net worth
4   Net income/total debt

GROUP III   DEBT/TOTAL ASSET RATIOS

1   Current liabilities/total assets
2   Long-term liabilities/total assets
3   Current plus long-term debt/total assets
4   Current plus long-term plus preferred stock/total assets

GROUP IV   LIQUID ASSET/TOTAL ASSET RATIOS

1   Cash/total assets
2   Quick assets/total assets
3   Current assets/total assets
4   Working capital/total assets

GROUP V   LIQUID ASSET/CURRENT DEBT RATIOS

1   Cash/current liabilities
2   Quick assets/current liabilities
3   Current ratio (current assets/current liabilities)

GROUP VI   (TURNOVER RATIOS)

1   Cash/sales
2   Accounts receivable/sales
3   Inventory/sales
4   Quick assets/sales
5   Current assets/sales
6   Net worth/sales
7   Total assets/sales
8   Cash interval (cash/fund expenditures for operations)
9   Defensive interval (defensive assets/fund expenditures for operations)
10 No-credit interval (defensive assets minus current liabilities/fund expenditures for operations).

Each of these ratios was tested for its predictive value in discriminating between two sets of data—79 companies that failed and 79 companies that did not fail. For comparison purposes each failing company is matched with another for the 5 years prior to the failure of the first company.

The best single predictor was the ratio of cash flow to total debt. Even it was not perfect and misclassified 22 percent of the firms 5 years in advance of failure. At 1 year in advance of failure, this ratio misclassified only 13 percent of the companies.

The other five ratios found to have the greatest predictive value were:

Net income to total assets
Total debt to total assets
Working capital to total assets
Current ratio
No-credit interval.

All these ratios but the last are either familiar or obvious. The no-credit interval ratio is defensive assets, such as cash and accounts receivable, less current liabilities, expressed as a ratio to operating expense less depreciation for the last period. This ratio is in effect the fraction of a year that the company could survive without any credit whatsoever. This measure, along with some related measures, dates back to an article written by Sorter and Benston in the October 1960 issue of *The Accounting Review*.

Beaver's work does not convert easily into a single summary number. It can, however, be converted into a series of letters and pluses and minuses which quickly communicate a company's condition and trend to the reader. The letter is used to represent the level of the ratio and a plus or minus sign to indicate the direction of the trend in the ratio. As an example of how these ratios have been converted into codes or hurdles, consider the ratio of cash flow to total debt. Using *level* as our first criteria, if a company has a ratio higher than 0.35 on average, we could fairly judge it adequate and give it a plus code. Were the ratio below 0.15, on average, it would be inadequate and given a minus code. Between 0.15 and 0.35 no comment would be appropriate. Using *trend* as our second criteria, a company would be awarded a plus if the ratio had increased for 3 or 4 years out of the last 4 years. The company would be given a minus if 3 or 4 years out of the 4 years had been down. For the in-between cases, no comment would be made.

Four of the six criteria from 1966 still seem to be valid. In the case of the working capital to total assets ratio and the current ratio, corporate treasures seem to have become more efficient and level cutoffs have had to be lowered.

The current cutoff points required to earn a plus or a minus are as follows:

	Level Test		Trend Test	
	To earn a +	To earn a −	To earn a +	To earn a −
Cash flow to debt	Above .35	Below .15	Up 3 or 4	Down 3 or 4
Net income to total assets	Above .04	Below .00	Up 3 or 4	Down 3 or 4
Total debt to total assets	Below .40	Above .55	Down 3 or 4	Up 3 or 4
Working capital to Total assets	Above .30	Below .20	Up 3 or 4	Down 3 or 4
Current ratio	Above 2.0	Below 1.5	Up 3 or 4	Down 3 or 4
No credit interval	Above .05	Below .05	Up 3 or 4	Down 3 or 4

In my actual tabulations on companies I have converted the pluses into letters. The good codes for the above six tests are F I D W C N. The "F" stands for cash flow to debt, the "I" for net income to total assets, and so forth. A company operating at a dangerous level would be awarded − − − − − −. Trend is expressed with in-between pluses and minuses. For example, a company with the letters F I D passes the first three level tests. If the trend is bad, it would be F − I − D −; if good, it would be F + I + D +. An endangered company with an improving trend may be − + − + − + − + − +, and so forth.

The obvious incompleteness in Beaver's work was a failure to combine these ratios into one measure that summarizes the score or degree of confidence in this forecast of failure. We examine the work of two people who have attempted to do this: Edward Altman and Jarrod Wilcox.

THE Z SCORE

Altman originally published his work in this field in an article entitled "Financial Ratios, Discriminant Analysis and the Prediction of Corporate Bankruptcy," in the September 1968 *Journal of Finance*. Since then, he has published widely on the subject, including a book *Corporate Bankruptcy in America in 1971*. Most recently, he and Wilcox were quoted extensively in the October 1975 issue of *Dun's Review*.

Without going into methodological details, Altman did his testing on about 22 variables (ratios) classified into five groupings: liquidity, profitability, leverage, solvency, and activity ratios. Five ratios were chosen from the 22, and his final discriminant function was as follows (a description of Altman's model can also be found in a prior paper in this book):

$$Z = .012_x + .014X_2 + .033X_3 + .006X_4 + .999X_5$$

where, X_1 = working capital/total assets
     X_2 = retained earnings/total assets
     X_3 = earnings before interest and taxes/total assets
     X_4 = market value equity/book value of total debt
     X_5 = sales/total assets
     Z = overall index

He concludes that any manufacturing company with a Z score of less than 1.81 is likely to go bankrupt. If the score is 2.675 or higher, it is likely to survive. He defines scores between 1.81 and 2.675 as being in a "zone of ignorance" analytically.

Altman is also careful to point out that the predictive powers of his model fall off sharply more than 2 years ahead of failure.

Others are beginning to pick up on the Z score, partly because it is useful and partly because of the *Dun's Review* article. Stephen Axelrod, Vice-President of Paine, Webber, Jackson, and Curtis prepared the following table on the Xerox Corporation as of November 11, 1975. Note, as he did, Xerox's declining Z score. Xerox is certainly not in danger of going bankrupt, but it is a maturing company. Note also the importance of variable D (X_4 in Altman's notation, or market value equity/book value of total debt).

Xerox Corporation
(million $, except share price)

Year	Working Capital	Retained Earnings	Pretax Income and Interest Changes	Sales	Assets	Debt	Shares Out	Year Price	Year Market Value
1975E	475.0	1,685.0	825.0	4,300.0	$4,500.0	1,700.0	78.9	65	5,128.5
1974	592.9	1,446.6	864.6	3,576.4	4,090.0	1,384.6	78.8	55	4,334.0
1973	437.0	1,195.2	735.8	2,989.7	3,102.1	806.9	78.7	123	9,680.1
1972	407.5	967.6	608.2	2,419.1	2,491.6	585.1	78.5	149	11,696.5
1971	383.9	786.4	507.7	1,961.4	2,156.1	532.6	78.0	125	9,750.0
1970	367.8	636.7	468.9	1,718.6	1,857.3	446.2	77.8	86	6,690.8
1969	257.8	500.0	414.5	1,482.9	$1,531.3	336.6	77.6	106	8,225.6

Year	Z	A	B	C	D	E
1975E	4.0	.13	.52	.60	1.8	.96
1974	4.1	.17	.49	.70	1.9	.87
1973	9.6	.17	.54	.78	7.2	.96
1972	14.5	.20	.54	.80	12.0	.97
1971	13.4	.21	.51	.78	11.0	.91
1970	11.5	.24	.48	.83	9.0	.92
1969	17.2	.20	.46	.89	14.7	.97

THE PROBABILITY OF RUIN

In Beaver's 1966 article, he argued that, if all else is held equal, four propositions can be stated:

1. The larger the reservoir (of money or assets), the smaller the probability of failure.
2. The larger the net liquid asset flow from operations (i.e., cash flow), the smaller the probability of failure.
3. The larger the amount of debt held, the greater the probability of failure.
4. The larger the fund expenditures for operations, the greater the probability of failure.

Wilcox noted the similarities of these propositions to the classical gambler's ruin problem. He combined this notion with an attempt to describe, in a theoretical sense, Beaver's work in an article entitled "A Simple Theory of Financial Ratios as Predictors of Failure" which was published in the Autumn 1971 issue of *Journal of Accounting Research*.

In that article he defined what he thought would be an adequate discriminator for finding very high-risk companies. Mathematically, it was

$$\left(\frac{1-X}{1+X}\right)^{Y} \qquad \text{where } X < 1, XY < 1$$

and where

$$X = \frac{\left(\begin{array}{c}\text{average net}\\ \text{income}\end{array}\right)\left(1 - \dfrac{\text{dividend}}{\text{payout ratio}}\right)\left(\begin{array}{c}\text{average proportion of net cash}\\ 1 - \text{flow less dividends reinvested}\\ \text{in illiquid assets}\end{array}\right)}{\substack{\text{standard deviation of (net cash flow less capital expenditures for illiquid}\\ \text{assets and less dividends)}}}$$

and

$$Y = \frac{\overline{\lambda_1}\,\overline{(\text{assets})} - \overline{\lambda_2}\,\overline{(\text{liabilities})}}{\substack{\text{standard deviation of net cash flow}\\ \text{less capital expenditures for illiquid}\\ \text{assets and less dividends.}}}$$

This equation has the property that the value of $(1 - X)/(1 + X)$ will be negative for a "good" company, so no measure of "goodness" is possible with this procedure. What is generated, though, is the probability of ruin for a marginal company. It normally varies between .00 and 1.00 and can be thought of as being somewhat like the weather forecast for the probability of rain.

Whi (this is an analogy that people can readily grasp, in practice the results are more of a switch like "rain" or "no rain," at least when working with companies that most of us have heard of.

PREDICTING FAILURE WITH IMPERFECT TOOLS

Part of my duties at the Continental Bank is to manage an indexed equity portfolio for one of the bank's important customers. In managing the fund, one of the problems is to avoid investing in securities that may go bankrupt. This is where Beaver, Altman, and Wilcox go to work.

Two fundamental rules of thumb in model building are to avoid intercorrelated variables and to add information where possible. It is really not necessary to have all the data on a company summarized in one number—what is needed is a predictive system that does not fail. Companies change their stripes very slowly. An examination of several companies may be useful. In all the Z-score and probability of failure computations 1 year's rentals have been added to the fixed assets. This has the effect of lowering the Z score and increasing the probability of ultimate failure for companies such as retailers that make extensive use of rental facilities. I have coined names in the examples, but the data are for actual companies listed on the New York Stock Exchange.

Cycleco—Manufacturer of a Cyclical Product:

Year Ending	Beaver Codes						Z Score	Probability of Ultimate Failure	Stock Price	Earnings per Share
	F	I	D	W	C	N				
1965	–	–	–	–	– W	C N		0.494	N.C.	10.12	
1966	–	–		–	W	C N		1.550	1.0000	6.87	0.17
1967	–	–		–	W	C N		1.708	1.0000	16.87	0.36
1968	–	–		–	W	C N		1.933	1.0000	18.25	0.68
1969	– +	–	+	–	+ W	C N		2.364	0.0485	17.75	0.78
1970	– +		+	–	+ W	C N		2.364	0.0001	18.75	0.99
1971	– +		+	–	+ W	C N		2.646	0.0000	37.12	1.37
1972	+	I	+		+ W	– C N		2.924	not calculated	37.25	1.86
1973		I			W	C N		2.800	0.0000	14.50	2.26
1974		I			W	C N		2.538	0.0001	9.00	2.06
1975		I			W	C N		2.512	0.0000	11.00	0.97

CYCLECO has traditionally managed its finances so that three ratios, W, C, and N (working capital to total assets, current ratio, and no-credit interval) remain intact. These may be fingerprints of the corporate finance officer. The improving trend in 1969 is particularly obvious in this company, and the company seems to be going along satisfactorily.

BRANCO—Brand Name Manufacturer:

Year Ending	Beaver Codes						Z Score	Probability of Ultimate Failure	Stock Price	Earnings Per Share
	F	I	D	W	C	N				
1965	F +	I	D +				2.547	N.A.	53.38	
1966	F	I	D +				2.347	Nom.	30.75	4.16
1967	F	I	D	−			2.110	Nom.	56.25	4.35
1968	F	I	D	−	−	−	2.388	1.00	56.00	6.23
1969	F	I	D	−	−	−	2.185	Nom.	34.38	2.09
1970	F		D	−	−	−	2.017	Nom.	28.00	(0.16)
1971			D	−	−	−	2.321	Nom.	28.63	1.67
1972			D	−	−	−	2.668	Nom.	41.00	4.27
1973			D	− +	− +	−	2.822	.008	15.65	4.80
1974			D	−	−	−	2.166	1.000	7.25	(0.92)
1975			D	−	−	−	2.299	1.000	10.13	(4.71)

N.A., Data not available: nom., very small.

BRANCO presents a problem to the financial analyst and the failure model builder. Only once (1973) in the period shown has the company been out of Altman's "zone of ignorance" on the upside. Of the Beaver codes, only one ratio (total debt to total assets) survives intact over this period, and even Wilcox's probability of ultimate failure is forecasting its demise. Without doubt, BRANCO's management deserves some sort of pat on the back for hanging in there all these years against very high odds. Will they make it? Yes, at least through this up cycle.

TRANCO—Transportation Company:

Year Ending	Beaver Codes						Z Score	Probability of Ultimate Failure	Stock Price	Earnings per Share
	F	I	D	W	C	N				
1965		I	−		−	−	1.591	N.A.	25.56	1.64
1966		I	−	+	−	−	1.688	1.00	27.38	2.31
1967		I	−		−	−	1.466	1.00	23.88	1.84
1968		I	−		−	−	1.336	1.00	29.25	1.46
1969	−		−		−	−	.984	1.00	11.63	(0.77)
1970	−	−	−	−	−	−	.852	1.00	12.13	(1.38)
1971	−	−	−		−	−	.856	1.00	15.25	(1.19)
1972	−	−	−		−	−	.960	1.00	9.00	(0.70)
1973	−	−	−		−	−	1.063	1.00	4.13	(0.45)
1974	−	−	−		−	−	.818	1.00	2.00	(2.09)
1975									5.25	(1.11)

TRANCO illustrates the need for specialized models for regulated and quasi-regulated industries. Existing models do not adequately allow for the degree of leverage that companies in this position can use and still survive. Even though absolute judgments may not be possible, the trend of the data on this company is not good.

HEAVYCO—Specialized Heavy Goods Manufacturer:

Year Ending	Beaver Codes F	I	D	W	C	N	Z Score	Probability of Ultimate Failure	Stock Price	Earnings per Share
1965						−	3.377	N.A.	56.75	
1966		I				−	3.593	0.0	48.12	5.16
1967		I				−	3.006	0.0	66.25	4.91
1968		I		−	−	−	3.477	0.0	46.12	2.83
1969		I	D	−	−	−	2.903	0.0	27.75	0.24
1970		−	D	−	−	−	2.566	0.7104	19.12	(0.62)
1971			D	−	−	−	2.251	0.0002	21.75	1.96
1972	−			−	−	−	2.342	0.0006	25.37	2.47
1973				−	−	−	2.640	0.005	20.00	3.84
1974		+		−	−	−	2.591	0.0097	19.25	4.88
1975		+	D	+	−	−	2.696	0.0079	37.62	7.62

Since Interactive Data does not keep information on companies that have gone over the edge, we are forced to look at companies that either are or were in trouble. This example represents a company that had severe problems in the 1969–1970 period and has since had a sharp rebound. The steady deterioration in Beaver codes gave a 1-year faster tip-off of trouble than did the Z score or the probability of ultimate failure number. The failure measure gave the fastest message that everything was once again alright.

TECHCO—High Technology Manufacturer:

Year Ending	Beaver Codes F	I	D	W	C	N	Z Score	Probability of Ultimate Failure	Stock Price	Earnings per Share
1965	F	I	D	W	C	N	2.328	0.0000	10.75	
1966	F −	I −	D	W −	C −	N −	1.689	0.0000	5.50	(0.25)
1967	F	I	D	W	C	N	2.842	0.0000	15.00	0.15
1968	F	I	D	W	C	N	3.271	0.0000	17.25	0.36
1969	F	I	D	W	C	N	3.636	0.0000	12.62	0.46
1970	F	I	D	W	C	N	3.441	0.0000	10.62	0.57
1971	F	I	D	W −	C −	N −	3.130	0.0000	10.62	0.64
1972	F	I	D	W	C	N	2.881	0.0002	6.25	0.35
1973	F	I	D	W	C	N	2.216	1.0000	1.62	(0.55)
1974	−	−	D −	W	C		1.166	1.0000	0.62	(1.38)
1975	−	−	−		C		2.276	1.0000	2.00	0.03

This company helps us to make at least two points. First, the Beaver codes sometimes do not flash early warnings; in 1966 and 1973, the company ran into heavy sailing, but the Beaver codes did not give any warning in the prior year. The Z score did somewhat better, but it may have been unduly influenced by the stock price action. The second point is that price action seems to have clearly led the corporate accounting reports, so there seems to be a place for good, traditional analytical methods of following companies too.

DIRECTIONS FOR FURTHER RESEARCH

Perhaps noting that there seems to be a place for traditional methods of analysis is a good place to end. But I should add that it seems easier to pin the tail on a company that may go down a lot than to identify a situation that might go up in price by 20 percent over the next year or so. It also does not make much sense to keep this work secret either. If this type of analysis were practiced more widely, two results would happen that are beneficial: (1) shares would be more efficiently priced, which is good for the index fund manager, and (2) companies could perhaps recognize a bad trend in time and reverse it, thereby helping society avoid the human pain and suffering that go along with bankruptcies.

This seems to be a rich vein for research funds. Wilcox has recommended that research be done on the three components of variance of net cash flows: (1) the variance of cash inflows, (2) the variance of cash outflows, and (3) especially the covariances of inflows and outflows. Beaver correctly points out that he did not deal with leases. More work needs to be done on different subsegments of the populations of companies. Altman did this with his railroad study—what about other regulated and semiregulated industries like utilities and banks? Inflation accounting, or more precisely the lack of it, introduces problems in analyzing companies, as do changes in tax-accounting practices. A computer-readable data base on bankrupt firms could be a gold mine to a university, yet Compusat and Interactive Data drop the companies as soon as they go under. Perhaps they could be persuaded to change their ways. In short, this is a "hot area" for research.

Marc P. Blum

The role in the law for models of business failure is budding. There is a potential for the development of such a role in regard to:

1. Aid in the making of a decision
2. Determination of whether a past decision process was reasonable.

After these roles have been discussed, the nature of models of business failure is briefly analyzed in order to discern their potential utility in a legal context.

AID IN MAKING DECISIONS

Models of business failure can be helpful in deciding whether a business firm is sufficiently weak economically that it should be allowed to complete a business combination otherwise offensive to antitrust laws or to laws governing regulated industries. This determination is usually made in accordance with the rationale of "the failing company doctrine," although upon occasion the doctrine is not involved by name. The failing company doctrine provides that two companies can complete an otherwise illegal business combination if, but for the business combination, one of the two companies would fail and there is no other good-faith "purchaser" for the failing company.[1] The failing company doctrine is one of the few affirmative defenses in an antitrust prosecution.

There are two distinguishable settings in which a model of business failure may aid a decision: regulated industry decisions made by the administrative agency concerned, for example, the Civil Aeronautics Board, and decisions made usually in regard to nonregulated industries by the governmental arms charged specifically with policing antitrust laws, the Antitrust Division of the Justice Department and the Federal Trade Commission. For simplicity, the former setting is referred to as regulatory and the latter as prosecutorial.

An understanding of the principal distinction between the regulatory and prosecutorial decision settings is a good clue to how a model of business failure can fit into a legal (or other) decision process. A regulatory agency is usually charged with the dual responsibility of ensuring adequate service to the public by the regulated industry, within the framework of not contributing unduly to monopolistic conditions, while a prosecutorial agency is usually concerned only with minimizing antitrust violations. As a result the decision process of a regulatory agency is likely to consider the penalty for having wrongly predicted a failed firm not to fail higher than a prosecutorial agency would. In other words, a regulatory agency is likelier than a prosecutorial agency to approve a merger that may better serve the public in the near term than failure of one of the merging parties.

Conversely, a regulatory agency is likely to consider the penalty for having wrongly predicted a nonfailed firm to fail lower than a prosecutorial agency would. In other words, a regulatory agency is likelier than a prosecutorial agency to approve a possibly unnecessary merger because the public would still be served by the combined resources of both merging parties.

A Supreme Court decision has recognized this distinction. In *United States* v. *Philadelphia National Bank*,[2] the Supreme Court indicated that the failing company doctrine would have a wider ambit when applied to possibly failing banks than it would in general commercial and industrial situations. This distinction has also been recognized by Congress in its passing of legislation to protect mergers of financially weak newpapers from antitrust prosecution.[3]

A reasonable decision can be reached only by considering both the probability of business failure, the assessment of which can be aided by a model of business failure, and the relative penalties for erroneous predictions, that is, for erroneously predicting that a failing firm will not fail and for erroneously predicting that a nonfailing firm will fail.

Regulatory Applications

A frequent example in the regulatory area is the allowance of mergers of weak banks with stronger banks, under the auspices of the Federal Reserve Board (for bank holding companies) or the Comptroller of the Currency (for national banks). In March 1976, the Federal Reserve Board reversed its ruling of November 10, 1975, and allowed Citicorp to acquire West Coast Credit Corporation, for the reason that the Seattle-based consumer finance company's economic situation had deteriorated to "at best a tenuous ability to survive."[4] Similarly, also in March, the Comptroller of the Currency approved the combination of the Continental Bank of Burien, Washington ($18 million in deposits) with the Puget Sound National Bank of Tacoma ($346 million in deposits and sixth largest in Washington State), and the Federal Reserve Board approved acquisition of the Security State Bank of Pompano Beach, Florida (deposits of $4,500,000), by the Landmark Banking Corporation of Ft. Lauderdale ($707,500,000 deposits and eighth largest in Florida).[5]

A nonbanking example is the Civil Aeronautics Board's allowance of United Air Lines, Inc.'s merger with Capital Airlines, Inc. in 1960.[6]

Prosecutorial Applications

Models of business failure can also be of direct aid in the prosecutorial decision process. For example, models can be consulted to determine whether an antitrust prosecution should be filed or whether a letter of clearance should be granted authorizing a business combination.

For instance, the preliminary results of a model of business failure were available to certain officials of the Justice Department during the making of its initial, and still outstanding, decision not to oppose the merger of White Motor and White Consolidated. This decision has recently become more famous, because on May 3, 1976, by a split board decision, the directors of White Consolidated decided not to go through with the acquisition, citing as one reason that the Justice Department had made "renewed inquiries" about the proposed transaction.[7]

Models could also be used during litigation but, until recently to my knowledge, they were not. Nevertheless, certain judicial opinions have taken into consideration data similar to those used in modern models of business failure. Courts have reviewed trends in financial ratios, for example. The Federal Trade Commission did so in 1960 in regard to Pillsbury Mills' proposed acquisition of the Ballard and Ballard Company,[8] and so did the Supreme Court in 1930 in regard to International Shoe's acquisition of the McElwain Company.[9] Such review is literally nonprobative if conducted outside the framework of a modeling process. It is not persuasive to look at the decline in a particular ratio, or lack thereof, to determine a failing condition. What must be analyzed is the performance of a particular firm's ratio in reference to the performance of that ratio for failing and nonfailing companies in the past. Then it must be determined whether the particular firm's ratio is more like that of companies that have failed than it is like that of companies that have not failed.

On May 20, 1976 a model of business failure was for the first time introduced in court. The case was *United States* v. *Black and Decker;* and the occasion was Black and Decker's invocation of the failing company doctrine to excuse its allegedly anticompetitive purchase, as a potential entrant into the gasoline-powered chain saw market, of McCulloch Corporation.

DETERMINING THE REASONABLENESS OF PAST DECISIONS

Models of business failure can also be used as a standard for assessing the reasonableness of past investment or credit extension decisions. There are two ways in which a model can be so used.

Assessing the Reasonableness of the Decision Itself

First, a model's prediction may be referred to by a court or administrative body as an aid in assessing the reasonableness of a past decision. However, a court typically brings to bear on such a decision many facts beyond those that a model of business failure takes into account. Also, if the model is based upon annual financial statements, the court may have access to more timely information from interim financial reports. Therefore, while it is possible that a court may look at a model in such a situation, it is not altogether likely to rely upon such a model.

Assessing the Reasonableness of the Decision Procedure

However, there is a second way in which a model of business failure can play a part in a court's assessment. A complainant may raise the question as to whether or not an investor or creditor's decision was reasonable since it was not made with regard to the prediction of a particular, well-known model of business failure. Thus the question presented is whether or not as a matter of prudent procedure the lender or investor used a sound model as a screening device. Of course, such lenders or investors could contend that they are in a situation analogous to that of the court discussed above, and that they customarily review many more factors than those upon which models are based. However, if it is the case that a particular investment was in a company predicted by a model to fail, and the investor or creditor gave that investment no unusual attention, it would be exposed to easy, later criticism that a particular investment that should have been flagged for special attention was not flagged. Here, all that is required to make the use of models of business failure widespread is the success of one such complainant in a court suit.

Legal contexts in which a model of business failure would be relevant to assessing the reasonableness of a past decision procedure are:

1. Trust and investment funds. Following the ancient trust rule that a trustee must be prudent with regard to each decision, trustees cannot afford to rely upon their overall investment performance. This is the lesson of *Bank of New York* v. *Spitzer*,[10] a recent case in which a trustee was held possibly liable for the consequences of four bad investments, in securities listed on the New York Stock Exchange, despite the fact that the fund as a whole had a reasonable performance. (On appeal the trustee, while possibly liable, was found in fact not to have made any unreasonable investment. It is also interesting to note that this case occurred in reference to a rising stock market.)

2. Banks and other financial institutitons. Here it should be noted that certain banks are now using models of business failure as a screening device as part of the loan decision (and investment fund management) process. Such banks are presumably protected already, provided that the models are sound and are reasonably applied,[11] for example, Jim McWilliams, of Continental Illinois, is in good legal shape.[12]

3. Securities industry. Professionals, such as investment bankers, lawyers, and accountants, are ever anxious to avoid risks and will be especially zealous converts to the use of models of business failure if one of them is involved in a lawsuit alleging, *inter alia,* that failure to consult a model was negligent. Models could be consulted by such professionals not only upon public issuance of securities, but also during compilation of annual financial statements, for example, public accountants could consult such models before deciding upon

going concern qualifications, as Altman has pointed out in the *Journal of Accountancy*.[13]

4.   The pension fund area should be treated separately, and not as a subset of trust or investment funds, because of the impact of the Employee Retirement Income Security Act of 1974 (ERISA).[14] ERISA has brought more persons within the definition of fiduciary, and more decisions within the rubric of investment decisions. Also, ERISA has established broad standards of cofiduciary liability and high standards of conduct, measuring investment decisions by the standard of a prudent qualified investor and not simply by the standard of a reasonable person who may not be an investment specialist. Furthermore, by mandating extensive disclosure of both investment performance and fiduciary liability to all of a plan's participants and beneficiaries, ERISA has enhanced the opportunity for a disgruntled individual to file suit.

Defensive Tactic: Routinize Use of Models

A reasonable solution for business concerned in this regard is to use models as screening devices. The success of this preventive measure depends upon the soundness of the model and the precision of its application, for example, to data similar to those upon which the model was built.

While the routine use of a model may provide persuasive evidence of the prudence of an investment or credit extension decision procedure, the model's probabilistic character must not be lost sight of. The model will flag the need for special documentation in some, but not all, doubtful cases.

THE NATURE OF MODELS

The question may be asked whether probabilistic creatures, such as models of business failure, can have proper roles in the eyes of the law. Resolution of this question requires a brief analysis of the nature of models.

Models are reasonable representations of reality, which are handier to work with than reality itself. A model of business failure is, to the extent that it relies upon accounting and other financial data, a model of symptoms of failure, not real-world causes of failure. There is no connection between cause and effect. Rather, there is a correlation, or association, between past data patterns for companies that failed and companies that did not fail, and this association is only as good as (1) the theoretical underpinning of the model, (2) the validity of the statistical test of the model, and (3) the reasonableness of extrapolation to the future from the past time period upon which the model is grounded.[15]

The necessity for an adequate validation procedure must be emphasized, particularly with reference to the use of powerful statistical techniques such as

discriminant analysis. An adequate validation procedure requires application of
the supposed model of business failure to completely fresh data, from which the
model was not derived, which is called the validation sample. The accuracy of
the model based on the validation sample represents a reasonable basis for
extrapolation to the future, given that the future is not expected to be
reasonably different from the past period tested. The accuracy of the model
computed with regard to the primary sample, which is the sample used to estimate the model parameters in the first place, is not a reasonable basis for
extrapolation. For instance, if the predictive accuracy of the primary sample is
98 percent and that of the validation sample is 75 percent, only the 75 percent
figure serves as a valid basis for extrapolation.

Once validated, it is necessary to fit a model of business failure into a decision procedure. A mere specification of the probability of failure of a business,
such as 95 percent, is insufficient for the making of a decision. The probability
of failure, whether 95 percent, higher, or lower, must be sufficiently grave and
imminent as to allow invocation of the failing company doctrine. The questions
of graveness and imminence can only be resolved by consideration of the relative penalties for erroneous decisions, as pointed out above in the discussion of
the regulatory and prosecutorial applications of models.[16]

With these qualifications in mind, the process of applying models of business
failure to a legal context is reasonable. What may seem tentative and uncertain
in such an application is not at all a defect in reasoning. Rather, it is merely
what seems tentative and uncertain when any entire decision procedure, including one not incorporating quantitative analysis, is made explicit.

CONCLUSION

In conclusion, there is a reasonable potential for future use of models of business failure in certain limited legal decision-making areas, such as the failing
company doctrine, and in regard to certain procedurally defensive applications,
in order to protect investment managers, lenders, and their professional
advisors from easy, later criticism that the results of a well-known model of
business failure were not flagged for proper attention. This defensive usage,
which is not yet prevalent, may become so quickly, if one lucky stockholder's
lawyer-brother wins a shareholder derivative suit in which inattention to such a
model is alleged.

To venture a prediction, resort to models of business failure as one element
in legal decision processes is likely to increase in frequency and sophistication.
This will be particularly likely if the proper use of models of business failure is
highlighted in the court's ultimate opinion in *United States* v. *Black and
Decker*. For instance, it may even be possible one day for the Antitrust Division

and the Federal Trade Commission to incorporate a model of business failure and a probabilistic decision rule into administrative determinations such as issuing letters of clearance for proposed business combinations.

The important questions facing real-world decision makers in this area are:

1. How does one select a particular model of business failure for a legal (or other) application? One interesting academic aspect of this question is: Can it be demonstrated that a multivariate model of business failure is better than a univariate approach?

2. How does one show that a model established several years ago, or even recently, is validly applicable to the legal (or other) decision at hand?

3. Is the expected accuracy of a model of commercial and industrial business failure in excess of some intuitively specified level, such as 95 percent, believable?

These problems are not peculiar to the legal context and must be addressed generally in any decision situation. This entails a critique of the relative merits of various models, which is beyond the scope of this article.

NOTES AND REFERENCES

1. *International Shoe Co.* v. *F.T.C.*, 280 U.S. 291 (1930), Marc Blum, "The Failing Company Doctrine", 16 Boston College Industrial and Commercial Law Review. Vol. 16, (1974), 75, 81.

2. 374 U.S. 321, 372 footnote 46 (1963).

3. Newspaper Preservation Act, 15 U.S.C. §§ 1801–04 (1970).

4. *Wall Street Journal,* March 23, 1976, p. 4.

5. *Wall Street Journal,* March 23, 1976, p. 30.

6. *Northwest Airlines, Inc.* v. *C.A.B.*, 303 F.2d 395, 402 (D.C. Cir. 1962).

7. *Wall Street Journal,* May 4, 1976, p. 6.

8. *Pillsbury Mills, Inc.*, 57 F.T.C. 1274, 1409 (1960).

9. Blum, *op. cit.*, note 1.

10. "The fact that this portfolio showed substantial overall increase in total value during the accounting period does not insulate the trustee from responsibility for imprudence with respect to individual investments for which it would otherwise be surcharged . . . To hold to the contrary would in effect be to assure fiduciary immunity in an advancing market such as marked the history of the accounting period here involved. The record of any individual investment is not to be viewed exclusively, of course, as though it were in its own water-tight compartment, since to some extent individual investment decisions may properly be affected by considerations of the performance of the fund as an entity, as in the instance, for example, of individual security decisions based in part on considerations of diversification of the fund or of capital transactions to achieve sound tax planning for the fund as a whole. The focus of inquiry, however, is nonetheless on the individual security as such and factors relating to the

entire portfolio are to be weighed only along with others in reviewing the prudence of the particular investment decisions." 35 N.Y. 2d 512, 517, 364 N.Y.S. 2d 164, 168, 323 N.E. 2d 700 (1974), followed in *In Re Will of Jacob W. Bayliss,* 80 Misc. 2d 491, 493, 363, N.Y.S. 2d 285 (1975) (". . . satisfactory results produced by proper investments do not serve to absolve trustees of any liability for investments that are invalidly made and result in a loss.").

11. Certain banks are already using Edward I. Altman's model; see "Corporate Bankruptcy Prediction and its Implication for Commercial Loan Evaluation," *The Journal of Commercial Bank Lending,* [1970], 12.

12. James D. McWilliams, "Failure Models and Investment Management," paper delivered on May 20, 1976 at the Salomon Brothers. Center Conference on Financial Crisis.

13. Edward I. Altman and Thomas McGough, "Evaluation of a company as a Going Concern," *Journal of Accounting* December 1974.

14. Public Law 93-406, Sept. 2, 1974, 88 Stat. 829; especially ERISA §§ 14, 404, and 405.

15. See generally, Marc Blum, "Failing Company Discriminant Analysis", *Journal of Accounting Research,* Vol. 12, No. 1 (Spring 1974), 1. Included among the extrapolation problems is one particularly important in the legal context, and unimportant, hence usually overlooked, in the commercial loan setting. In the law, type II error (wrongly predicting a nonfailing firm to fail) is sometimes more important to avoid than type I error (wrongly predicting a failing firm not to fail); type I error is far more important to avoid in the commercial loan setting, and type II error is of little concern there. See Blum, *op. cit.,* note 1, pp. 109–111. The extrapolation problem concerns type II error and arises when a model of business failure is based upon a paired sample design with frequency of failed and nonfailed firms different from their populations in a particular decision situation. For example, Altman (*op. cit.* notes 11 and 13), Deakin, ["A Discriminant Analysis of Predictors of Business Failure," *Journal of Accounting Research,* Vol. 10 (Spring 1972), pp. 167–179), Blum, and Beaver (citations in this note) studied paired samples, whereas the real world is often assumed to have on the order of 100 nonfailed for every failed firm; see Altman, "The Z-Score Bankruptcy Model: Past, Present and Future," p. 10, footnote 7, paper delivered at the Salomon Brothers Center Conference on Financial Crises (May 20, 1976). Generalization about the expected error of the prediction "failure" from such a model, simply from the expected type II error, is not reasonable; see, for example, O. Maurice Joy and John O. Tollefson, "On the Financial Implications of Discriminant Analysis," *Journal of Financial and Quantitative Analysis,* December 1975, pp. 723, 733, footnote 9. For example, if a split sample of 100 firms each has an expected type II error of 5 percent, the expected error of the prediction "failure" is 5 percent also. However, if the nonfailed firms in a real-world decision situation number 10,000 and the failed firms number 100, the expected type II error remains 5 percent, but the expected error in the prediction "failure" increases from 5 to 84 percent (95 of the 100 failed firms and 5 percent, that is, 500, of the nonfailed firms will be predicted to fail; the expected error of the prediction "failure" is then 500 erroneous predictions divided by 595 total predictions of failure, or 84 percent). This point was acknowledged by William H. Beaver in his article, "Financial Ratios as Predictors of Failure," *Empirical Research in Accounting: Selected Studies,* 1966, Supplement to *Journal of Accounting Research,* Vol. 4 (1966), 71, 99 footnote 39, and in his "Reply to Professor Neter," following the article, p. 123; John Neter had raised this point in his "Discussion of Financial Ratios as Predictors of Failure," appearing after Beaver's article, pp. 112, 115–117. This point has also been noted by Altman, "The Z-Score Bankruptcy Model", p. 7, footnote 5, and Edward B. Deakin, "Business Failure Prediction: An Empirical Analysis", Working Paper 76–13, Bureau of Business Research, University of Texas, November 1975, pp. 2–5 (also published in this volume).

16. Decision rules derived from Bayesian probability theory are discussed in Blum, *op. cit.,* note 1, pp. 109–113; William H. Beaver, "Financial Ratios as Predictors of Failure", *Empirical Research in Accounting: Selected Studies,* 1966, Supplement to *Journal of Accounting Research,* Vol. 4 (1966), 71, 95–98, and in Neter's comment, pp. 116–117; Henry A. Kennedy, "A Behavioral Study of the Usefulness of Four Financial Ratios", *Journal of Accounting Research,* Vol. 13, No. 1 (Spring 1975), 97.

PART TWO

The Fragile Financial Environment and Endangered Financial Markets

The American Financial Environment— Fragile or Resilient?

ARNOLD W. SAMETZ

Minsky, author of the first paper in this group, has written early and often on the subject of financial crisis and has developed a model of crisis development and resolution.[1] And most important for our purposes, the differing viewpoints of the other papers—more financial market-oriented than macroeconomic—are clarified and deepened on initial reading by comparison with Minsky's views. However, the articles by Kaufman, by Wallich, and by Wright have differences among them which are just as important distinguishing features as their mutual distinctions from Minsky's approach.

In Minsky's model, a robust financial environment inevitably develops into a fragile one as the consequence of private, decentralized financing of real capital assets during the cyclical upsurge. Even if the boom is short-circuited by an imposed recession, a financial crisis still develops because of the falloff in cash inflows, which in turn leads to accelerated deflation and depression. If accelerating inflation is extended in a last-gasp effort to keep the fragile financial structure from collapsing, cash outflows for external finance soar, impairing liquidity. Thus, just as recessions cannot in Minsky's world forever postpone the onset of crises, neither can inflation.

There is no real disagreement with respect to expressing cyclical financial pressures in terms of sectoral flows of funds and the structure of financial assets

[1] See Sinai's article for a review and appreciation and a listing of Minsky's work.

and liabilities. The monetarist's view of the financial world simply never comes up; there seems to be an unspoken consensus that the supply of money is simply one element in financial flows and stocks. In other words, financial crises are essentially structural imbalances and cannot be explicated in terms of any one financial asset.[2]

Thus while all agree that crises originate in unsustainable developments in the sequence of financing—from internal to external finance and within external, from long-term to short-term sources—Minsky is alone in suggesting that the sequence must in time be followed through (rising interest rates and falling sales, etc.) to its bitter panic-depressive end. But in addition to this extension of Keynes-Kalecki macrofinancial thought, Minsky's description of the euphoric financial sequence en route to the boom is both colorful and insightful. To express the sequence in terms of hedge, speculative, and Ponzi finance is to highlight the key causal element: the timing and other relationships between *expected* net cash inflows and required cash outflows to creditors.

Once the Ponzi finance stage has become general—with current interest expenses exceeding current net income, so that only more borrowing to pay interest (or a sudden rise in cash inflows) can stave off financial collapse—a crisis is inevitable. In effect, Kaufman and Wallich and Wright all find effective means that are and have been capable of preventing Ponzi finance from becoming general.[3] The adjectives "resilient" and "adaptable" (if not "robust") are as frequently applied by them to describe the financial environment as are "fragile" and "rigid."

Kaufman, reviewing the three financial stringencies of the last decade (1966, 1969–1970, 1974–1975), sees each as having a different cause and none developing into a general crisis, but he notes that each was successively more severe. In other words, crises first developed among depository institutions via disintermediation, then in the commercial paper market, and most recently in the municipals markets; but the crises did not spread, as the financial system proved resilient: Financial management policies (both private and public) proved appropriately adjustable.

However, Kaufman fears that a fourth financial crisis, if it comes about too soon—owing, say, to increasingly flexible financial markets spreading initial stringencies rapidly and widely throughout the system—may well lead to

---

[2] This is not to say that the conference was antimonetarist; it was simply nonmonetarist in that the central concern—the *composition* of financial assets and their *flows* between segmented imperfect financial markets—cannot be explicated within a monetarist framework, much as modern inflation cannot be explicated within the traditional Keynesian framework.

[3] Not only do they challenge the inevitability of the sequence from financial fragility to financial crisis, and especially then on to general deflation and depression, they also consider the onset of fragility itself to be as likely "contrived" (i.e., due to bad policy) as natural or irresistible.

general government credit allocation and thus to a fundamental change in the nature of the financial system.

This result, which would fit easily into Minsky's framework, is, however, not viewed by Kaufman as likely, much less inevitable. But he makes an interesting and strong case against fully liberated financial markets as likely to induce the opposite extreme—controlled financial markets. The variety of constraints and frictions in our segmented financial markets have allowed us to prevent financial stringencies from developing into general crises, as the piper is paid in the real sector (say, by curtailment of investment and borrowing by nonfinancial corporations) and in the pressured financial sector (say, by interest ceilings and curtailment of lending and borrowing). Then, during the pause, financial structure can be rebalanced and liquidity rebuilt. Moreover, as a consequence of these restrictions—and this plays a highly significant solo role in all the papers except Minsky's—the national level of inflation will be curtailed, which in turn, for a variety of reasons, will ease the pressures for hedged speculative finance to evolve into a Ponzi pattern.

Wallich's view that the system's resilience has successfully been tested is based upon the fact that private financial policies reversed the financing sequence that ends in financial crises and collapses, while public policy refrained from the monetary ease required to refloat the system, which in turn would have allowed financial managers to try another round of increasingly expensive and shorter-term debt. Wallich's fundamental point is that borrowers' (and lenders') expectations, while dependent on all past experience, are especially influenced by the *recent* past, and that recent experience has been sufficiently scary to increase the aversion to risk substantially. Indeed Wallich is optimistic with respect to the timing of the fourth crisis, because he sees the risk factor as working in reverse now: Risk premiums have increased sharply and are causing firms generally to retreat to a less exposed credit position for the longer haul.[4] This is to say that the financial sequence is being retraced back toward cautious hedge financing.

Wright projects to the future the resilience that Wallich portrayed for the 1975–1976 period. By cataloging the causes of past and recent crises, Wright adds weight to Kaufman's case for eclecticism in modeling financial stress. And by treating the crises of 1907 through 1974–1975 as a continuum, Wright implicitly supports Minsky's systematic approach.

But Wright's analysis of crises is unique in its fundamental dependence on the achievements of private innovative finance and public antiinflationary policy. His advocacy of innovative flexibility[5] stands in contrast to Kaufman's

[4] Towards this end, Wallich proposes that the tax deductability of interest be removed, which would further reduce the pressure to increase risk via debt versus equity financing.

[5] But he reminds us that the Real Estate Investment Trust (REIT) was an innovation, though surely not an anticrisis one.

views, and his emphasis on inflation itself—not merely as part of crisis evolution—as a main cause of crises, parts him from Minsky's views. And finally,
Wright sees some of the disintermediation impacts of Federal Reserve policy as
harsh, though the underlying blame is attached to rate rigidities and ceilings.

Recent crises, according to Wright, have been overcome by a combination of
government action (legislation, the Federal Reserve and federal credit
agencies), private innovation in instruments and markets, and investor losses.
Since these experiences have reduced the willingness to take risk, mismanagement of both financial and nonfinancial corporations (as exhibited in undercapitalization and bankruptcy) is less likely to be a cause of future crises. But
the possibilities of mismanagement in the international sphere is more likely.
Finally, although our public policy activities and their viability as crises
averters have earned good grades, the greatest danger will arise if an outburst
of double-digit inflation is renewed.

The *discussants* are particularly incisive and concise and, like this introduc-
tory overview, tend toward comparative analysis and criticism. It suffices
therefore to note here that *their* communality rests on two principal issues:

1.   Preference for an eclectic crises theory with special emphasis on the role
of unanticipated inflation-multi-caused and highly irregular—in inducing
financial instability, stress, and crises.
2.   The key role of corporate financial management.

For example, Lintner sees no trend toward increasing financial instability in
the economy. Bosworth stresses the heavy responsibility of falling corporate
profits and retentions in inducing unusual financial strain. Von Furstenberg
reminds us that a crises theory can be expressed in terms of velocity or other
talismen of monetary theories of the cycle. Sinai agrees with Minsky that
financial stress is an endogenous process but adds that financial system institutional errors and shocks intensify it to a crisis level but can be anticipated by
appropriate econometric analysis and offset by appropriate policy.

With respect to national policy, Bosworth emphasizes the crisis-inducing
role of instability of interest rates, that is, the shift of monetary policy toward
concentration on monetary aggregates, leaving interest rates "to take the hind-
most." Lintner stresses the need for prudent or noninflationary monetary and
fiscal policies to break expectations of cumulative waves of increasing inflation.
Von Furstenberg is particularly concerned with altering business accounting
standards to allow for business adjustments to inflation, which in turn would
improve business capacity to finance internally, that is, to reduce pressures on
(external) financial markets. Sinai would not depend on institutional innovation and restructuring to prevent crisis. Rather, via modeling financial

instability and simulating the process, he specifies the necessary conditions for avoiding credit crunches—stabilized inflation, moderated business expansion, balance sheet restructuring, no stop-go policies, and cushioned external shocks—conditions that are primarily endogenous but are affected by external policy measures. About most of these conditions, Sinai (like Wright and Kaufman) is quite optimistic: ". . . current prospects for a relatively long period of financial stability are quite good."

My own impression of these papers is that a consensus is developed that the concept of "crisis inevitability" has few supporters either in theory or in practice. In contrast to the Minsky approach, the other papers stress the "therapeutic" effects of learning by experience: the development of "conservative" financial policies in the *private* sector, and the evolution toward "correct" *public* monetary and fiscal policies.

6.
A Theory of
Systemic Fragility

HYMAN P. MINSKY

My aim is to explore why we have had three near or incipient financial crises since 1966, whereas no such episodes occurred in the first 20 years after World War II. The argument that follows is that a fragile financial structure, which is a precondition for a financial crisis, now exists and that the emergence of a fragile financial structure, out of the robust structure that ruled at the end of World War II, resulted from the processes by which investment and positions in the stock of capital assets are financed in our economy.

Although the theory is stated in terms of robust and fragile financial states and the progression between them, in truth there is a continuum between these polar states. From flow of funds accounts, numbers can be derived indicating that the economy is on a robustness-fragility scale, but these numbers measure changes and trends and cannot tell us what will happen. This is so because institutions, usages, and policy interventions are important in determining how any fragile (or incipient crisis) financial situation will develop: Our economy is a historical and not a mechanical system. In order to understand our economy we have to leave the easy world of econometrics, simulations, and computer printouts and enter the tough world in which institutions, usages, and policy affect what happens.

Because of space limitations, I will have to make many of my points by assertion rather than by detailed argument. However, this expository form should clearly reveal the forest, even if the trees are vague and imprecise. This is not a numbers paper. I have given some of the numbers elsewhere.[1]

To put my argument bluntly, the incipient financial crises of 1966, 1969–1970, and 1974–1975 were neither accidents nor the result of policy errors, but the result of the normal functioning of our particular economy. The cumulative changes that occurred in the financial structure over 1945–1965 resulted from profit-seeking activity in our economy, an economy that uses decentralized markets not only to produce and distribute but also to deal in capital assets and finance investment. As a result of normal market behavior the extraordinarily robust financial structure inherited from World War II, in which a financial crisis was a virtual impossibility, was transformed into the fragile structure we now have, in which the periodic triggering of a financial crisis is well nigh certain.

The past decade has shown that in our economy, with a big government and passably effective lender-of-last-resort operations by the Federal Reserve, the FDIC, and explicit or implicit consortia of giant banks, a cumulative debt deflation need not follow upon an incipient financial crisis but can be aborted. However, in our economy success in aborting an embryonic financial crisis leaves a residue which virtually ensures that a period of accelerating inflation will follow.

The resilience the economy showed in 1975 was due to an accidental but crudely apt fiscal policy—money was literally thrown at the economy—combined with successful lender-of-last-resort operations. The recovery over the four quarters (1975-II–1976-I) cannot be imputed to either an inherent resilience of our monetary and financial system or to a self-equilibrating property of the income-generating mechanism. In a trivial and uninteresting sense 1974–1975 vindicates Keynes.

SOME DEFINITIONS

In what follows we deal with our economy. Our economy is a capitalist economy with sophisticated and complex financial institutions and usages.

Financial fragility is an attribute of the financial system. In a fragile financial system continued normal functioning can be disrupted by some not unusual event. *Systemic fragility* means that the development of a fragile financial structure results from the normal functioning of our economy; financial fragility and thus the susceptibility of our economy to disruption is not

[1] H. P. Minsky, "Financial Resources in a Fragile Financial Environment," *Challenge*, July–August 1975, presents some data on the trends of financial variables which are relevant to our theoretical formulation.

due to either accidents or policy errors. Therefore a theory of systemic fragility endeavors to explain why our economy endogenously develops fragile or crisis-prone financial structures.

Once fragile financial structures exist, the incoherent behavior characteristic of a financial crisis can develop. Incoherent behavior occurs when the reaction to a disturbance amplifies rather than dampens the initial disturbance. A financial crisis starts when some unit cannot refinance its position through normal channels and is forced to raise cash by unconventional instruments or by trying to sell out its position. Inasmuch as the assets in position have thin markets (a characteristic of positions that are financed rather than traded), excess supply leads to a sharp price break. Once this occurs, the initial disequilibrium is made worse. Other units experience a decrease in asset values and thus have difficulty in making position. History, as well as the theory of the determination of capital asset prices, indicates that a financial crisis is a necessary and apparently sufficient condition for a deep depression. Thus an economy with systemic financial fragility has a deep depression from time to time.[2]

PARADIGMS IN ECONOMICS

About 200 years ago Adam Smith set two problems for economics. One was to explain why a decentralized market mechanism yields a coherent result. The second was to explain why one country is richer or poorer than another—or why a country grows richer or poorer over time.

The response to Smith's first problem is the substance of pure economic theory. Pure theory shows that within barter paradigm models decentralized markets lead, under quite restrictive assumptions, to a coherent result. Barter paradigm models focus on trade and simple production. They abstract from time, money, uncertainty, history, policy, capital assets of the kind we know exist, and the financial institutions and usages associated with "Wall Street." Economic theory has not shown and *has not attempted to show* that an economy with the capital asset, monetary, and financial characteristics of our economy is coherent. As a result of the limitations of standard theory, it is not legitimate to add money onto a "barter" paradigm model of the economy, as is done by both the quantity theorists and the standard Keynesians, and then draw inferences about the behavior of our economy.

[2] Irving Fisher, "The Debt-Deflation Theory of Great Depressions," *Econometrica*, October 1933, pp. 337–357. Evans Clark, ed., *The Internal Debts of the United States* (New York: MacMillan), 1933. A. G. Hart, et al. *Debts and Recovery 1929–37* (New York:, The Twentieth Century Fund), 1938.

Smith's second problem, to explain the relative richness or poverty of different countries or of one country over time, has been answered in terms of differential endowments of capital assets. These differential endowments are the result of past accumulation. Accumulation depends upon an ability to generate and allocate effectively a surplus. In our economy the surplus is extracted and allocated by the market processes that finance investment and the government processes that determine taxes and spending.

"Wall Street" will serve as the label for the institutions and usages that generate and allocate the finance for investment and for positions in the inherited stock of capital assets. In our economy the behavior of "Wall Street" is a determinant of the pace and direction of investment. A model of the economy from the perspective of "Wall Street" differs from the standard model of economic theory in that it first sees a network of financial interrelations and cash flows and then a production and distribution mechanism. A "Wall Street" paradigm is a better starting point for theorizing about our type of economy than the "barter" paradigm of conventional theory.[3]

From the perspective of "Wall Street," economic theory has to explain the prices of capital assets and equity shares, instruments which have value only because they are expected to be profitable or to pay dividends over some future period. A further problem of economic theory is to determine the relation, if any, between the prices of existing capital assets and the prices of current output and the effect, if any, that various alignments of these two sets of prices have upon the behavior of the economy.

The prices of capital assets are determined by expected future profits and portfolio preferences. Portfolio preferences and relative supplies determine the prices of various capital and financial assets, which differ in the incomes they are expected to yield, carrying costs, and liquidity. Money is an asset, with a particular yield, carrying costs, and liquidity characteristics, whose price is always one. The money prices of other assets are determined by their special characteristics and their relative scarcity.

Money therefore directly affects the price level of various capital assets and financial assets—it does not directly affect the price level of current output. The proximate determinant of the price level of current output is the money wage rate and, roughly speaking, the weight of disposable incomes derived from government activity and the production of investment goods in total disposable income.[4] Thus the proximate determinants of the two price levels are quite different.

[3] Hyman P. Minsky, *John Maynard Keynes* (New York: Columbia University Press), 1975, contains a fuller statement of the theory I am "asserting" here.

[4] M. Kalecki, J. Robinson, N. Kaldor, P. Davidson, J. Kregal, and S. Weintraub build on such a relation. For an introduction and guide to the material, see either J. Kregal, *The Reconstruction of Political Economy* (London: MacMillan), 1973, or P. Davidson, *Money and the Real World*, (New York: John Wiley), 1972.

The money wage rate is a dominant determinant of the supply price of investment output. The price of a capital asset is a determinant of the demand price of a comparable investment good. Given that the price level of capital assets and investment output are based upon quite different principles, it is not surprising that, at times, they can and do get out of "alignment." This is especially so when, as is true for our economy, positions in capital assets, as well as the investment output in the process of being produced, are debt-financed, so that changes in financing terms affect both the supply price of investment outputs with significant gestation periods as well as the market valuation of capital assets.

THE DIMENSIONS OF FINANCIAL FRAGILITY

Introduction

To put meat upon a "Wall Street" paradigm approach to economic theory, a precise statement of the determinants of the robustness or fragility of a financial structure is necessary. One determinant of the robustness-fragility of a financial system is the mix of hedge, speculative, and Ponzi finance in the economy. Another determinant of robustness-fragility is the weight of cash or near-cash assets in portfolios: the liquidity narrowly defined, of various classes of units. A third determinant is the extent to which ongoing investment is debt-financed.[5]

A financial contract is a money today–money tomorrow deal. Money today–money tomorrow deals are a pervasive reality in our economy. Such deals—in the form of money loans, bonds, bank deposits, equity shares, insurance contracts, mortgages, and so on—are the essence of financial businesses. In addition, in our economy, capital assets—plants, equipment, housing, commercial estates, and inventories—are particular and essential money today–money tomorrow contracts. Capital assets are best thought of as a special type of financial instrument. Whereas in the world of finance the money tomorrow part of the contract is a commitment of some household, business firm, or government unit, in the capital asset "contract" the money tomorrow is the gross profit income of some business enterprise operating with its particular management in specific markets and in a particular economic context.

Capital assets therefore yield cash flows over time, the cash flows depending upon how the demand for outputs that use the services of the particular capital asset develops. Positions in such capital assets are financed by combinations of

---

[5] H. P. Minsky, "The Modelling of Financial Instability: An Introduction," *Modelling and Simulation*, Vol. 5 (Pittsburgh: Instrument Society of America, 1974, pp. 267–273, gives a semi-mathematical statement of what follows.

debts and equities. The cash flow problem of a unit owning capital assets can be characterized as a balancing of the cash receipts from operations and the cash payments due to debts. In a "Wall Street" paradigm model, all units are like a banker who maximizes profits under liquidity and solvency constraints.

Hedge, Speculative, and Ponzi Finance

The liabilities of a unit state the dated, demand, or contigent cash payments it has to make; these cash payments are on account of principal and interest. The cash to make such payments can be on hand or obtained from the cash flow due to (1) the operations of the unit, (2) the fulfillment by others of owned contracts, (3) the sale of an asset, or (4) the issuance of debt. There are limitations to the sale of some assets; for business corporations the capital assets used in production, and for financial units some assets with thin markets, are difficult to sell to raise cash. Such assets are the unit's position.

If a unit's cash flow commitments on debts are such that over each significant period the cash receipts are expected to exceed the cash payments by a significant margin, the unit is said to be engaged in hedge financing. A household whose monthly income far exceeds the monthly payment on a home mortgage and has few other debts payments is a hedge financing unit. A profitable firm that has virtually no short-term debt and which has mainly equity liabilities is a hedge financing unit.

A speculative financing unit has cash flow payments over some periods— typically near term—that exceed the cash flows expected over this period. This situation usually arises because the principal amount of some debt is due; contractual and demand cash flow commitments are on account of both principal and interest. However, the present value of the cash flow expected to accrue to the firm from owned assets exceeds the present value of contractual cash payments. A speculative financing unit has a positive net worth, even though in some near-term periods cash payment commitments exceed the cash flow from operations. What both the borrower and the lender expect—and they expected it when the deal was set up—is that the debtor will be able to refinance his or her position. New debts will be "sold" or "issued" to raise funds that will be used to pay maturing debts.

A Ponzi financing unit is a speculative financing unit for which the interest portion of its cash payment commitments exceeds its net income cash receipts. A Ponzi unit has to increase its debt in order to meet commitments on outstanding instruments. Units engaged in Ponzi finance may have a negative net worth in any honest computation of present values; however, units may engage in Ponzi finance with substantial net worths if accruals account for a large part of their income.

Whereas units that engage in hedge finance are vulnerable only to what happens in the market for their product (or whether the terms on owned contracts are fulfilled), units that engage in speculative or Ponzi finance are also vulnerable to changes in financial markets.

Commercial banks and depository institutions, such as savings banks of various kinds, typically engage in speculative finance: The term to maturity of their debts is shorter than that of their assets. They need to attract or purchase deposits continually in order to meet withdrawals; "liability management" banking is more speculative than "asset management" banking. The shorter term of debts than of assets in banking means that banks are vulnerable to financial market developments; untoward developments can increase the carrying costs of assets in position without necessarily improving their cash flows.[6]

Present Values of Cash Flows

One difference between units that engage in hedge and speculative finance is that the present value of a hedge financing operation is always positive regardless of the movement of interest rates, whereas the present value of any speculative financing unit, for which the surplus cash flows come later than the deficit cash flows, is positive or negative depending upon the ruling pattern of interest rates. For units that engage in speculative finance a rise in both short- and long-term interest rates can transform a positive present value into a negative present value.

Furthermore, a rise in interest rates can transform a speculative unit into a Ponzi financing unit, in that upon refinancing the cost of carrying position can exceed the income from the assets in position.

The fragility of the financial system depends upon the number of factors that can amplify initial disturbances. Hedge, speculative, and Ponzi financing units alike are vulnerable to events that reduce the cash flows from assets. A decrease in income from operations, or a default or restructuring of the debts owed to a unit, can transform a hedge financing unit into a speculative financing unit. For things to go wrong with a hedge financing unit something first has to go wrong someplace else in the economy—unless the hedge characteristics of the initial financing were based upon unrealistic euphoric expectations with respect to markets and their growth. However, speculative and Ponzi finance units are vulnerable to changes in interest rates. Increases in interest rates increase cash flow commitments without increasing receipts. Furthermore, as they must continuously refinance their positions, they are vulnerable to financial market disruptions. The greater the weight of speculative finance in the total financial structure, the greater the fragility of the financial structure.

[6] Henry Simons, *Economic Policy for a Free Society* (Chicago: University of Chicago Press), 1948, discusses this flaw in finance.

The Thrust to Speculative Finance

That our economy transits from a robust to a fragile financial structure is evident from data and from history, which contains numerous examples of financial crises. What we need to add to our ability to point at data and events and say, "This is what we mean," is an argument as to why such changes take place. Why is it that the volume of short-term indebtedness tends to increase and the holdings of cash assets tend to decrease until the financial structure becomes sufficiently fragile so that a financial crisis or near financial crises occur?

Our economy is characterized by private ownership of capital assets and the existence of a wide variety of financial instruments which finance ownership and control over these capital assets. In particular, in our economy, as it is currently organized, an overwhelming proportion of the capital assets are owned by corporations, and their equity shares, bonds, and short-term indebtedness are the assets households either own directly or through the intermediation of some financial institution.

Each collection of assets—financial or capital—is characterized by two explicit and one implicit cash flow. One explicit cash flow is the income—for capital assets the quasi-rents—it yields. The other explicit cash flow is the carrying costs. The implicit cash flow is the liquidity yield, which is the value of the insurance some assets provide because they can easily be turned into cash in order to fulfill payment obligations. Money, which is the unit in which debts are denominated, is the "premier" example of a liquid asset, but other financial instruments such as U.S. Treasury debt and commercial paper can have considerable liquidity as long as the market for these assets functions. However, for assets other than money that have liquidity attributes, the possibility exists that when the liquidity is really needed some price concession will have to be made to acquire money; they will sell at a discount relative to money.

As a result of the various mixes of yield, carrying cost, and liquidity that assets embody—and the yields, carrying costs, and liquidity of assets differ in how assured they are—the relative prices of assets are determined. Given that the price of money is always one, asset prices in money are determined.

The yields—or quasi-rents—of the items in the stock of capital assets are determined by the functioning of the economy. In a simple formulation the gross profits after taxes are determined by the expenditures on investment.[7] However, if the quantity of money and near monies is plentiful, the yield on assets that embody a fair amount of liquidity will be low. If investment is proceeding apace in an economy with a robust financial structure, short-term

[7] See Kalecki et. al.

interest rates will be significantly lower than the yield on capital assets and the expected yield from newly produced capital assets, that is, investment.

Under a regime of robust finance the rate pattern, even during periods of only reasonably active investment, is such that one can make on the carry by financing positions, in both long-term financial assets and capital assets, by short-term debt. Given that financial institutions and usages are such that the supply of bank financing is within significant limits determined by the interaction of bankers and their customers, and given the existence of a wide spectrum of financial instruments, a substitution of liquid assets for money in portfolios will yield funds to finance positions in assets.

Such an endogenous increase in money and liquid assets pushes up the price of capital assets relative to the price of money, liquid assets, and current output. The increase in the price of capital assets increases the difference between capital asset and investment goods prices. Given the robustness of finance and the elasticity of short-term financing, an increase in the rate of investment will follow. Once again, simplifying the story a bit, this increases the yield from the existing items in the stock of capital assets.

Fundamentally, while the constraints through the techniques of production may define the acceptable sets of production techniques, acceptable financing techniques depend upon the current subjective preferences of bankers and businesspeople and their current views about the prospects of the economy. In the financial structure that ruled in the 1950s, businesspeople and bankers were correct in being willing to increase their short-term indebtedness. The only problem is that success breeds a disregard for the possibility of failure; the combination of the successful operation of the economy over a long stretch and the absence of serious financial difficulties over a substantial period led to the development of a "euphoric" economy in which short-term financing of long positions became a way of life to many organizations.[8]

Inasmuch as institutions, usages, and personnel changed between the financial trauma of the 1930s and the 1960s, it was quite natural for central bankers, government officials, bankers, businesspeople, and even economists to begin to. believe that a new era had arrived. The warnings that nothing basic had changed, that we still could reach a breaking point, and that a deep depression was still possible, were ignored. As the doubters of permanent prosperity did not have printouts to prove the validity of their views, it was quite proper to ignore arguments drawn from theory, history, and institutional analysis. Nevertheless, it is evident that in a world of uncertainty, capital assets with a long gestation period, private ownership, and "Wall Street," successful functioning of the economy, within an initially robust financial structure, leads

[8] H. P. Minsky, "Financial Instability Revisited: The Economics of Disaster," *Reappraisal of the Federal Reserve Discount Mechanism,* Vol. 3, (June 1972), 95–136.

to an increase in short-term speculative finance, so that the financial structure becomes even more fragile as time elapses.

"Cash Kickers" and Margins of Safety

Borrowing and lending take place on the basis of various margins of safety. One margin of safety is the excess of expected cash receipts over cash payment commitments for all time periods. This margin of safety exists for units that engage in hedge financing but does not exist for units that engage in speculative finance. A second margin of safety is the excess of the present value of assets over the present value of liabilities. This margin of safety exists for units that engage in both hedge and speculative financing, but as the markets for the assets in portfolios are often very thin, the excess of present value may well evaporate if the need to sell assets to meet payment commitments ever arises. A third margin of safety is the holding of "cash kickers," money and liquid financial assets that are superfluous to operations, so that a small shortfall in cash receipts or an unexpected need to make payments does not disrupt normal functioning.

From the above overview of margins of safety, it is apparent that units—and economies—that are heavily into speculative finance should keep large cash kickers. Commercial banks are inherently speculative organizations and the reserves banks keep are cash kickers. However, as we look at our economy, it is evident that, the greater the volume of speculative finance relative to total financial interrelations, the smaller the cash kickers. One or more of three things will have to change for this to be so: views about or the importance attached to various uncertainties diminish, the payoffs from speculative finance increase, and the costs of carrying cash increase. In the later stages of the development of a fragile financial situation a speculative boom—in the stock market, in tulips, in Florida real estate—is likely to occur, reflecting increased short-term payoffs from speculative finance and a downgrading of uncertainties. These subjective changes make the development of an investment boom, especially a boom in investments with extended gestations periods, likely.

Conclusions

The above has been sketchy. The theory of the working of our economy based upon emphasizing finance rather than barter is complex and departs from standard theory at many points. But the major difference is in the conclusion. Within standard economic theory the financial crises and big depressions of history are anomalies. The economic theory of the 1920s could not explain the 1930s. Hence Keynes' effort to construct a new theory that made the anomaly a usual event; his view of "the general theory" was that it explained why our economy was so liable to fluctuations.[9]

The development of economic theory over the postwar period neglected financial considerations in determining the behavior of the economy, so that the instability of the past decade is an anomaly. Obviously, a theory that cannot explain what is happening except by appealing to errors or accidents is unsatisfactory. Current standard economic theory—the so-called neoclassical synthesis—does not even address the problems represented by the crisis-prone behavior of our economy.

INVESTMENT PROGRAMS AS FINANCIAL CONTRACTS

The financing of investment during its gestation period is another determinant of the robustness or fragility of the financial structure. Some unit—whether it be the ultimate user of the capital asset, the contractor, or the supplier of non-human inputs—has to make payments for labor and raw materials as an investment project progresses from its initial conception to completion. An investment program involves commitments to pay cash as the work progresses, and thus it is like a debt.

The funds for these payments can come from a number of sources: gross profits of the purchaser, bank loans, long-term bonds, new equities, and so on. When an investment project has a long gestation period, like a nuclear power plant or a condominium complex, funds to make such progress payments may be required over several years and are frozen in the project until it is completed. The cost and the present value of an investment project while it is in process vary with financial market conditions.

As it starts an investment project a unit can raise all the external funds it feels it will require for the project with long-term debt, so that upon completion of the project the cash flows from its operation will fulfill the debt commitments. Such financing is a form of hedge financing. However, for an investing unit such hedge equivalent financing carries conjectural elements not present in the financing of in-being capital assets; the amount of external financing required depends upon the internal funds generated, the returns earned upon the initial excess short-term funds depend upon money market conditions, and the cost of the project depends upon the time it takes for completion. As we all know, engineers and architects estimates of time for completion of projects are almost as error-prone as economists' forecasts; even prior financing has speculative elements.

[9] J. M. Keynes, "The General Theory of Employment," *Quarterly Journal of Economics,* Vol. 51 (February 1937), 209–223.

Even though raising funds for investment projects by prior financing is possible, a sequential financing strategy is more usual. Different sources of funds are tapped as investment proceeds. In our economy, where large continuing corporations do a large part of the investing, it is impossible to segregate the funds needed by a particular project from the financing and refinancing needs of the corporation as a whole. However, the gestation period financing of investment involves commitments to pay cash at specified dates or stages and a parallel need to raise cash, which constitutes a particularly inelastic demand for funds. Thus the costs of investment output, the present value of a project, and the overall financial structure of a unit which deficit finances investment projects are sensitive to money market changes. Furthermore, a run-up of the costs of investment output while in progress tends to strip an investing unit of its liquid assets.

The extent of sequential and external financing of investment over the gestation period is a determinant of the overall speculative posture of the financial structure and thus of the fragility of the financial system. Any lengthening of the gestation period of investment, any substantial increase in the price level of inputs to investment relative to prices of output in general, any increase in the ratio of external to internal funds in the financing of investment, and, once short-term funds are used to finance investment goods in process, any increase in short-term interest rates increases the extent of speculative finance in the economy and thus the fragility of the financial structure. If speculative finance in general makes a financial structure fragile, then the speculative or sequential financing of investment is a particularly sensitive part of the fragile financial structure. Whenever investment greatly exceeds the internal corporate cash flows available to finance investment, the economy is most susceptible to the emergence of an incipient financial crisis.

The split between construction and takeout financing for housing and commercial construction was of particular importance in the incipient financial crisis of 1974–1975. Housing—and this is true of condominium projects—involves a separation between the unit that finances the investment and the unit that owns the finished capital asset. In fact, the investment is typically completed before the sale of units is arranged. Thus any failure of sales to take place as scheduled raises the cost of the project by the carrying costs on the investment. High interest rates and a slowdown of sales guarantee that difficulties, such as still plague banks with respect to the Real Estate Investment Trusts (REITs), will occur, and high long-term rates are a guarantee that a slowdown of sales will occur.

If the gestation period of investment is long, and if a substantial part of the cost of a project is front-loaded, a rise in short- and long-term interest rates during the gestation period of a project can transform an initial positive present value into a negative present value. If bankers are alert, such developments should lead to a cutting off of funds and the abandonment of the project—at least until lower interest rates and a writing down of the sunk costs to a fair market value make it feasible to proceed.

But even short of the transformation of a positive present value into a negative present value, interest rate changes, which raise the cost of the finished capital asset and lower the completion date present value of the capital asset, lead to a reduction in the margin of safety underlying the particular deal. Three dimensions of the margin of safety have been identified: the excess of the value of assets over liabilities, the excess of cash flow receipts over payments, and cash kickers in the asset structure. All three are adversely affected by a rise in interest rates.

Whenever margins of safety are eroded, financing terms can be expected to reflect the increased uncertainty that lenders bear. Contractual interest rates are one dimension of financing terms. When the margin of safety for a unit deteriorates, its financing terms increase beyond what takes place in measured market rates. Not only does the premium over market rate increase, but the liquidity security and maintenance of net worth provisions become more constraining even as increased prime rates decrease margins of safety. But these financing codicils, while designed to protect lenders, make the position of debtors worse—if only by constraining their freedom of action. Thus, once financial fragility becomes significant, it seems as if an inexorable trend toward ever-increasing fragility is begun.

A BRIEF CONCLUSION

There are two possible channels by which money market changes can affect income and employment: by diminishing aggregate demand by decreasing investment by first increasing interest rates (or directly decreasing spending if we accept monetarist contentions), and by inducing financial disturbances. Whenever money market changes lead to present value reversals or appreciable decreases in the margins of safety, the possibility exists that refinancing will not be available, that is, that an incipient financial crisis will be triggered. Furthermore, if refinancing is achieved (perhaps because bankers are "responsible") in spite of adverse cash flow commitments which make the present value of expected cash flow receipts and commitments either uncomfortably close to or below the present value of cash payments, a variety of Ponzi financing will emerge as important in the financial picture.

Ponzi finance, considered a joke played on gullible Bostonians, is ever present in a world in which speculative finance exists and in which the costs due to debts can exceed concurrent receipts from operations. If true current interest rate computations lead to negative or too-small-for-comfort net worths, borrowing to pay financial commitments becomes a form of Ponzi finance. Once Ponzi financing becomes a significant portion of the financial structure, either we go through a debt deflation and a serious depression or we float the debt off by generating significant increases in the expected cash flows from operating capital assets, increases that may be possible only through inflation. To float off the debt we now have, we need to have significant profit inflation even as privately financed investment is constrained to corporate cash flows. This can be achieved by having a large government deficit, such as we have had and are continuing to have, together with strong borrowers' and lenders' risk aversion, which ruled in 1975 and is apparently easing now.

AN ASIDE ON MONETARY POLICY

If the economy is characterized by a dominance of hedge finance, so that few firms can be adversely affected by rapidly rising and high interest rates, if investment is largely internally financed, and if units are liquid, in that portfolios contain a large value of financial assets that are superfluous to operations, interest rates cannot move very much. Under these circumstances it is safe for the Federal Reserve to adopt a money quantity rule. Sharp variations in interest rates will not occur, and if they do occur nothing much will happen.

If a large body of speculative finance exists, if corporate fixed investment is, to a large extent, financed by external funds, and if units have been largely stripped of liquidity, interest rates can move sharply and Federal Reserve actions must be constrained by a concern about the movement of interest rates. If the liquidity of private deficit financing units (investing corporations) has been impaired, interest rates—especially short rates—can move quickly and range widely. Because the payment commitments on ongoing investment projects are inelastic with respect to interest rate changes, a short fall of the supply of finance leads to large increases in interest rates. Given the existence of speculative finance, these higher interest rates are quickly written into financing contracts. Under a regime of speculative and fragile financial situations it is dangerous for the Federal Reserve to wear blinders which make the quantity of money rather than financial market conditions the proximate objective of monetary policy.

It is a paradox that, when financial conditions were such that the Federal Reserve could safely ignore interest rates, a fear of money market disturbances was a constraint upon its operations,[9] whereas now, when financial conditions are such that higher interest rates can trigger reversals of present value, erosions of margins of safety, and explosions of Ponzi finance, monetary policy increasingly emphasizes the quantity of money and deemphasizes the significance of interest rate variations.

The only universal rule for Federal Reserve policy is that it cannot be dictated by any universal rule. Federal Reserve policy must adapt to the actual conditions in financial markets. The Federal Reserve must recognize that its responsibilities extend beyond the behavior of institutions labeled banks and statistical constructs labeled the money supply. The Federal Reserve must accept the responsibility to be the lender of last resort to financial markets as they exist.

Federal Reserve economic policy duties can be divided into two spheres. Monetary policy involves the day-to-day operations within a for now coherent set of financial markets. Lender-of-last-resort responsibilities are intermittent interventions designed to abort a threatening incipient financial crisis.

When the financial structure is robust, the need for lender-of-last-resort interventions is unlikely to arise; the Federal Reserve is free to think only about monetary policy actions. Furthermore, these actions need not be constrained by any fear that a financial crisis can be set off. When the financial structure is fragile, lender-of-last-resort responsibilities become important and should be dominant in determining Federal Reserve action. Furthermore, because the range of variation of interest rates is greater, Federal Reserve actions need to be constrained by the knowledge that large and rapid increases in interest rates can trigger a financial crisis.

In the context of a fragile financial structure, a money supply strategy such as has been identified with the monetarists is a particularly inept exercise of Federal Reserve power. Once a fragile financial structure exists, Federal Reserve policy should try to induce behavior that tends to diminish the weight of speculative finance in the economy. This may very well require some control over the liability structures and asset/equity ratios of giant corporations and banks. At present the Federal Reserve has no power to affect such variables. My conjecture is that after the next "near miss" with respect to a financial crisis, the development of such controls will move onto the agenda for reform.

7.
Financial Crises: Market Impact, Consequences, and Adaptability

HENRY KAUFMAN

Just the words alone—financial crises—make most people cringe. It is not the history books' retelling of the crash of 1929 or the panic of 1907 that most of us recall when we hear these words, but rather the so-called crises of the past decade. These were the credit crunch of 1966 and the crises of 1969–1970 and of 1974–1975. I attempt in this article to discuss the increasing instability during this period from a market viewpoint and the problems associated with adapting our credit system to the stresses and strains of financial crises.

If we apply Webster's definition of a crisis as a condition of instability or a stage in a sequence of events at which the trend of all future events for better or worse is determined, it is doubtful that we can classify all three postwar periods of stringencies as crises, at least not in the classical sense. In none of these three crises did the markets ever stand still or completely malfunction. While acute stringencies prevailed in some sectors, new-issue volume was large and, secondary markets were active throughout, even during the most tense moments. Thus the crises were concentrated in specific sectors and, in many instances, in specific issues. There were no bank holidays or closings of organized stock exchanges, although foreign exchange markets were closed from time to time to allow for a realignment of currencies.

Regardless of how history will classify these periods, they did cast a shadow of doubt on our ability to achieve effective stabilization policies. This is reinforced by the fact that the 1966 credit crunch was mild compared with the 1969–1970 crisis, which in turn was not as acute as the crisis of 1974. Moreover, the financial crises of 1969–1970 and of 1974–1975 coincided with the terminal stages of the last two economic expansions and early months of recession. None of the cyclical swings of the 1950s or early 1960s had any tinge of crisis. Does this suggest that financial crises are the only way of eliminating new excesses in the future and that a return to mild cyclical behavior in economic activity is unlikely? No wonder these mounting shocks have raised fears that the next crisis will be far more severe than what has occurred to date in the postwar years.

Besides the increasing severity of the financial problems, there are other differences among these three crises. Disintermediation came on the scene in 1966. It was experienced by all deposit institutions as well as life insurance companies. By the time the last crisis was in full bloom in 1974, however, disintermediation was still a problem for savings banks, savings and loan associations, and life insurance companies, but not for commercial banks. In fact, commercial bank credit increased by 9 percent in 1974 as compared with 6 percent in 1969–1970 and 5 percent in 1966. Moreover, the commercial bank share of credit market financing remained extraordinarily high in 1974, while in comparable earlier periods it had contracted. Nevertheless, banks were not without problems in 1974.

The problem of the quality of credit was not the distinguishing feature of the 1966 credit crunch, partly because the so-called artificial market constraints slowed credit creation quickly. The sharp deterioration of credit quality was one of the highlights of the last two crises. It surfaced in the corporate sector in 1970 and was dramatized by the bankruptcy of Penn Central. This bankruptcy and other credit problems contributed to an extraordinary preference for high-quality securities. This preference intensified even more in the last crisis. There was not only concern about the credit quality of the corporate sector, which deepened when the credit ratings of many corporations were reduced, but also about the strength of our commercial banking system and of several state and local governments. The 1974 crisis also had an international look to it. Besides some of the dramatic banking problems in Europe, including the Herstatt debacle and the plight of smaller banks in London, there was an uneasiness about the burgeoning Eurodollar market, the uncertainty surrounding the ability of the financial markets to recirculate the surplus of OPEC and the rapidly rising debt structure outside the United States, especially of underdeveloped nations.

The interest rate structures at the peak periods of stringencies provide little comfort. As shown in Table 1, interest rate peaks were successively higher dur-

Table 1 Selected Long-Term Interest Rates during the Last Three Major Credit Stringencies

	Approximate Peak Yields (%)		
	1966	1970	1974
U.S. governments	5.05	7.59	8.75
New Aa utilities	6.15	9.40	10.60
Prime municipals	4.25	7.00	6.80

	Approximate Rise in Yields during 12 Months Prior to Reaching Peak Yields (in B.P.)[a]		
	1966	1970	1974
U.S. governments	+78	+126	+149
New Aa utilities	+148	+160	+295
Prime municipals	+90	+120	+160

	Quality Yield Spreads (in B.P.)					
	1966		1970		1974–1975	
	Max.	Prior	Max.	Prior	Max.	Prior
Corporates						
A versus AAA new utilities (est.)	35	13	70	29	160	26
A versus AAA new industrial (est.)	35	18	50	26	115	28
Municipals, A versus AAA	50	30	115	55	80	25

	Average Monthly Yield Range (in B.P.)		
	1966	1970	1974–1975
U.S. governments	13	38	21
New Aa utilities	19	33	44
Prime municipals	15	34	21

[a] 100 B.P. (basis points) = 1 percent.

ing each of the three crises. Peak yields for new issues of AA-rated utility bonds were about 6.15 percent in 1966, 9.40 percent in 1970, and 10.60 percent in 1974. The yield spread between high-quality and medium-quality issues widened dramatically, reflecting virtually the denial of credit to lesser-rated borrowers. The yield spread between new AAA- and A-rated industrial bonds reached a peak of approximately 35 basis points in 1966, 50 basis points in

1970, and 115 basis points in 1975. Naturally, the yield spread between AAA-rated and Baa issues was even wider. Most of the weaker credits were denied access to the market in 1974 and 1975. In addition, credit markets were highly volatile during the years of crises. For example, the average monthly yield swing for new AA utility bonds was 19 basis points in 1966, 33 basis points in 1969–1970, and 44 basis points in 1975.

While we can take considerable comfort from the resiliency of the market-place during the three postwar crises, escalating crises are dangerous and trigger far-reaching changes eventually. Assume for a moment that another crisis more intense than the last will envelop us within the next 4 or 5 years. What will the markets be confronted with?

1.   The volume of credit market debt would have increased very rapidly by the time the crisis reached full bloom, and a new group of speculative excesses would be visible.

2.   A crisis more intense than that of 1974–1975 would raise interest rates to new postwar highs, well above the double-digit interest rates of 1974.

3.   In the money market, the issuance of commercial paper and negotiable certificates of deposit would be entirely the domain of the largest corporations and banks.

4.   The quality of all sorts of credit would deteriorate again. Insolvencies would increase sharply and would be even more spectacular than those of the 1970 and 1974 vintage.

5.   Under these conditions, the yield spread between high-grade and medium-grade bonds would rise above the 300 basis points that prevailed during the crisis days of the 1970s.

6.   The issuance of long-term bonds would be limited in the private sector to AAA- and AA-rated borrowers. The pressure on banks to finance the rest would be very strong.

7.   A more severe credit crisis than we have experienced to date in the postwar years would put financial institutions, particularly deposit-type, in an extremely precarious position. The quality of their asset structure would weaken, which would hinder substantially their ability to attract outside capital. These circumstances suggest that financial institutions would have to pay a very high premium to obtain bond money over highly rated business corporations and over the obligations of the U.S. government. This is because high-grade business corporations can offer substantial asset protection besides their earning power, which financial institutions, being highly leveraged, cannot.

8.   Investors would probably begin to show a greater preference for the direct obligations of the U.S. government than for the federally sponsored agencies. This preference was not great during the crises to date.

9. The next financial crisis in the United States would probably trigger a massive involvement by the federal government in business and finance. Credit allocation schemes would flourish. Strong pressures would be exerted to extend credit to maintain jobs, even though the borrowers involved may not be credit worthy by today's standards in American credit markets. We need only look at the extent to which the credit decisions of some European institutions were circumscribed by official edicts or governmental persuasion to obtain a sense of what may happen here.

Now, at least part of what I have just catalogued transpired in one way or the other during the past two crises. Can it happen soon again with even greater fervor? It really depends on whether one thinks that crises have a telling impact on people. I think that some crises do. The pain inflicted by a financial crisis is supposed to encourage a return to prudence in the making of financial and economic decisions. It is quite obvious the 1966 credit crunch and the 1970 financial crisis failed to achieve this objective. This may have been both because the marketplace failed to see the new risks and because the authorities may have preferred to try to avoid new unpleasantness. Otherwise, the dramatic financial events thereafter would not have materialized. The harbingers of a financial crisis are massive debt creation fueled by a high inflation rate, a willingness by business and others to increase leverage substantially, and financial institutions and others willing to extend credit readily and aggressively at increasingly liberal terms. Concurrently, a liberal monetary policy is a basic prerequisite. The drift toward a financial crisis can also be recognized by the trend toward a more loquacious financial language. During the past decade or so, this language included such terms as "off-balance sheet financing," "liability management," "conglomeration," "synergism," "bonds as substitute for equity capital," just to mention a few.

Neither this language nor some of the other manifestations just mentioned are with us today. Perhaps a new generation of bankers, business people, and policymakers have learned some enduring lessons from the recent financial stresses. Perhaps corporate officers may long hesitate to enlarge borrowings at the cost of lower credit ratings, and perhaps bankers' criteria for lending and investing will show improved objectivity. If so, liquidity preferences will increase sharply and quickly when adverse developments appear in the future, thereby either nipping the financial crisis in the early stages or preventing it from turning into a full-fledged financial hurricane.

I should now like to discuss the ability of financial markets to adapt to financial crises. Thus far, we have done reasonably well. It is doubtful, however, that financial markets can adapt to financial crises of increasing intensity. Several efforts, however, are underway that are supposed to give markets greater resiliency. These include flexible credit instruments, the cross-fertilization of markets by giving broader lending and investing powers to individual institutional groups, the removal of interest rate ceilings, increasing depositor protection, and government programs. The new flexible instruments such as the floating prime rate and the variable mortgage rate are supposed to protect the profit margins of financial institutions when interest rates rise sharply, as occurs in a financial crisis, and therefore to help maintain their viability. By giving broader lending and investing powers to specialized institutions, financial competition is supposed to improve the distribution of credit as well as the strength of the institutions involved. Finally, government programs such as the federal credit agencies or the proposed new Reconstruction Finance Corporation will limit the secondary or tertiary impact of credit stringencies.

I have various reservations about such approaches as a way of increasing institutional resiliency during future financial difficulties. The floating rate lending arrangements encourage both lender and borrower to accelerate the debt creation process, which is after all the genesis of most financial crises. The lender is encouraged to make loans because the floating rate removes the money rate risk from the lending arrangement, while the borrower consoles himself with the notion that the high interest rates required may be only temporary. Under these conditions, the larger the volume of loans, the greater the lender's profit, because he or she supposedly has locked in a fixed profit margin. The cross-fertilization of financial institutions and the removal of interest rate ceilings also encourages rapid debt expansion.

When there is financial friction blocking the movement of funds, market participants are forced to desist more quickly, but when there is virtually none, a highly combative showdown takes place, which raises interest rates sharply and exposes the marginal in the system. Is it really logical to assume that a consumer, a marginal business, or a heavily debt-burdened city can outbid either the U.S. government or the large and better-rated corporations? Most government financial programs are supposed to ease the burden of the financially oppressed during credit stringencies. Their success has been marginal in most instances. Witness the many government programs designed to shelter housing financing, but still housing starts contracted from peak to trough by 49 percent from 1963 to 1966, by 39 percent from 1969 to 1970, and by 62 percent from 1973 to 1974. At the same time, the federal credit agencies have heightened the battle in the credit markets in the crisis period and have weakened the marginal which were not protected by the federal umbrella.

There is another aspect of most of these measures aimed at supposedly strengthening our financial system against future shocks, which deserves to be mentioned. In highly liberated financial markets, financial institutions try to pass the pain of financial stress on to the real world without the institutions themselves having to absorb any of it. This is the essence of bank liability management and of such lending techniques as variable interest rate deals.

These are approaches, however, that hardly slow the creation of debt or arrest the deterioration in credit quality. Of course, financial institutions cannot escape the penalties of excessive debt creation, but a highly liberated system provides many illusionary trappings which initially suggest that they can. Similarly, the problem is compounded by supervisory or regulatory agencies unwilling to expose large institutions to the risk of the marketplace and by enlarged protection for depositors and other creditors of financial institutions.

Thus it seems that most of these well-intentioned proposals to increase the resiliency of the financial system will actually increase susceptibility of the system to financial crises, unless the formulation and implementation of monetary policy improve significantly. There seem to be only a few choices, and none offer the best of all possible worlds. One is liberated financial markets, which will bring forth the entrepreneurial spirit of its participants. This may result in increasing competitive struggles, followed by more financial concentration and, in the end, more government intervention again unless the efficiency of monetary policy improves vastly. However, there are the more structured markets with all their supposed inefficiencies. In the past, however, they have helped to slow quickly debt creation, because the institutions themselves experienced loss of profitability early. In the current and prospective environment, where constraints are diminishing and where many structural changes in the marketplace have occurred, monetary policy, to be effective, may have to engineer mini crises or at least have the market perceive the actual risk of such events if financial crises of increasing intensity are to be avoided.

8.
Framework for
Financial
Resiliency

HENRY C. WALLICH

The American economy, having passed through a long period during which risks were escalating, now seems to be clearly in the process of reducing financial risks. The data that accompanied the escalation phase are familiar. Nonfinancial enterprises increased the ratio of external to total financing from the low levels of the 1950s; within external financing they increased the role of debt relative to equity and, within debt, that of short-term to total debt. Cash and liquid assets declined in relation to short-term liabilities.

For the banking system, an analogous process meant diminishing capital ratios, increasing reliance on purchased funds, increasing "maturity intermediation" (transformation of short-term liabilities into long-term assets), and reducing the proportion of secondary liquid assets.

Most of these trends, in part displayed in Tables 1 through 4, had been continuing with only minor interruptions since the end of World War II, at which time the economy was perhaps overly liquid as a result of financial consolidation in the 1930s and the exigencies of wartime finance. In point of fact, it is difficult to indicate a historical period when the financial structure was "right."

A process of rebuilding liquidity and restructuring balance sheets has been underway for most nonfinancial and financial enterprises for well over a year. We do not know how far it will go. We do know that similar reversals in 1967 and 1970 were no more than interruptions of a longer trend toward higher risks. I believe that the present phase of consolidation is different. The shock waves that emanated from the events of 1973 and 1974 seem to have set in motion a trend toward greater financial caution, which promises to achieve a much more satisfactory degree of financial consolidation than has occurred on previous occasions.

The financial system is not condemned to move toward ever higher degrees of risk, with ever greater reliance on government to stave off ultimate calamity. On the contrary, the degree of risk taking in an economy fluctuates in long-term cycles, extending over a series of business cycles, and the elevation of risk exposure on one side of this cycle produces results that induce an extended period of movement toward safer financial configurations. If we think of insolvency as the ultimate brink toward which the escalation of risk leads, the early part of the long-term cycle represents an exploration of approaches to the brink. Nobody quite knows where it is. Some bold spirits press forward and, if they are observed not to fall over, others conclude that the terrain is safe and follow. Eventually some do go over, and the rest, having suffered a severe scare, fall back. The scare occasioned by the latest exhibitions of financial brinkmanship has been sufficient to induce a very sizable retreat toward safer ground.

It is this process of approach and retreat that I examine in somewhat more detail here. Underlying the process is a hypothesis that people's expectations of a major calamity are formed, much like other expectations, on the basis of a weighted sum of past experiences. Recent experience under such a hypothesis typically receives high weight, and experience far in the past low weight. If a major financial crisis, such as the 1930s, is only a few years behind, heavy weighting of recent past experience will make firms and households cautious. As the experience fades into the past, it receives diminishing weight relative to more recent experience when nothing adverse happened. Thus the restraint of experience diminishes over several relatively mild business cycles until the resulting escalation of risk leads to a new crisis and the process begins once more.

Within this framework, I examine some of the mechanisms and elements in the post-World War II environment that propelled business firms and banks in the direction of higher risk as recollections of past calamities faded. Three types of mechanisms were at work: (1) genuine changes in the degree of risk, especially as a result of government action of various sorts, (2) a change in perception, in a downward direction, of the probability of particular events, when the actual probabilities had not declined, and (3) changes in attitudes toward risk, that is, a reduction in risk aversion.

I begin by examining case 1, representing changes in objective reality that imply a reduction in risk. Government has had a reasonable, although far from complete, degree of success in using countercyclical fiscal and monetary policies

Table 1 Internal and External Sources of Funds of Nonfinancial Corporations[a]

End of Year or Quarter[b]	Retained Profits After IVA and CCA[c]	Capital Consumption Allowance[d]	Gross Internal Funds[e]	Short-Term Debt[f]	Long Term Debt[g]	Net Equity Issues[h]
		Annual Flows (billion of $)				
1946	3.2	4.6	7.8	6.0	3.5	1.0
1947	6.9	5.7	12.6	7.9	5.2	1.1
1948	11.9	6.8	18.7	3.2	5.2	1.0
1949	11.3	7.8	19.1	−3.6	2.9	1.2
1950	9.3	8.6	17.9	18.4	4.0	1.3
1951	9.9	10.0	19.9	8.0	5.8	2.1
1952	9.9	11.2	21.1	−0.2	5.8	2.3
1953	8.2	12.9	21.1	0.3	4.0	1.8
1954	8.7	14.6	23.3	−0.4	4.5	1.6
1955	12.2	17.0	29.2	15.4	6.1	1.7
1956	10.5	18.4	28.9	5.6	7.5	2.3
1957	10.3	20.3	30.6	1.0	8.5	2.4
1958	8.1	21.4	29.5	1.6	8.1	2.0
1959	12.1	22.9	35.0	10.5	7.5	2.1
1960	10.2	24.2	34.4	4.3	7.1	1.4
1961	10.2	25.4	35.6	8.0	8.7	2.1
1962	13.0	28.4	41.4	6.6	10.2	0.4
1963	14.9	29.5	44.4	11.8	10.1	−0.3
1964	19.3	30.7	50.0	11.3	9.8	1.1
1965	23.4	32.6	55.9	21.4	13.4	*
1966	25.0	35.4	60.4	16.7	18.3	1.3
1967	22.2	38.9	61.1	8.9	21.2	2.4
1968	19.5	42.6	62.1	29.9	22.2	−0.2
1969	14.3	47.3	61.6	32.5	21.5	3.4
1970	6.0	52.7	58.7	11.4	27.0	5.7
1971	10.3	57.7	68.0	9.9	31.1	11.4
1972	18.2	62.0	80.2	25.2	33.2	10.9
1973	15.7	68.1	83.8	44.4	39.8	7.4
1974	0.1	77.6	77.7	53.1	44.6	4.1
1975	15.2	88.6	103.8	−3.7	33.9	9.9
1976-I	25.2	94.8	120.0	37.3	24.6	7.2
Averages:						
1946–1950	8.5	6.7	15.2	6.4	4.2	1.1
1951–1955	9.8	13.1	22.9	4.6	5.2	1.9
1956–1960	10.2	21.4	31.7	4.6	7.7	2.0
1961–1965	16.2	29.3	45.5	11.8	10.4	0.8
1966–1970	17.4	43.4	60.8	19.9	22.0	2.5
1971–1975	11.9	70.8	82.7	25.8	36.5	8.7

to reduce business risk from major recessions. Even in 1973–1974 it took the combined interaction of food shortages, the oil crisis, a simultaneous cyclical downturn throughout the industrialized world, and the accumulated maladjustments of previous years, including almost 10 years of inflation, to produce the most severe recession of the postwar period. In addition to the risk reduction resulting from macroeconomic stabilization, the government has employed microeconomic measures to limit economic and financial risks for individuals and businesses, among them programs for income maintenance, governmental assistance to small businesses and farmers and even large firms in distress, lender-of-last-resort facilities, deposit insurance, mortgage insurance and guarantees, and stock market credit regulation.

Bank supervision and regulation should also be added to this list, since measures of this kind cannot achieve total protection. Regulation, by its nature, cannot cover all contingencies. Some avenues toward excessive risk taking are likely to remain open. If the regulated erroneously conclude that everything not marked dangerous is therefore necessarily safe, they may be misled. Likewise, if the regulated are prepared to accept a certain degree of risk in their operations, regulation that limits particular forms of risk will not keep them from achieving their preferred risk exposure. It will merely foreclose for them their preferred forms of risk, leaving open others that are second best. Thus regulation may lead the regulated toward the selection of risks they regard as suboptimal in kind, even if appropriate in degree.

Next I turn to what seems to be a tendency to reevaluate, that is, change the perception of, risks that in an objective sense are really invariant. This arises,

---

Source: Flow of Funds Section, Board of Governors of the Federal Reserve System.

[a] Nonfarm corporations.

[b] Numbers for first quarter 1976 are preliminary and are at seasonally adjusted annual rates.

[c] Retained profits are on the old NIA basis through 1961—reflect only the inventory valuation adjustment (IVA)—and are on the new NIA basis after 1961—reflect the inventory valuation adjustment plus the capital consumption adjustment (CCA) for underdepreciation. Retained profits include foreign branch profits.

[d] The capital consumption allowance is from the NIA and is primarily tabulated by the IRS from tax returns filed by nonfinancial corporations.

[e] Gross internal funds: retained profits after IVA and (since 1962) CCA plus capital consumption allowance. Totals may not add because of rounding.

[f] Short-term debt: commercial paper, acceptances, finance company loans, U.S. government loans, construction loans, 60 percent of bank loans Not Elsewhere Classified (N.E.C.), profit taxes payable, trade debt, and miscellaneous liabilities.

[g] Long-term debt: tax-exempt and corporate bonds, multifamily and commercial mortgages, and 40 percent of bank loans N.E.C.

[h] Net equity issues: new equity issues less equity retirements.

[i] Less than 0.05.

Table 2 External Sources of Funds of Nonfinancial Corporations: Percentage Distribution of Annual Flows[a]

End Year or Quarter[b]	External Sources of Funds (billion $)[c]	Percent		
		Short-Term Debt/ External Sources[a]	Long-Term Debt/ External Sources[a]	Net Equity Issues/ External Sources[a]
1946	10.5	57.1	33.3	9.5
1947	14.2	55.6	36.6	7.7
1948	9.4	34.0	55.3	10.6
1949	0.5	n.m.	n.m.	n.m.
1950	23.7	77.6	16.9	5.5
1951	15.9	50.3	36.5	13.2
1952	7.9	−2.5	73.4	29.1
1953	6.1	4.9	65.6	29.5
1954	5.7	−7.0	78.9	28.1
1955	23.2	66.4	26.3	7.3
1956	15.4	36.4	48.7	14.9
1957	11.9	8.4	71.4	20.2
1958	11.7	13.7	69.2	17.1
1959	20.1	52.2	37.3	10.4
1960	12.8	33.6	55.5	10.9
1961	18.8	42.5	46.3	11.2
1962	17.2	38.4	59.3	2.3
1963	21.6	54.6	46.8	−1.4
1964	22.2	50.9	44.1	5.0

164

1965	34.8	61.5	38.5	e
1966	35.3	46.0	50.4	3.6
1967	32.5	27.4	65.2	7.4
1968	5.9	57.6	42.8	-0.4
1969	57.4	56.6	37.5	5.9
1970	44.1	25.8	61.2	12.9
1971	52.4	18.9	59.4	21.7
1972	60.3	36.4	47.9	15.7
1973	9.6	48.5	43.4	8.1
1974	10.8	52.2	43.8	4.0
1975	49.1	-9.2	84.5	24.7
1976-I	69.1	54.0	35.6	10.4
Averages				
1946–1950	1.7	56.1	35.5	8.3
1951–1955	1.8	22.4	56.1	21.4
1956–1960	1.4	28.8	56.4	14.7
1961–1965	22.9	49.6	47.0	4.3
1966–1970	44.4	42.7	51.4	5.9
1971–1975	7.0	29.3	55.8	14.8

Source: Flow of Funds Section, Board of Governors of the Federal Reserve System.

[a] Nonfarm corporations.

[b] Numbers for first quarter 1976 are preliminary and are at seasonally adjusted annual rates.

[c] External source of funds: short-term debt, long-term debt and net equity issues. See Table 1 for these data.

[d] See the footnotes to Table 1 for the definition of this item. n.m. not meaningful.

[e] Less than 0.05.

166

Table 3 Total Sources of Funds of Nonfinancial Corporations: Percentage Distribution of Annual Flows[a]

End of Year or Quarter[b]	Total Sources of Funds (billion $)[c]	Gross Internal Funds/ Total Sources[d]	Memo: Ret. Profits/ Total Sources[d]	Percent Short-Term Debt/ Total Sources[d]	Long-Term Debt/ Total Sources[d]	Total Debt/ Total Sources[e]	Net Equity Issues/ Total Sources[a]
1946	18.3	42.6	17.5	32.8	19.1	51.9	5.5
1947	26.8	47.0	25.7	29.5	19.4	48.9	4.1
1948	28.1	66.6	42.3	11.4	18.5	29.9	3.6
1949	19.6	97.5	57.6	-18.4	14.8	-3.5	6.1
1950	41.6	43.0	22.3	44.2	9.6	53.8	3.1
1951	35.8	55.6	27.6	22.3	16.2	38.5	5.9
1952	29.0	72.8	34.1	-0.7	20.0	-19.3	7.9
1953	27.2	77.6	30.1	1.1	14.7	15.8	6.6
1954	29.0	80.3	30.0	-1.3	15.5	-14.1	5.5
1955	52.4	55.7	23.3	29.4	11.6	41.0	3.2
1956	44.3	65.2	23.7	12.6	16.9	29.6	5.2
1957	42.5	72.0	24.2	2.4	20.0	22.3	5.7
1958	41.2	71.6	19.7	3.9	19.7	23.5	4.9
1959	55.1	63.5	22.0	19.1	13.6	32.7	3.8
1960	47.2	72.9	21.6	9.1	15.0	24.2	3.0
1961	54.4	65.4	18.7	14.7	16.0	30.7	3.9

1962	58.6	70.7	22.2	11.3	17.4	28.7	0.7
1963	66.0	67.3	22.5	17.9	15.3	33.2	-0.5
1964	72.2	69.3	26.7	15.6	13.6	29.2	1.5
1965	90.7	61.6	25.8	23.6	14.8	38.4	f
1966	96.7	62.5	25.9	17.3	18.9	36.2	1.3
1967	93.6	65.3	23.7	9.5	22.5	32.2	2.6
1968	114.0	54.5	17.1	26.2	19.5	45.7	-0.2
1969	119.0	51.8	12.0	27.3	18.1	45.4	2.9
1970	102.8	57.1	5.8	11.1	26.3	37.4	5.5
1971	120.4	56.5	8.6	8.2	25.8	34.1	9.5
1972	149.5	53.7	12.2	16.9	22.2	39.1	7.3
1973	175.4	47.8	9.0	25.3	22.7	48.0	4.2
1974	179.5	43.3	0.1	29.6	24.9	54.4	2.3
1975	143.9	72.1	10.6	2.6	23.6	-21.0	6.9
1976-I	189.1	63.5	13.3	19.7	13.0	32.7	3.8

Source: Flow of Funds Section, Board of Governors of the Federal Reserve System.

a Nonfarm corporations.

b Numbers for first quarter 1976 are preliminary and are at seasonally adjusted annual rates.

c Total sources of funds: gross internal funds plus external sources of funds. See Tables 1 and 2 for data and definitions.

d See Table 1 for data and definition.

e Total debt: short-term debt plus long-term debt. Totals may not add because of rounding. See Table 1 for data and definitions.

f Less than 0.05.

Table 4 Selected Outstandings and Ratios of Nonfinancial Corporations[a]

End of Year or Quarter[b]	Outstandings (billion $)					Ratios of Outstandings			
	Liquid Assets[c]	Short-Term Debt[d]	Total Debt[e]	Historical Cost Equity[f]	Current Cost Equity[g]	Liquid Assets/ Short-Term Debt	Short-Term Debt/ Total Debt	Historical Cost Equity/ Total Capitalization[h]	Current Cost Equity/ Total Capitalization[h]
1946	33.5	41.5	80.5	96.5	113.3	0.807	0.516	0.545	0.585
1947	35.1	49.5	93.7	110.6	133.9	0.709	0.528	0.541	0.588
1948	36.3	52.5	102.2	124.5	148.9	0.691	0.514	0.549	0.593
1949	39.4	49.0	101.5	136.0	155.7	0.804	0.483	0.573	0.605
1950	44.0	67.7	124.1	151.6	173.8	0.650	0.546	0.550	0.583
1951	46.7	75.9	138.1	168.0	192.2	0.615	0.550	0.549	0.582
1952	46.6	75.8	143.8	179.1	202.0	0.615	0.527	0.555	0.584
1953	48.6	76.6	148.5	191.5	214.9	0.634	0.516	0.563	0.591
1954	48.9	76.4	152.9	201.0	222.5	0.640	0.500	0.568	0.593
1955	54.2	92.0	174.5	216.3	245.3	0.589	0.527	0.554	0.584
1956	49.7	97.8	187.8	231.2	269.0	0.508	0.521	0.552	0.589
1957	49.2	98.8	197.4	244.8	286.6	0.498	0.501	0.554	0.592
1958	51.7	100.6	207.4	255.2	297.2	0.514	0.485	0.552	0.589
1959	57.1	111.7	225.9	269.8	313.2	0.511	0.494	0.544	0.581
1960	53.0	116.1	237.6	281.0	320.0	0.457	0.489	0.542	0.574
1961	56.5	122.0	253.2	292.4	329.5	0.459	0.486	0.535	0.565
1962	59.6	129.8	270.2	308.2	343.7	0.459	0.480	0.533	0.560
1963	64.2	141.8	292.3	322.6	359.1	0.453	0.485	0.525	0.551
1964	65.1	153.5	313.7	342.6	380.6	0.424	0.489	0.522	0.548

1965	67.8	175.3	348.9	364.9	405.8	0.387	0.502	0.511	0.538
1966	64.1	192.0	383.9	392.2	439.3	0.334	0.500	0.505	0.534
1967	68.8	201.6	414.6	418.3	473.7	0.341	0.486	0.502	0.533
1968	76.7	231.3	466.6	439.6	508.2	0.332	0.496	0.485	0.521
1969	78.9	26?.9	520.7	466.7	553.4	0.299	0.507	0.473	0.515
1970	78.5	275.8	559.6	485.7	595.5	0.285	0.493	0.465	0.516
1971	89.1	285.4	600.4	514.0	643.3	0.312	0.475	0.462	0.517
1972	93.1	310.7	658.6	548.3	701.3	0.300	0.472	0.454	0.516
1973	100.1	356.0	748.8	598.6	780.1	0.281	0.475	0.444	0.512
1974	113.1	412.0	844.3	653.5	922.2	0.275	0.488	0.436	0.522
1975	132.4	408.4	874.7	646.0	1002.1	0.324	0.467	0.425	0.534
1976-I	133.2	412.6	883.2	n.a.	n.a.	0.323	0.467	n.a.	n.a.

Source: Flow of Funds Section, Board of Governors of the Federal Reserve System.

a Nonfarm corporations; n.a., not available.

b Numbers for first quarter 1976 are preliminary.

c Liquid assets: demand deposits, currency, time deposits, U.S. government securities, state and local obligations, commercial paper, and security R.P.'s.

d Short-term debt: see footnotes to Table 1 for a definition.

e Total debt: short-term debt plus long-term debt. See footnotes to Table 1 for definitions

f Historical cost equity represents the capital stock of nonfinancial corporations using historical cost accounting. Financial assets are valued at par or book value, while fixed assets and inventories are valued at historical cost after deducting depreciation on a straight-line basis, which is the most common accounting method used in published statements of condition. The number for 1975 is preliminary.

g Current cost equity represents the capital stock of nonfinancial corporations using current cost accounting. Financial assets are valued at par or book value, while fixed assets are valued at current prices after deducting depreciation on a double declining balance basis. The number for 1975 is preliminary.

h Total capitalization is the sum of total debt plus historical cost equity when the numerator of the ratio is historical cost equity and is the sum of total debt plus current cost equity when the numerator is current cost equity.

first, because asset markets, like other markets, sometimes develop imperfections. Some assets are not always valued correctly, and innovative operators may then be able to take advantage of this. Their success, however, can spawn imitators whose actions may contribute to an overevaluation of assets that originally were not undervalued. There are many obvious examples of this in the history of the stock and real estate markets.

Second, a tendency to underestimate risk may occur because the ultimate consequences of excessive risk do not materialize immediately. In terms of probability, a high-risk operation may work out well several times or for a considerable period before the failure whose probability was underestimated occurs. In the interim, erroneous assessments of the true risk may proliferate.

Third, excessive risk taking can result from the tendency of portfolio managers to justify their decisions by reference to the decisions of others similarly situated, rather than by use of objective criteria. When a peer group is employed to represent the standard of sound practice, there is no real check on a developing trend toward riskier portfolios.

Fourth, managers of investments, financial and real, probably tend to underestimate covariance within portfolios or assets or projects they manage. For the expert whose job it is to evaluate the risk and return of a particular asset, the specific risk of that asset very easily comes to dominate his or her assessment of general market risk. In the event, as we have often seen, market risk may dominate, as most factors tend to go up and down together, and the result will be excessive risk taking.

Fifth, even when risk is recognized and a risk premium demanded, it may not always give the protection expected. It is one thing to invest in a B bond and receive a risk premium of 1 percent per year for 30 years. It is quite another to receive the same premium rate on a 90-day certificate of deposit. There is in effect no reasonable risk premium that could compensate for substantial risk in a short-term asset. A belief to the contrary is likely to lead to excessive risk taking.

From the discussion of changing perception, that is, reevaluation, of objectively unchanging risks, I now turn to the possibility that fundamental attitudes toward risk may change over time, leading to a greater willingness to accept risks that are correctly evaluated as such. It should be borne in mind that risk aversion is not necessarily good and that risk neutrality is not necessarily bad. Much economic theorizing postulates risk neutrality on the part of the firm and risk aversion on the part of individuals as ultimate wealth owners. In the long run, one may assume, a sample of risk-neutral firms will outcompete a sample of risk-averse firms, even though a higher percentage of the risk neutrals may fall by the wayside.

First, a firm's willingness to accept risk may increase over time as older executives who experienced the last big crisis retire.

Furthermore, the attitude of managers toward risk tends to depend on the structure of penalties and rewards. A manager who expects to be penalized for losses but not to be greatly rewarded for gains is very cautious. Another who has a chance to make it big if he wins, and thinks he can always find another job if he misses, leans in the other direction. The increased use of stock options and management bonuses may encourage this attitude. It appears that, in the investment business at least, the structure of rewards and penalties was moving in the second direction before recent calamities struck.

Finally, there may be a tendency to accept greater risk with respect to the investment of money derived from past gains than with respect to the original investment.

These situations, although based only upon casual empiricism, seem to provide at least a partial explanation of behavior observed in the not-too-distant past. If my basic hypothesis is right—the highest weight in the formation of expectations attaches to recent, often traumatic, experience—most of the mechanisms pushing for greater risk taking are now operating in reverse. The bright young men have learned a lesson, or perhaps they are gone altogether. Greatly increased risk premiums indicate a heightened awareness among investors as to the risk being assumed. These premiums in turn create an incentive for firms to move to less exposed positions. The location of the brink has been thoroughly explored, and some have fallen over. The question is how far the retreat from the brink will go and how long it will last.

There is no signpost telling us where danger ends and safety begins. There are only more safe and less safe positions. A fully informed investing public accurately gauging economic risk makes asset choices which guide firms to positions reflecting public preferences. We should bear in mind that a universal effort to achieve maximum safety may send us on a long and thirsty journey, as each of the travelers tries to improve liquidity or protect solvency by forcing a less advantageous position on the rest.

Improvement in balance sheet structures, both of nonfinancial and financial corporations, is obviously very much needed. I conclude with a short account of a few measures government has taken, and a few it could take, to shorten and ease the trip, and to reduce artificial incentives to riskier financial structures.

First, the monetary authority has not sought to resolve liquidity and solvency problems by inflating the economy. The rate of growth of the money supply M_1 has been moderate over the last 2 years and the Federal Reserve plans to keep it that way. We have learned, moreover, that whatever power inflation might have had in the past to float the economy off any financial shoals has vanished today. Inflation has revealed itself as a threat to liquidity and solvency.

What government has done of late through its fiscal policy is to take on some of the burden of debt that needed to be incurred if savings were to be invested and jobs protected. Over the entire postwar period, however, the federal government has been the one sector that has sharply reduced its debt relative to its income. As a result, all other sectors together have found their debt/income ratios rising. While this may have been an additional factor making for higher risk, I do not accept for a moment the implication that the government should increase its debt in order to spare the private sector the need to increase its own. The private sector can live with higher debt/income ratios than those of the late 1940s and the 1950s. But the substitution of public for private debt capacity during the recent recession has been beneficial for the restructuring process as well as for the maintenance of income levels. I need hardly add that what is beneficial during a recession may become a threat as recovery advances.

I have in the past examined two devices that may reduce the economy's inherent pressure toward escalating risk. One is a change in our tax system designed to eliminate the tax bias toward debt and against equity. We can achieve this by reducing the tax deductibility of interest, thereby increasing the tax base so that the corporate tax on dividends and profit retentions may be simultaneously reduced. If the same tax rate were applied to income going into interest payments, dividend payments, and profit retentions, the tax system would be neutral with regard to the corporate choice between equity and debt. The problems of phasing into such a system—it can only be done gradually— are not inconsiderable, but can most likely be solved.

A second reduction in our financial risk exposure applies to the banking system. The present insurance of $40,000 per deposit protects 63 percent of the dollar value of deposits in insured banks, but leaves particularly large banks vulnerable to withdrawal of deposits in excess of $40,000. The historical loss experience, even including the U.S. National Bank of San Diego and the Franklin National Bank of New York, indicates that it would cost little to raise the level of insurance even up to 100 percent. Doing so, in addition to provid: ing insurance, would also help to minimize liquidity problems such as arose in the case of Franklin National, where a rapid runoff of certificates of deposit forced the Federal Reserve to substitute its credit for that of large depositors. However, it may not be wise to go to 100 percent insurance, even if some of the inherent regulatory problems would be dealt with by graduated premiums. Full deposit insurance may eliminate the discipline now exerted over banks by the marketplace. Nor is insurance a full substitute for a continued effort by banks to improve their capital positions. Nevertheless, enlarged deposit insurance is one of the avenues open to the government to increase the safety of our financial structure.

9. A Projected Resilient Financial Environment

KENNETH M. WRIGHT

DEFINITIONS OF RESILIENCY

The term "resiliency" is not part of the usual lexicon of economics and therefore requires examination at the outset. The dictionary definition of resiliency emphasizes the word "elasticity" which is a traditional concept in economics but in a far different sense. Elasticity refers to the relation between the price and the quantity purchased or offered, that is, the shape of a demand or supply curve. We are considering extreme cases in which shifts in demand or supply schedules move beyond the normal range, where demand-supply schedules fail to intersect, with a consequent discontinuity in markets.

One way to define a financial crisis may be to speak of a situation in which buyers and sellers are unable to find a price at which markets will clear, leading to a breakdown in the market system. An example is the inability of bond issuers to obtain bids on new offerings, for whatever reason. In this context, resiliency refers to the ability to absorb or recover from the shock that has produced market discontinuity. To return to a secondary dictionary definition, resiliency is the capability "to recover its size and shape after deformation, especially by compressive stresses." One is reminded of the physical effect of hitting a golf ball or tennis ball, but a better analogy may be a trampoline. In the trampoline analogy, one may go on to consider such factors as the strength and condition of the canvas, the tautness of the lashings, and the stability of the frame. But I do not wish to introduce a new "trampoline school" of economics, so I will not press the analogy further. In plain language, I consider resiliency the ability to recover from a financial crisis without a cumulative worsening of or permanent damage to the functioning of markets.

My approach in this paper is institutional and impressionistic, rather than theoretical and quantitative. In this way, I hope to disarm my critics who may prefer to attack this problem with multivariant regressions and econometric models. Still, I hope to provide enough of a systematic analysis to lay a foundation for more rigid examination by others using more sophisticated techniques.

REVIEWS OF PAST FINANCIAL CRISES

To lay the groundwork for analysis, it may be helpful to review briefly the major financial crises of the past 75 years and the responses that took place, designed either to correct the problem promptly or to forestall a recurrence.

An early example is the Panic of 1907 which resulted from an institutional inelasticity in the money supply and led directly to the establishment of the Federal Reserve system in 1913. Next, the stock market collapse of 1929–1931 led to the establishment of the Securities Exchange Commission to prevent fraudulent stock exchange practices and also to Federal Reserve margin requirements to curb the excessive use of credit in the stock market. A third well-known crisis was the run on the banks that led to the Bank Holiday of 1933, followed by establishment of the Federal Deposit Insurance Corporation to restore confidence and to insure small deposits. Fourth, the collapse of the residential mortgage market during the Great Depression led to the Federal Housing Administration (FHA) insurance system and development of the self-amortizing mortgage. Finally, widespread corporate bankruptcies in the depression years led to establishment of the Reconstruction Finance Corporation (RFC) to inject new capital into private business through loans or purchases of preferred stock.

It is noteworthy in all these instances that the response to each form of financial market breakdown was through governmental action, which obviously came too late to end the crisis but did provide a new framework to soften the impact in case of a recurrence. A good part of the market resiliency that exists in our present markets must be attributed to the presence of these new governmental agencies.

In the first two decades after World War II, we somehow avoided any major financial crises worthy of the name. We did see a major adjustment in market practices and attitudes after the U.S. Treasury–Federal Reserve Accord of 1951 and the unpegging of government bond prices. It was at this time that the term "resiliency" came into use in financial circles, as part of the phrase "depth, breadth, and resiliency," to describe the U.S. Treasury bill market where Federal Reserve open market operations were confined under the "bills only" doctrine of the time. U.S. Treasury coupon markets were deemed to be "too thin" to absorb the weight of open market operations without untoward effects on prices.

The 1945–1965 period did have its share of dramatic episodes, such as the bankruptcy of certain finance companies and the infamous "salad oil scandal" which led to unexpected losses by many investors. But these did not assume the magnitude of a true crisis with national impacts of the type we have seen in the past decade. Perhaps some scholar should examine the market environment that enabled us to fare so well over these two decades in contrast to the recurrent financial crises after 1965.

CATALOG OF FINANCIAL CRISES OF 1965–1975

Rather than a chronological review, it seems preferable to classify the many crises of this period according to their major or proximate cause, using illustrations under each category and noting the effects on market participants and/or the public. Against this background, a second classification is later set forth according to the method used to resolve or overcome the crisis, using flashbacks to specific cases noted in the first classification. The organization of these categories may appear loose and arbitrary, sometimes using the same example in two places, but it serves to form a basis for applying the lessons from this experience to the outlook for future resiliency of the financial system.

Corporate Mismanagement Leading to Actual or Imminent Bankruptcies

Under this heading are included Penn Central, Lockheed, the Franklin National Bank of New York, and the Real Estate Investment Trusts (REITs).[1] The Penn Central collapse not only threatened the loss of rail service in the northeast but led to more cautious investor attitudes toward other railroads and airlines. Another repercussion was widespread doubt as to the ability of corporate issuers of commercial paper to roll over such obligations, as noted later. In the Lockheed case, the threatened bankruptcy raised questions concerning the

---

[1] Some might include W. T. Grant because of its size, but it has been ignored here because its repercussions were not as broad or as deep.

continuity of regional employment and the ability to complete private and military contracts. The collapse of Franklin National not only led to heavy depositor withdrawals but also threw suspicion on other commercial banks and raised international concern over the soundness of the U.S. banking system. The REITs came to disaster through overleveraging, with short-term debt positions that could not be sustained when interest rates rose sharply and the demand for real estate began to slacken. Speculative inventory of unsold construction projects, both residential and commercial, is in the process of liquidation at substantial losses to the REITs and to their creditors.

Fiscal Mismanagement by Governmental Entities

The leading example under this heading is obviously New York City, which found itself unable to roll over its obligations even at penalty rates and required special financing on a nonmarket basis from local financial institutions. This crisis not only threatened the continuity of public services in New York City, but the potential collapse of the market values of its obligations jeopardized the financial position of a great many commercial banks with large holdings of such New York City issues. Additionally, widespread investor concern arose over a wide spectrum of state and local government issues, with a consequent inability of some borrowers to market their obligations on a normal basis over a period of several weeks. Investors seeking to unload holdings of lower-rated municipal issues encountered difficulty in finding bids for such offerings in the disorderly market that prevailed for a time.

It is tempting to include under this heading fiscal mismanagement by the federal government, but I resist the temptation except to note that the steep climb to unscaled heights of required U.S. Treasury deficit financing obviously raises serious questions of potential financial crisis, unless other sectors of the financial market have the capability to adapt. Perhaps one demonstration that our financial system is extraordinarily resilient is the very fact that federal debt was increased by $85 billion in one calendar year without disastrous consequences for the rest of the financial system.

Impact of Inflation on the Level of Interest Rates

Largely because of high rates of inflation, interest rates have risen to the highest levels of the last 100 years, climbing above 8 percent on high-grade corporate bonds in 1969, and above 10 percent in 1974. The very height of interest rate levels has created a climate of greater financial tension and potential crisis throughout the financial system over the past decade. Many investment projects have become infeasible with borrowing costs at these high levels, causing plans to be scrapped or projects to be abandoned in midstream.

High interest rates have added greatly to the burden of fixed debt charges carried by corporate business and home buyers, a burden that will not be worked off for many years.

In addition to raising interest rates, the presence or expectation of high-rate inflation has called into question the viability of fixed income obligations themselves and the feasibility of continuing to borrow or lend through traditional debt instruments of mortgages and bonds. About 5 years ago, serious concerns were voiced over the willingness of individual savers and/or institutional lenders to be locked into fixed dollar investments in which real purchasing power of the principal and interest might be cut in half within a decade and more severely impaired over the 20- to 25-year maturity of the instrument.

The severe market imbalances and adjustments required under conditions of high inflation rates have not brought on a financial crisis in the traditional sense of precipitous breaks in market continuity. But they have produced severe strains and dislocations throughout the financial world, with innumerable shocks to business concerns and institutions which would not have occurred at lower levels of inflation. Perhaps most important to the question of financial crisis is that the emergence of high-rate inflation has led to antiinflation policy actions by the government, which in turn have triggered financial crises on repeated occasions, as shown in the next section.

Impact of Government Policy Changes

To combat rising inflation, Federal Reserve policy has periodically shifted toward monetary restraint, often quite severe, with sharp upward movements in interest rate levels as a result. The financial crises created by these actions largely fall under the heading of "disintermediation," with large-scale deposit drains from depositary thrift institutions and also policy loan drains at life insurance companies. This is not to say that the Federal Reserve was mistaken or unjustified in taking action that raised the levels of market interest rates. However, by working within a financial framework replete with fixed interest rate ceilings at many points, the inevitable result was to shift the flow of market funds away from lower-rate outlets to the high-rate market instruments that became available to a wide range of individual investors. The culprit in these unhappy episodes was the very presence of rate rigidities or limits, though the Federal Reserve was obviously aware of their existence and the market consequences. Among the offending rate limits were the deposit rate ceilings at thrift institutions, the fixed interest rate on life insurance policy loans, the usury law ceilings in many states, and the legal limits on borrowing costs of many state and local jurisdictions. The mortgage rate ceilings of the FHA and Veterans Administration had created a somewhat similar problem during the 1950s, but rapid administrative adjustments in rate ceilings in recent years have ameliorated this situation.

It should be noted that the proximate cause of crises under this heading has been the widening differential between market rates and controlled rates, as distinct from the effects upon the financial system of generally high interest rates created by the expectation of high-rate inflation.

Government actions to resist inflation through monetary restraint seem also to have increased the volatility of market interest rates, with sharper swings during the past 10 years than over the previous 20 years. Such volatility has led many borrowers to be caught in a sudden squeeze of sharply higher rates, as in the notable case of REITs which could not afford to roll over their short-term borrowings as they had expected or to obtain longer-term takeout financing at rate levels projected for their projects.

General Loss of Confidence

This factor is often mentioned as the cause of financial crises, and it is certainly visible in a number of specific cases. However, loss of confidence is probably a secondary effect of a more fundamental cause, often creating acute difficulties for institutions or businesses not immediately involved in the original crisis.

Among the illustrations that seem to fit this category are the difficulties of the commercial paper market in the days and weeks immediately after the failure of Penn Central; the markets for municipal bond issues outside New York City, when bids were very hard to find for sellers of new or seasoned municipal debt; and the loss of confidence in a wide range of commercial banks after the failure of Franklin National generated doubts about bank solvency generally and the safety of negotiable certificates of deposit in specific instances. In each of these cases, the difficulty spread from a specific crisis to a more generalized situation of reduced confidence which disrupted the normal functioning of markets at least for a time.

MEANS OF RESOLVING RECENT FINANCIAL CRISES

Despite this recitation of horrors, the U.S. financial system has survived and recovered, which is the most pertinent and impressive demonstration of our resiliency. One might ask whether it would have been possible for our financial market system to weather these storms under the conditions that prevailed in the 1920s or 1930s, and also whether such repeated crises could have been overcome in other advanced nations during the 1965–1975 decade. Probably not. This section examines how these U.S. financial crises were overcome or resolved, leaving scars perhaps, but without permanent damage to the system.

Again, we proceed with a catalog of differing solutions with reference to the various crises cited above.

New Federal Legislation

New legislation by the federal government was the principal means of resolving financial crises in the cases of Lockheed, Penn Central, and New York City. This involved extensions of government credit or reorganization under government auspices based in each case on ad hoc legislation. It is useful to observe that none of these legislative solutions involved a wider range of corporations or the establishment of new programs, as seen during the depression years. Still, suggestions were offered that such broader programs were needed to ensure continuity of vital public services and to permit prompt resolution of future crises, perhaps with an RFC-type entity for corporations, as well as broader use of federal credit or guarantees to backstop state and local financial difficulties in credit markets.

Federal Reserve Actions

While the Federal Reserve system has been identified as a proximate cause of recurrent financial crises under the heading of "disintermediation," it has also played a role in resolving several financial crises through the use of special techniques or by assuming a role beyond its narrower functions. Even during the first disintermediation of 1966, the Federal Reserve took special steps to provide added liquidity for institutions affected by cash flow drains, in order to avoid disorderly markets that might be created by the wholesale dumping of marketable assets. As opportunities arose, the Federal Reserve also led the way in adjusting rate ceilings upward among the banks and thrift institutions to bring them more into line with the higher prevailing level of interest rates. In the commercial paper crisis of June–July 1970, the Federal Reserve stepped forward to avoid a serious liquidity squeeze by making bank credit readily available to corporations that could not roll over their commercial paper, hence substituting bank borrowings for intercorporate borrowings during this troubled period. In the Franklin National crisis, the Federal Reserve entered into special arrangements including an advance of $1.7 billion to bolster the liquidity of that institution, and furthermore acquired Franklin National's foreign exchange position to prevent dishonoring of those contracts. In the New York City crisis, the Federal Reserve relaxed its credit policy during the fall of 1975, partly to avoid a state of financial stringency among commercial banks threatened with the possibility of a default on a sizable portion of their securities portfolios. In short, the central banking authorities have played an active role in softening the impact of U.S. financial crises, especially on those parts of the financial system not immediately involved in the origins of the crises. Such imaginative and flexible attitudes by the central bank act as one of the bulwarks of the resiliency of our financial system, by providing liquidity when needed to forestall, or shorten the duration of, disorderly market conditions.

The Role of Federal Credit Agencies

It is often taken for granted that certain federal agencies play a role in smoothing out financial disruptions. The Federal Reserve itself is the key source of liquidity, though at a price, for the commercial banking system. Additionally, the Federal Home Loan Bank system provides borrowing facilities to its member savings and loan associations and has been instrumental in cushioning the impact of disintermediation on repeated occasions. The mortgage credit agencies—Federal National Mortgage Association (FNMA) and Government National Mortgage Association (GNMA)—helped to stabilize the mortgage market during periods of stress by providing secondary markets for mortgage loans and maintaining a flow of housing credit when private institutional sources were in a state of disarray. Finally, the FDIC has continued to be a source of comfort in bank failures, playing a major role in protecting the interests of depositors, including the difficult case of Franklin National. The support framework provided by these government agencies should not be neglected in any analysis of resiliency, though their roles are now considered traditional and expected. Without them, we certainly would have seen different results in the past 10 years.

Innovation of Market Techniques and Instruments

As noted earlier, high-rate inflation has threatened the viability of fixed dollar debt markets, in the fear that even high interest rates could not adequately compensate longer-term investors for declining real values. In the period since 1965, a host of innovations has been developed or revived, in large part to overcome investor concern over the high level or volatility of market interest rates. Convertible debt issues became very popular in 1969–1970, allowing corporations to hold down fixed interest charges while providing investors with a stock market option which had considerable appeal in the days when common stock was considered a workable inflation hedge. In the mortgage field, variable mortgage rates were designed (and put into use in a few jurisdictions) to allow interest rates and portfolio returns to fluctuate more closely with changing market rates. In the commercial mortgage field, the high interest rates and tight money generated by rising inflation in 1969 led to widespread use of income participation or contingent interest features on top of fixed contract interest rates in order to provide lenders with a higher return from "a piece of the action" then expected from rising rental revenues. Still another innovation has been floating rate notes tied to movements in short-term U.S. Treasury bill rates, issued by some banks and industrial corporations with considerable initial success among investors who sought an inflation hedge in this form in the belief that higher inflation would be offset in part by higher interest payments. Volatility of rate levels has also led to adoption of the floating prime rate among commercial banks, enabling them to better balance out the current cost of short-term funds raised through certificates of deposit against business loans made for longer periods. Another innovation in response to very high short-term rates and an inverted yield curve has been the money market funds that enable individual investors to channel savings into U.S. Treasury bills and other short-term instruments when the yields against savings deposit rates or long-term bond yields became favorable.

Market Losses by Investors

I do not wish to leave the impression that financial crises have been resolved in all instances by the salvation of government rescue operations, or the timely intervention of government agencies, or ingenious innovations in market practices. Severe losses have often been suffered by private investors who have paid the full penalty for taking market risks. The emergence of unforeseen events, misjudgments of credit worthiness, or yielding to speculative temptations have brought disaster to both borrowers and lenders in many instances, including cases not enumerated here. The scars of these experiences have undoubtedly led to more cautious attitudes, both by the loss takers and by unscathed bystanders, as to the practices they will follow to avoid such mistakes in the future. In this sense, market participants may now be less tolerant of exposure to risk and thereby reduce the probability of future crises arising from speculation or financial overextension.

THE OUTLOOK FOR FUTURE RESILIENCY

Based on the pattern of analysis used for past financial crises, the outlook for resiliency in the decade ahead may be divided according to (1) the potential for emergence of future crises, and (2) the ability of our financial system to respond promptly and efficiently in overcoming such crises. One underlying thought is the possibility that the harsh lessons of the past decade may encourage business and government policies designed to avoid crises and therefore demand less resiliency from the system. If the reverse is true, and the history of the past decade means that our financial system has become more crisis-prone, more adequate response mechanisms will be needed to retain the resiliency we prize so highly.

Potential Sources of Future Crises

How vulnerable is the U.S. financial system to major crises over the next decade? While our vision is always blurred on such matters, there are several areas that may be examined for possible answers. First, in the area of corporate mismanagement, the dramatic cases of corporate bankruptcies witnessed in the past few years seem to have encouraged a new sense of business conservatism and caution which could forestall the imprudent practices that have led to bankruptcies and financial crises. After all, the hard lessons of the depression years imbued the business community with a cautious attitude that apparently helped to keep us free of major bankruptcies for two decades after World War II.

A second potential source of crisis is undercapitalization of business and/or banking institutions. Broader concern has been expressed about the substantial erosion of debt/equity ratios and deposit/capital ratios, which leaves a thin margin for businesses or banks to absorb unforeseen shocks. It is interesting to note that this factor was not a visible cause of the crises of the 1965–1976 decade, but there is a danger that we have run out our string on thin capitalization. The possible vulnerability in this area should be corrected through a change in the tax treatment of dividend payments as against interest payments by corporations, to better equalize the comparative costs of raising capital through the debt-versus-equity route.

A third factor that presents cause for concern is the international payments area, which was not covered in my analysis of recent financial crises but could readily qualify by reason of the dollar devaluations after 1971 and the later concern over petrodollar recycling. There can be little question that the international payments system is now less stable than it was earlier and the possibility of unforeseeable major shocks over the next decade is much higher. As American business and financial relationships have moved increasingly into the international sphere, this involvement has become a far greater source of potential crisis. Despite the weakening of the dollar, our currency still remains a key currency in international trade and capital movements. If the experience of the pound sterling over the past century is any guide, a currency that wears this mantle must expect to face crises that will impact the domestic financial system from time to time. It is by no means apparent that we have the response mechanism in place that would allow us to quickly overcome the effects of crises originating in the international sphere.

Fourth, and perhaps most important, is the potential force of renewed high-rate inflation within the next decade. A great many of the financial ills of the past decade have stemmed directly or indirectly from inflation and, while the current view is that inflation rates will average somewhat lower in the years immediately ahead, there are probably few who would rule out absolutely an outburst of double-digit inflation rates at some point within the next decade. Government policy responses of curbing excess demand and restricting the growth of credit could impose severe financial stress in some markets, as they have in the past. As noted above, however, the financial strains produced by antiinflation policies have often resulted from the interaction of such policies with fixed interest rate ceilings. To reduce our vulnerability to the potential of high inflation, and the restrictive government policies provoked thereby, it seems clearly advisable to remove fixed interest rate ceilings to the greatest extent possible, in order to allow greater flexibility within the market system and more rapid adjustment to financial strains as they arise.

Ability to Respond to Financial Crises

We already have in place an impressive array of governmental agencies which can operate effectively to cushion against the shock of financial crises and to prevent a pervasive loss of confidence or a cumulative worsening of financial debacles. These include the Federal Reserve, the FDIC, the Federal Home Loan Banks, the Securities Exchange Commission, and a variety of federal credit agencies. They have served us well in the past, and they seem likely to continue their good performance in the future. It may prove necessary, however, to develop still further tools for these agencies, particularly to withstand shocks from the international payments system where the U.S. Treasury and Federal Reserve are most deeply involved at present.

Defense against widespread corporate bankruptcies has not been developed in a generalized way, along the lines of the RFC of the depression years. Specific cases such as Lockheed and Penn Central were dealt with by specific legislation. Unless our economy becomes involved in a generalized business downturn threatening a cumulative impact of the depression variety, it seems inadvisable to construct such a safety net as a national program. In a very real sense, the best means of avoiding financial losses is to leave open the possibility of losses, so that managers and financiers will approach their decisions with the risk of loss clearly in mind. Stated another way, there is a danger that a widespread reliance on government bail-outs will give rise to business and financial decisions that create the occasion for such bail-outs.

The ability of the U.S. financial system to innovate, especially under the pressure of changing market conditions, is a very real source of strength and resiliency. But it should also be remembered that the REITs were themselves a type of innovation that ultimately came to disaster under unforeseen conditions of high and volatile interest rates. Nevertheless, innovations that allow markets to function under adverse conditions, by creating new instruments or new channels for credit, represent a fundamental means for overcoming or forestalling financial impasses or crises.

Summing up, I submit that the prospects for adequate financial resiliency in the next decade are reasonably good, though not fully ensured. We should be alert to the need for new policy tools and for enhanced market flexibility through the removal of interest rate ceilings. In the last analysis, the ability of our financial system to withstand and overcome financial crises rests on our determination to avoid the conditions that lead to crises, particularly high rates of inflation. The objectives of balanced and sustainable economic growth, along with reasonable price stability, remain the indispensable ingredients for a financial system that can effectively serve our private and social needs without recurrent crises.

Discussion

Barry Bosworth

All four of these papers are concerned with the causes and implications of financial crises. Yet the paper by Hyman Minsky differs sharply in tone from the others, since he sees the tendency toward financial instability as being inherent in the structure of modern financial markets. It emphasizes a view of financial markets that is primarily concerned with the process of moving funds between savers and investors rather than the supply and demand of money. In addition, it reflects a concern with financial asset structures in addition to interest rates. Implicitly, the latter condition reflects the existence of substantial imperfections in the markets for capital assets—particularly the limited nature of resale markets for highly specialized physical capital. This is in sharp contrast to the neoclassical approach in which capital is simply another variable factor—like labor—which can be bought and sold. The existence of a variety of financial assets (such as short-term debt, long-term debt, and equity) provides a means of allocating the risks associated with the ownership of long-term specialized physical assets which cannot be easily resold.

However, I wonder to what extent the recent problems of our financial system can be traced to the inherent trends stressed by Minsky, as opposed to an alternative explanation which emphasizes the increased instability of nominal interest rates and the sharp decline in the rate of return on physical capital since 1966.

The basic structure of the U.S. financial system developed during a postwar period (prior to 1966) of low inflation and relative stability of nominal interest rates. The expectation of limited variability of future interest rates led to the belief that the extention of liquidity to savers was of low risk, even though such funds were committed by intermediaries to long-term business and mortgage debt. But recent sharp fluctuations in inflation rates, together with a more volatile monetary policy, have resulted in substantial increases in nominal interest rates—a type of risk that cannot be fully arbitraged away, although its burden can be shifted among savers, intermediaries, and investors. The result has been periodic financial crises brought about by the withdrawal of liquid deposit funds from financial intermediaries. Many of these problems can be handled through a natural evolution of financial markets, as the institutions place a higher price on liquidity and correspondingly widen the interest rate margin between short-term savings instruments and long-term debt.

The second major change in the behavior of the system has been the sharp decline in corporate saving rates because of a lower profit share of the gross national product. This decline in business saving has been offset by higher household saving rates. The result, however, is that a larger proportion of investment must be financed through capital markets. Since much of this increased external financing has been in the form of fixed debt, corporations have become increasingly vulnerable to the decline in cash flow that accompanies a recession as severe as that of 1974.

The financial structures of other countries have accommodated a far greater degree of reliance upon debt versus equity financing, but this has been at the cost of a far more intimate relationship between financial institutions and the firms they finance. The alternative within the United States may be a revival of interest in new equity issues rather than fixed interest instruments as a means of attracting external funds. The proposal of Wallich and of Wright to equalize the tax incentives for equity versus debt financing would stimulate such a development. In addition, there is some evidence that the trend of a falling profit share may be ending, and the contribution of internal funds is likely to be greater in future years.

Finally, the increased severity of recent financial crises reflects the interplay between reforms designed to improve the resiliency of financial intermediaries (particularly in the mortgage market) and a Federal Reserve determined to have an impact on the real sector. Efforts to maintain the housing market in the face of high interest rates only induce the Federal Reserve to push interest rates even higher at those times when they believe aggregate demand should be restrained. Thus the severity of the next financial crisis can only be measured by the obstinacy of the Federal Reserve.

While the arguments of Minsky about excessive risk taking are persuasive (and are echoed in large part by Wallich), inflation, an intensified use of monetary policy, and the growth of external debt have been important aspects of the recent crises. I am doubtful that they fit completely within a framework of increasing risk. I am, however, sympathetic to Minsky's arguments for a broader frame of reference for the guidance of monetary policy, in contrast to Wallich's emphasis upon money supply growth.

I tend to agree more with the conclusion of Wright that we do not face a serious special problem of financial instability. Some of the problems that have emerged are likely to be met by continuing evolution within private markets. Instead our financial crises are primarily a reflection of problems in other more fundamental areas: our inability to find an acceptable solution to inflation and futile efforts of the Federal Reserve to solve the inflation problem by periodic bouts of extreme monetary restraint.

Allen Sinai[1]

INTRODUCTION

Financial instability has always been a characteristic of the American economy. From the "financial panics" of 1873, 1893, and 1907 to the "crunches" of the postwar period, episodes of collapsing financial institutions, market rigidities, monetary policy errors, disruptions in flows of funds, and severe economic dislocation have appeared. The recurring pathology of the financial environment and its effects upon "real" behavior thus cannot be questioned. Understanding the nature and evolution of financial phenomena is critical to improving the performance of the American economy.

Despite repeated trauma from financial disturbances, systematic study of the financial environment, in the same sense that other topics have been formally analyzed by economists, has been sparse.[2] The papers in this part of the book provide a welcome attempt to examine the financial processes that so importantly affect the economy.

Several groups of questions should be raised. First, are endogenous processes responsible for financial crises and instability? If so, what are they, how do they evolve, and what determines their cyclical patterns? Can a theory that is grounded in the decision making of economic units and testable by appeal to data be developed to predict financial instability? Standard economic theory does not explain financial flow of funds cycles. This first set of issues is the concern of Minsky.

---

[1] The final version of this paper has benefited from the comments of Hyman P. Minsky.

[2] A path-breaking work is by Fisher (1933). Friedman and Schwartz (1963a,b) present a landmark, but superficial view of cause and effect from financial disturbances. Hicks (1950) recognizes the potential importance of endogenous financial factors in the trade cycle, but his treatment is highly aggregative. Minsky (1963, 1964, 1969, 1972, 1974, 1975a,b) attempts to describe the endogenous development of financial instability and offers a definition of fragile finance. Sinai (1976a) is concerned with the systematic factors in four postwar credit crunch periods and suggests a framework for analyzing episodes of financial instability (Sinai, 1975). Sinai and Brinner (1975) explore the causes and evolution of financial instability during the postwar period with the financial system of the DRI model of the U.S. economy. Temin (1976) is concerned with the role of money in the Great Depression.

Second, is financial instability primarily the result of inadequate financial institutions, market imperfections, mismanagement of internal affairs by households and corporations, external shocks, central bank policy errors, and profligate governments? Does the existing legal and institutional framework serve to intensify or cushion episodes of financial instability? Wright and Kaufman discuss these questions in their papers.

Finally, how can the periodic bouts of financial instability be prevented? Are there now sufficient feedback mechanisms to dampen the impacts of financial disturbances, or is the economy nonresilient? Is this better done through institutional change or by improving our comprehension of underlying processes? And what are the future prospects for financial crises? All of the authors address these issues.

My remarks are directed toward an evaluation of the papers in this part of the book in terms of the above questions. Some observations on the nature, causes and prospects for financial instability also are offered in a concluding section.

FINANCIAL INSTABILITY: AN ENDOGENOUS PROCESS?

Minsky (1963, 1964, 1969, 1972, 1975a,b) has previously attempted to explain the endogenous development of financial crises. His perceptions have been exceptional, especially considering when they were advanced.

In Minsky's current paper, "A Theory of Systemic Fragility," several key ideas are offered. Among them are (1) the conditions underlying a financial crisis develop endogenously, manifesting themselves in a "fragile financial structure;" (2) a "Wall Street" paradigm, rather than the more standard income-expenditure approach, is a useful framework for analyzing the behavior of the U.S. economy; (3) decision-making economic units can finance by hedge or speculative methods, depending on whether near-term cash flow payments fall short of or exceed near-term expected cash receipts; in an extreme form of speculative finance called Ponzi financing, interest payments exceed cash inflows, and additional debt must continually be sold; (4) the divergence between the market valuation of capital assets and current replacement costs determines the rate of investment; (5) sustained economic expansion over a run of years brings an increase in speculative and Ponzi financing, relative to hedge finance, laying the basis for fragile finance and financial crises.

These notions may be critical to understanding the nature of financial instability, but unfortunately Minsky fails to integrate them into the unified theory that would be necessary "to explore why we have had three near or incipient financial crises since 1966." The "theory" presented in the paper is a series of concepts, insightful and appealing when taken separately, but never concretely applied to explain the 1966, 1969–1970, and 1973–1974 experiences.[3]

The major shortcoming of the analysis is the failure to elucidate the continuous process by which financial positions evolve into a "fragile financial structure," with potential negative effects on expenditures. It is one thing to *define* the robustness-fragility of the financial system in terms of certain characteristics, but another actually to *specify* the dynamic endogenous processes that lead to financial crises at specific times. For example, Minsky does not clearly show how autonomous changes in business expenditures may generate particular modes of financing, affect a firm's balance sheet structure and liquidity, cause fragile finance or balance sheet instability, and then reactions in corporate spending through a negative feedback loop. No attempt is made to analyze similar interactions between uses and sources of funds for other sectors such as households, financial units, or governments. Neither do we learn how speculative or Ponzi financing units evolve from a robust position, only that Ponzi finance exists and is quite sensitive to outside disruptions. The reasons for the 1966, 1969–1970, and 1973–1974 incipient financial crises are never explicitly tied to the theory, so that at the end of the paper the notion of "systemic fragility" still cannot be applied to actual events.

Finally, the Minsky conception lacks the predictive content required for empirical testing. The structure of the theory does not lend itself to validation or refutation. Nor can the degree of financial fragility be measured to determine how near a crisis is. Indeed, Minsky denies that flow-of-funds data can be useful in prediction and downgrades the role of econometrics in understanding our economy. His rationale is that "institutions, usages, and policy interventions are important in determining how any fragile (or incipient crisis) financial situation will develop; our economy is an historical and not a mechanical system."

While the last statement is undoubtedly true, it provides an incorrect basis for dismissing the usefulness of econometrics for analyzing flow-of-funds cycles. On the contrary, econometric modeling and simulation offer the most promising method for determining the impact of the factors mentioned by Minsky on the evolution of financial crises.[4]

---

[3] See Sinai (1976a) for a discussion of postwar credit crunches.

[4] The DRI econometric model of the United States is explicitly concerned with the contribution of balance sheet positions, liquidity, and flows of funds to expenditures in times of financial stress. A large number of sectoral flow-of-funds behavioral equations for households, nonfinancial corporations, commercial banks, savings and loan associations, mutual savings banks, and life insurance companies interact simultaneously with consumption, investment, housing, and state and local government expenditures. The results of model simulations, as applied to the capital shortage issue, appear in Sinai and Brinner (1975, Chap. 5), demonstrating how a financial crisis could arise during the next decade. Institutions, external shocks, and policy interventions play an important role, and their effects are analyzed within the framework of the model.

My suggestion is to use a framework that organizes the economy by sector, that is, households, firms, commercial banks, savings and loan associations, mutual savings banks, life insurance companies, the central bank, state and local governments, the federal government, and rest of the world.[5] Defining sectoral balance sheets of financial assets, liabilities, and physical assets (where relevant), long-run demand functions for each item can be obtained from maximizing an objective function defined over the balance sheet of each sector, subject to constraints. In general, the target levels of the various assets or liabilities depend upon own and alternative rates of return (or costs), uncontrollable assets or liabilities, and net worth.

By admitting short-run disequilibria and interrelated balance sheet adjustments in all assets and liabilities, equations describing sectoral uses and sources of funds can be derived. Uses include consumption by households, investment by firms, and loans and investments by financial institutions. Sources are the current cash flows or "new money" for each sector, increased liabilities, or sales of assets. In this framework, uses (including expenditures) and sources (including cash flow generated by current activities) of funds' decisions are simultaneous and interrelated.

The expenditure and financing activities so determined result in endogenous changes in the balance sheet of each sector. During an economic expansion each sector evolves to a more speculative position in terms of measures defined on the balance sheet, as flows of internal funds become inadequate to support planned outlays. Assets are drawn down, borrowing is increased, and interest rates move higher. For households, the ratio of financial assets to liabilities declines, and debt repayment grows relative to disposable income. Firms' debt service burdens become increasingly onerous, the ratio of short- to long-term debt rises, the proportion of financial assets to short-term liabilities declines, and the debt/equity ratio moves higher. Financial institutions experience rising loan/deposit ratios. Policy intervention to restrain the expansion intensifies the growing weakness in balance sheets. Balance sheet instability and weakened liquidity eventually constrain the expenditures or uses of funds in each sector.

In fact, such a framework has been incorporated in the Data Resources, Inc. (DRI) model of the U.S. economy since 1974. Although only a beginning in the macroeconometrics of sectoral flow of funds, the model shows that economic expansion endogenously generates more risky balance sheets for households, corporations, and financial institutions. Strong negative feedback effects of rising interest rates, declining liquidity, and weakened balance sheet positions are found in consumption, investment, and government spending. Cyclical processes in finance are generated interactively with "real" sector dynamics, in

---

[5] See Brimmer and Sinai (1976), Sinai (1975), and Sinai and Brinner (1975) for further explanation and application.

what are labeled "flow-of-funds cycles." Measures of balance sheet instability are defined and their evolution traced, with cyclical counterparts to Minsky's hedge, speculative, and Ponzi finance. Other causes of financial fragility also have been identified.[6] From this work has come an enhanced understanding of the major factors that account for financial instability.[7]

Briefly turning to some other aspects of the Minsky paper:

1.   The effects of inflation are omitted. There is a strong correlation between the accelerating inflation of the last decade and increased sectoral financial instability. Also, the tremendous surge in liquidity since the last quarter of 1974 has coincided with diminishing rates of inflation. The DRI model shows pronounced effects of changes in inflation on liquidity ratios such as household financial assets to liabilities, corporate debt to equity, short- to long-term debt, and cash flow to outlays. To the extent inflation is endemic to the economy, it should play a role in "systemic fragility."

2.   More episodes of financial disruption have occurred in the postwar period than 1966, 1969–1970, and 1973–1974. Many characteristics of financial instability also appeared in 1955–1957 and 1959–1960.[8] There have been five crunch periods in the past 20 years, not just those mentioned by Minsky.

3.   It is not clear that a fragile financial structure currently exists, or that threats of a severe financial crisis are inevitable, as Minsky seems to suggest. The U.S. economy is in the midst of the greatest period of liquidity rebuilding since the depression. There is now a financial capital surplus, not a shortage.[9] For example, various measures of nonfinancial corporate liquidity and balance sheet strength indicate the most substantial improvement in postwar history.[10] Cash flow has been near 100 percent of corporate expenditures since 1974-IV and should remain close to 90 percent through 1976. The ratio of financial assets to short-term liabilities was 0.65 in 1976-I, up from 0.51 in 1974-IV. Short-term liabilities as a proportion of total outstanding debt was 33.7 percent in 1976-I, compared with a peak of 38.2 percent in 1974-IV. The debt burden proxy relative to cash flow was down to 29.4 percent in 1976-I; the peak was 44 percent in 1974-III. Finally, the debt/equity ratio has shown sustained declines for the first time in many years. Current DRI forecasts show no worsening in these ratios at least through 1978, along with 6.2, 5.7, and 4.0 percent annual rates of growth in real gross national product, inflation rates between 5 and 6 percent, a slow unwinding of the unemployment rate to 6.1

[6] Most important is acceleration in the rate of inflation.
[7] See Sinai and Brinner (1975, Chap. 5).
[8] See Sinai (1976a).
[9] See Sinai (1976b) for a discussion.
[10] See the appendix for charts and a table of these measures.

percent in early 1978, and cautious attitudes toward spending by households, corporations and governments.

4. Minsky's discussion of how a financial crisis starts is too limited. Each bout of financial instability since 1955 has been characterized by a rather pervasive breakdown of flows of funds, with subsequent distress sales and collapse, sector by sector. The process applies more generally than only in the corporate sector, which is the last to become disrupted.

5. Not enough credit is given to the ability of contemporary macroeconomics to address the crisis-prone behavior of our economy. Since the late 1960's the MPS model has contained a detailed model of financial flows to housing and the potential for collapse in that sector. At DRI, we have been concerned with financial instability since early 1973 and subsequently have dealt with the issue in the model's structure.[11] Detiorating balance sheets and disruptions in flows of funds affect consumption, fixed investment, housing, and state and local government expenditures—directly and through interest rate effects.

FINANCIAL INSTABILITY: THE ROLE OF INSTITUTIONS AND THE RESILIENCY OF THE FINANCIAL SYSTEM

Wright stresses the response of institutions to financial crises throughout U.S. economic history and notes their beneficial nature. Also, he views the causes of financial crises as less endogenous and process-oriented than Minsky, reminding us that the institutional environment can be an important aspect of financial instability.[12] The cases of corporate mismanagement, unbridled government spending, and errors in policy associated with financial crises could be symptomatic. The tendency toward institutional "correction" and survival of the U.S. financial system is cited optimistically for the prospect of future resiliency.

However, the institutional reactions following each episode of financial instability can be likened to medicating a patient with a chronic, but poorly understood, illness. The symptoms can be tested after the fact, but the underlying problems remain to engender subsequent difficulties. Certainly, the institutional environment can intensify financial crises or perhaps cushion them. But optimism clearly is unwarranted on institutional grounds, since financial

[11] A number of papers are available, including Brimmer and Sinai (1976), Fromm and Sinai (1974), Sinai (1975, 1976a), and Sinai and Brinner (1975).

[12] One consequence of inflation, duly noted by Wright, is the lagged endogenous response of monetary policy. The seeds of financial crisis are sewn before the Federal Reserve enters the scene, however. The monetary authority does not so much create a crisis, but may intensify or provide the final blow to an already fragile financial structure.

instability worsened from 1965 to 1974 in spite of numerous financial innovations.

As for resiliency, survival and recovery of the economy is insufficient evidence to demonstrate the existence of this property. The U.S. financial system would be resilient if the economic costs of periodic financial crises were held to a minimum through endogenous economy and institutional responses. The costs of financial instability during past years have been great in terms of lost production, excess unemployment, and balance sheet difficulties. A sanguine outlook, based on extrapolating the patchwork response of institutions, thus is inappropriate.

The other major problem with the Wright analysis concerns whether some of the factors identified as proximate causes of financial crises are actually effects. Corporate bankruptcies result from a long period of overextension and evolving financial fragility. Mismanagement is essentially a consequence of aggressive, albeit misguided, profit-maximizing behavior. Government fiscal mismanagement generally has not been blamed for any specific financial crisis, except indirectly through effects on inflation. Only worsening inflation is clearly a potential cause of financial instability, and not just because of "impacts on interest rates."

Kaufman is less optimistic about resiliency, arguing that removing "financial frictions of the past" may increase the susceptibility of the system to financial crises. However, Wright feels that interest rate ceilings and similar factors have been a major cause of financial instability. My belief is that interrupted flows of funds to households and eventually corporations, occasioned by ever-widening yield differentials, have figured importantly in exacerbating financial instability. A flexible system of interest rates is likely to be more effective in gradually slowing the economy than the discrete changes of the past, even if yields rise to unprecedented levels.

FINANCIAL INSTABILITY: PROSPECTS AND PREVENTION

Despite the frequent bouts of financial crises during the past decade, three of the four authors are optimistic that severe problems can be avoided in the foreseeable future. Wright feels that the existing institutional framework, Federal Reserve actions, congressional legislation, responses of federal credit agencies, and financial innovation can prevent a severe crisis. Kaufman believes a new restraint may arise on the part of decision makers because of "lessons from the recent financial stresses." Wallich argues that the economy has reached a trough in a cycle of risk taking and escalating financial difficulties, driving participants away from the brink of insolvency. The present phase of consolidation and reliquification is thought to be a reversal of the long-time trend toward financial instability. Only Minsky seems to believe that threats of severe financial disaster are inevitable.

Let me add my vote to the majority, but with some qualification and explanation. Prevention of financial crises is not a matter of changing tax laws (Wallich and Wright), financial innovation (Wright), or Federal Reserve behavior (Kaufman).[13] Like the various stages in business fluctuations, periods of financial stress are probably inevitable, associated with acceleration toward full employment in both the private and public sectors. Fundamentally, financial instability is an integral part of the business cycle, amenable to macroeconomic analysis and policy. But so is reliquification, the recovery from financial instability. The presence of systematic financial processes augers well for the eventual prevention of financial crises, since understanding is a prerequisite to devising preventive policies.

The modeling of financial instability in the DRI macroeconometric model has permitted the identification, through simulation analysis, of some necessary conditions for avoiding credit crunches during the next 5 years. First, the rate of inflation must stabilize or decline, even if prices remain at very high levels. Second, monetary and fiscal policy has to refrain from the "stop-go" applications that so often have occurred. Third business expansion should be moderate and well-balanced, so that sectoral uses of funds do not outpace the sources. Fourth, the endogenous processes of liquidity rebuilding and balance sheet restructuring need to continue, in order to provide a cushion for later funding. Finally, severe external shocks such as wars, commodity shortages, oil embargos, and Watergate must not recur. Unexpected perturbations reverberate through the economy, creating havoc in the reactions of policymakers.

Almost all these key factors are endogenous to the U.S. economy, although each can be affected by external policy measures. Control of inflation and reliquification are perhaps the most important. Currently, the necessary conditions listed above are being satisfied. If their existence continues or is not seriously violated, a repeat of the previous decade's financial crises is unlikely.

CONCLUDING OBSERVATIONS

None of the papers or comments can fully answer the questions raised in the first section of this article. Considerable work and analysis remain to be

---

[13] At the margin, appropriate measures in these areas can ease financial stress. See Brimmer and Sinai (1976) for an analysis of tax-incentive effects on corporate liquidity and balance sheet strength.

performed. But on the basis of the papers presented here and my own research, I offer some tentative conclusions.

First, financial instability is an endogenous process, rooted in the cyclical evolution of risky balance sheet positions for various decision-making units. Expenditure and finance decisions together determine the pattern and degree of financial stress, with major contributions from public policy and existing institutions.

Second, the institutional environment can intensify the endogenous progression of financial instability and sometimes even precipitate crises. But the basic causal factors are not amenable to financial innovation and institutional restructuring, since they are rooted in the behavioral processes of the economy.

Third, the recurring credit crunches of the past 10 years are *prima facie* evidence that reliance on innovations in institutions is insufficient to prevent destabilizing financial strains from arising. If by resiliency, survival is meant, then the economy is indeed resilient. But this is not enough, for the costs of near crises are too great. The increasing severity of credit crunches hardly suggests institutions as the major means for alleviating financial instability.

Fourth, an important contemporary cause of financial instability is accelerating inflation. Rising prices raise nominal demands for funds, hinder savings flows, cause higher interest rates, distort the relative costs of various financial modes, induce speculative behavior, and eventually bring restrictive monetary policies. Other factors are erratic fiscal or monetary policy, the pace and balance of economic expansion, external shocks (whether political or economic) and the economy's reaction to them, and attitudes toward spending by households, corporations, and government.

Fifth, the current prospects for a relatively long period of financial stability are quite good, given the exceptional restoration of balance sheet strength and liquidity that has occurred throughout the economy in the last year. Corporate balance sheets have made an amazing turnaround, not yet fully recognized by many observers. Households, financial institutions, and even government have improved their financial positions. Severe financial strains are unlikely in the current situation of capital surplus, and the cushion of liquidity being accumulated could last for several years. Decision makers in all sectors are showing the restrained behavior that, if maintained, could prevent any recurrence of sustained financial imbalances.

Finally, economists must turn to developing an analytical framework for flow-of-funds cycles, the counterpart to the national income fluctuations in traditional macroeconomics. Only after the realization that simultaneous processes in expenditures and finance exist can models be constructed that will trace the business cycle completely, including episodes of disaggregated financial instability.

REFERENCES

Brimmer, A. F. and A. Sinai, "The Effects of Tax Policy on Capital Formation, Corporate Liquidity, and the Availability of Investible Funds: A Simulation Study," *Journal of Finance,* Vol. 31 (May 1976), 287–308.

Fisher, I., "The Debt-Deflation Theory of Great Depressions," *Econometrica,* Vol. 1 (October 1933), 337–357.

Friedman, M. and A. J. Schwartz, *A Monetary History of the United States, 1897–1960* Princeton, N.J.: Princeton University Press, 1963.

Friedman, M. and A. J. Schwartz, "Money and Business Cycles," *Review of Economics and Statistics,* Vol. 45 (February 1963), 32–64.

Fromm, G. and G. Sinai, "A Policy Simulation Model of Deposit Flows, Mortgage Sector Activity, and Housing", presented at Econometric Society Meeting, December 1974.

Hicks, J. R., *A Contribution to the Theory of the Trade Cycle* (New York: Oxford University Press), 1950.

Minsky, H. P., "Financial Crisis, Financial Systems, and the Performance of the Economy," in *Private Capital Markets, Commission on Money and Credit* Englewood Cliffs, N.J.: Prentice-Hall, 1963, pp. 173–380.

Minsky, H. P., "Longer Waves in Financial Relations: Financial Factors in the More Severe Recessions," *American Economic Review,* Vol. 54 (May 1964), 324–335.

Minsky, H. P., "Private Sector Asset Management and the Effectiveness of Monetary Policy: Theory and Practice," *Journal of Finance,* Vol. 24 (May 1969), 223–238.

Minsky, H. P., "Financial Instability Revisited: The Economics of Disaster," *Reappraisal of the Federal Reserve Discount Mechanism,* Vol. 3 (June 1972), 97–136.

Minsky, H. P., "The Modeling of Financial Instability: An Introduction," Fifth Annual Pittsburgh Conference on Modeling and Simulation, Proceedings, April 1974, pp. 354–364.

Minsky, H. P., "Financial Instability, the Current Dilemma, and the Structure of Banking and Finance," *Compendium of Major Issues in Bank Regulation,* Committee on Banking, Housing and Urban Affairs, 94th Congress, 1st Session, United States Senate, August 1975, pp. 311–353.

Minsky, H. P., "Financial Resources in a Fragile Financial Environment," *Challenge,* July–August 1975, pp. 6–13.

Sinai, A., "The Integration of Financial Instability in Large-Scale Macroeconomic Models," paper presented at the Midwest Economic Association Annual Meeting, Chicago, Illinois, April 1975.

Sinai, A., "Credit Crunches—An Analysis of the Postwar Experience," in O. Eckstein (ed.), *Parameters and Policies in the U.S. Economy* (Amsterdam: North-Holland), 1976a, pp. 244–274.

Sinai, A., "The Prospects of a Capital Shortage in the U.S.," *Euromoney,* May 1976b, 94–100. Reprinted as DRI Economic Studies Series No. 24, Data Resources, Lexington, Mass.

Sinai, A. and R. E. Brinner, *The Capital Shortage: Near-Term Outlook and Long-Term Prospects* (Lexington, Mass.: Data Resources), 1975.

Temin, P., *Did Monetary Forces Cause the Great Depression?* New York: Norton), 1976.

APPENDIX   MEASURES OF LIQUIDITY AND BALANCE SHEET STRENGTH: NONFINANCIAL CORPORATIONS (HISTORY AND FORECAST)

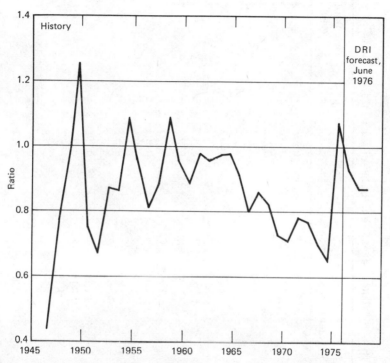

Figure 1   Ratio of cash flow to expenditures: nonfinancial corporations. Cash flow equals the sum of retained earnings, foreign branch profits, capital consumption allowances, and inventory valuation adjustment. Capital outlays equal the sum of plant and equipment expenditures, inventory accumulation, and residential construction. *Sources:* Federal Reserve Board, Data Resources, Inc.

Table 1 Measures of Liquidity and Balance Sheet Strength: Nonfinancial Corporations

Year	Cash Flow/ Capital Outlays[a]	Financial Assets/ Short-Term Liabilities[b]	Short-Term/ Total Liabilities[c]	Debt Burden Proxy/ Cash Flow[a]	Debt/ Equity[e]
1946	0.438	2.845	0.255		0.234
1947	0.734	2.331	0.280		0.254
1948	0.923	1.999	0.292		0.264
1949	1.253	2.091	0.283		0.247
1950	0.747	2.587	0.253	← NA →	0.260
1951	0.667	2.290	0.274		0.260
1952	0.870	1.904	0.291		0.269
1953	0.862	1.895	0.286		0.264
1954	1.085	1.927	0.269		0.262
1955	0.931	1.854	0.284	0.084	0.267
1956	0.810	1.435	0.305	0.101	0.276
1957	0.887	1.347	0.296	0.113	0.280
1958	1.091	1.415	0.277	0.130	0.281
1959	0.954	1.389	0.289	0.130	0.284
1960	0.888	1.164	0.298	0.145	0.288
1961	0.979	1.195	0.289	0.152	0.289
1962	0.958	1.197	0.286	0.136	0.291
1963	0.971	1.198	0.288	0.138	0.294
1964	0.978	1.095	0.299	0.124	0.295
1965	0.909	0.960	0.322	0.124	0.303
1966	0.799	0.801	0.329	0.141	0.312
1967	0.861	0.783	0.326	0.166	0.323

1968	0.823	0.759	0.335	0.197	0.339
1969	0.726	0.660	0.355	0.272	0.356
1970	0.707	0.613	0.347	0.318	0.369
1971	0.780	0.663	0.329	0.310	0.378
1972	0.768	0.624	0.332	0.285	0.392
1973	0.696	0.551	0.357	0.324	0.417
1974	0.647	0.509	0.382	0.406	0.450
1975	1.074	0.634	0.343	0.337	0.437
1976F	0.934	0.671	0.334	0.286	0.425
1977F	0.871	0.617	0.344	0.285	0.426
1978F	0.874	0.595	0.336	0.276	0.420

Sources: Federal Reserve Board and Data Resources, Inc (DRI).

[a] Cash flow equals the sum of retained earnings, foreign branch profits, capital consumption allowances, and inventory valuation adjustment. Capital outlays equal the sum of plant and equipment expenditures, inventory accumulation, and residential construction.

[b] Financial assets equal the sum of money, deposits, U.S. government bonds, state and local bonds, and commercial paper. Short-term liabilities equal the sum of bank loans, open-market paper, finance company loans, and U.S. government loans.

[c] Total liabilities equal the sum of short-term liabilities, bonds, and mortgages.

[d] Debt burden proxy equals the sum of the weighted average of past new issue rates multiplied by the beginning-of-period level of bonds, the weighted average of past prime rates multiplied by the beginning-of-period level of bank loans, and the weighted average of past 4- to 6-month commercial paper rates multiplied by the beginning-of-period level of open-market paper.

[e] Debt equals the sum of bank loans, mortgages, bonds, open-market paper, finance company loans, and miscellaneous liabilities. Equity equals the difference between total assets and total liabilities. Total assets equal the sum of financial assets, physical assets (gross stocks), and other miscellaneous assets. Total liabilities equal short-term liabilities, long-term liabilities, and other miscellaneous liabilities.

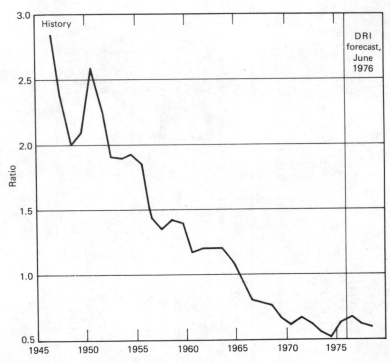

Figure 2 Ratio of financial assets to short-term liabilities: nonfinancial corporations. Financial assets equal the sum of money, deposits, U.S. government bonds, state and local bonds, and commercial paper. Short-term liabilities equal the sum of bank loans, open-market paper, finance company loans, and U.S. government loans. *Sources:* Federal Reserve Board, Data Resources, Inc.

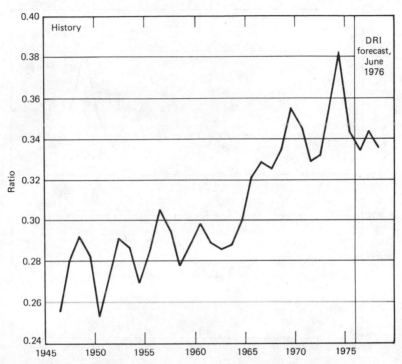

Figure 3 Ratio of short-term to total liabilities: nonfinancial corporations. Short-term liabilities equal the sum of bank loans, open-market paper, finance company loans, and U.S. government loans. Total liabilities equal the sum of short-term liabilities, bonds, and mortgages. *Sources:* Federal Reserve Board, Data Resources, Inc.

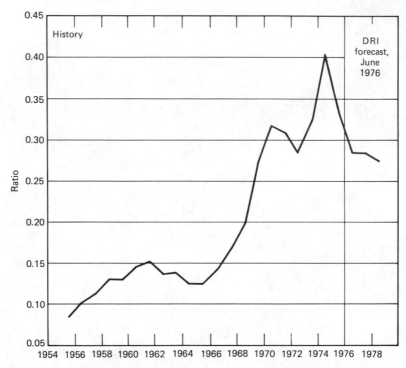

Figure 4 Ratio of debt burden proxy to cash flow: nonfinancial corporations. Debt burden proxy equals the sum of the weighted average of past new issue rates multiplied by the beginning-of-period level of bonds, the weighted average of past prime rates multiplied by the beginning-of-period level of bank loans, and the weighted average of past 4- to 6-month commercial paper rates multiplied by the beginning-of-period level of open-market paper. *Source:* Federal Reserve Board, Data Resources, Inc.

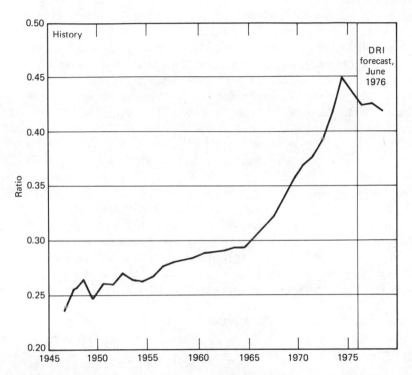

Figure 5 Ratio of debt to equity: nonfinancial corporations. Debt equals the sum of bank loans, mortgages, bonds, open-market paper, finance company loans, and miscellaneous liabilities. Equity equals the difference between total assets and total liabilities. Total assets equal the sum of financial assets, physical assets (gross stocks), and other miscellaneous assets. Total liabilities equal short-term liabilities, long-term liabilities, and other miscellaneous liabilities. *Sources:* Federal Reserve Board, Data Resources, Inc.

John Lintner

The papers by Minsky, Kaufman, Wallich, and Wright nicely complement each other in providing a useful review and analysis of the susceptibility of our financial markets to strain and crisis and some of the steps that can be taken to make them more surely viable and resilient in the future. Rather than undertake any detailed or systematic critical review of these papers as such, I focus my discussion on just a few matters, which will hopefully provide some useful additional perspectives on these important issues.

When the first three decades of our postwar history (1945–1974) are viewed as a whole, the overall trends suggest progressive and even accelerating declines if virtually every one of the readily available measures of financial strength and resiliency. In Minsky's vivid terminology, over this long period, we moved from a highly conservative "fully hedged" posture into an increasingly speculative position which—whether or not it was Ponziesque—was at least so taut, strained, and fragile as to raise spectors of crisis and possible widespread collapse. Apart from some cyclical fluctuation, the ratio of liquid financial assets to current liabilities of nonfinancial corporations declined to lower and lower levels over these three decades, while their ratios of short-term to total liabilities and both total and long-term debt to equity rose higher and higher over much of the period. Along with this progressive weakening in the usual measures of the robustness of balance sheet positions, there was also a marked deterioration between the earlier and later years of the period in several important flow relationships such as the fraction of all financing provided from equity sources (internal and external combined), the ratio of internal cash flow to capital outlays, and the ratio of debt service to earnings or total internally generated funds. Over the same period, there was a marked and continuing decline in the ratio of the capital funds of commercial banks to their liabilities and, particularly in the later years, a significant increase in classified assets and problem loans.

Minsky regards this transformation of the extraordinarily robust financial structure inherited from World War II into "the fragile structure we now have, in which the periodic triggering of a financial crisis is well nigh certain" as being "as result of normal market behavior," and he offers "a theory of systemic fragility [which] endeavors to explain why our economy endogenously develops fragile or crisis-prone financial structures." My own view is considerably different.

Everyone agrees that the balance sheet ratios usually used in assessing financial soundness were extraordinarily distorted by the exogenous impact of World War II. With most normal investment outlets shut off, debt ratios were reduced far below normal levels, and tremendous amounts of redundant liquidity were accumulated *faut de mieux*. The general reductions in liquidity

ratios between the end of the war and the mid-1960s reflected the gradual
wringing out of redundant positions, along with reductions in desired ratios as
increasingly effective methods of cash management and new technology were
introduced. Similarly, it appears that the increases in debt ratios on balance
sheets up until roughly 10 years ago should be regarded as essentially reflecting
a gradual asymptotic approach to more normal and still fully sustainable
financial structures—a normalization rather than a worrisome deterioration—
and in particular, *not* as establishing an endogenous *trend* with any momentum
of its own which would be extrapolated on into the future. In the same vein,
rather than being an extension of earlier trends toward fragile financial structures, I regard most of the progressive, stepwise *further* weakening of most
balance sheet and flow measures of financial strength over the years 1966–1974
as being due to the impact of successive, larger and larger increments of unanticipated inflation during this period.

In this view, *neither* the marked distortions of more normal financial standards and structures on the side of excessive robustness in the late 1940s and
early 1950s *nor* the marked distortions from these norms in the late 1960s and
early 1970s should be attributed to the endogenous normal market behavior of
financial institutions or the financial policies of nonfinancial corporations. Both
were largely the responses of these sectors to extraordinarily stressful circumstances external to them. If it had not been for World War II, the balance
sheets of these financial and nonfinancial private institutions would have looked
much more normal in the late 1940s and early 1950s than they did. In the
same view, *if* much more prudent fiscal policies and more responsible and stable monetary policies had been adhered to in the years after 1965, and other
external and exogenous shocks exacerbating the inflation had not occurred,
these balance sheet and flow relations would again have been much more
normal in 1973 and 1974.

The evidence is clear that the waves of increasing inflation after 1965 led to a
substantial erosion of corporate profitability and successive reductions in the
purchasing power value of gross business savings. At the same time they forced
firms to rely more heavily on outside capital for their financing—and not
merely because of taxes on inventory profits and the difference between replacement and historical cost depreciation as often thought.[1] Moreover, inflation
drastically reduced equity prices, sharply raised interest rates, and forced an
increasing fraction of all financing onto the debt markets, doubly impairing

---

[1] See J. Lintner "Inflation and Security Returns," Presidential Address to the American Finance
Association, *Journal of Finance,* May 1975, pp. 259–280, especially pp. 268–276. Other evidence
on the impact of our recent inflation on corporate profits and the financial structure can be found in
J. Lintner, "Savings and Investment for Future Growth," in *Answers to Inflation and Recession:
Economic Policies for a Modern Society* (New York: The Conference Board), 1975.

coverage ratios. It seems fair to say that without the distortions directly attributable to a decade of accelerating inflation, the financial strains and crisis of these later years would have been largely avoided.

This is not an appropriate occasion to enter into a thorough discussion of the causes of this debilitating and crisis-inducing inflation, but it seems clear from studies made that the price stability we enjoyed in the earlier 1960s was destroyed by the unsound *public* financial policies that led to the overheating of the economy after 1965. The Council of Economic Advisor's analyses show that real gross national product was running above their (perhaps optimistically calculated) "potential" output for *four* consecutive years, 1965–1969. In this context, the villain was not the Vietnam War nor the Great Society programs as such, but the fact that *neither* was financed by timely tax increases large enough to keep overall supplies and demands in the economy in balance. This publicly induced overheating of the economy initiated the inflation that then resulted in a classic wage-price spiral in the context of an accommodative monetary policy. These growing inflationary problems were of course accentuated by the international feedback mechanisms incident to the regimen of fixed exchange rates before 1971 and the delayed impact of the resulting devaluation of the dollar. Finally, after inflation rates and expectations of further inflation had risen to a high level, exogenous shocks (worldwide crop shortages, the oil embargo, and the action of an external cartel quadrupling oil prices) further exacerbated the situation. Their effects, however, would have been much less severe if inflation had not already been proceeding at a high and accelerating rate—and it would not have been if responsible noninflationary fiscal and monetary policies had been in place over the preceding decade. Experience since 1973 has also confirmed the efficacy of floating exchange rates to protect an economy from imported inflation. *Given* flexible exchange rates *and* responsible noninflationary fiscal and monetary policies, the endogenous operation of our economy would not have produced any substantial inflation during the late 1960s and early 1970s—and in the absence of such inflation the financial crises of 1973–1975 would have been easily manageable.

This of course does not imply that, in the context of a noninflationary fiscal and monetary policy, our financial markets will always move on an utterly placid course with no localized strains, excesses, or defaults. A large fraction of final demands in the private economy involve durable goods and long-lived real assets (housing, plant and equipment, structures, etc.) subject to stock adjustment processes which inevitably produce fluctuations except under unrealistically idealized "steady-state" assumptions. Moreover, as Wallich and Kaufman usefully emphasize, there will of course be recurring waves of undue optimism and changes in attitudes toward risk, which will affect financing patterns in the private economy. Wallich is on sound ground in saying that people's assessments of risks and rewards seem to be formed on the basis of a weighted sum of past experience, with greater weight on the more recent experience. For a time after a major financial crisis, firms, households, and lenders turn cautious but, as the untoward experience fades in the past, its restraint diminishes. After several relatively mild business cycles there clearly tends to be an escalation of risk which leads to disappointed expectations and at least localized losses.

Whether this normal endogenous escalation of risk leads to a new crisis of substantial severity and generality under modern conditions depends very heavily on whether it occurs in the context of increasing inflation. Both specific prices and general price levels of course move up and down to some extent with cyclical fluctuations in business activity. Nevertheless, *if* fiscal and monetary policies are maintained on a sufficiently restrained and even keel as to eliminate cumulative increases in inflation rates from cycle to cycle, such endogenous increases in risk within the private sector are not likely to lead to serious and widespread distortions in our financial structure which would threaten its viability. As Wright emphasizes, we now have the Federal Reserve in place as a lender of last resort, along with all the other institutional supports and reforms growing out of the 1930s, and a growing body of knowledge of how to avert or reverse any incipient, cumulative, deflationary spiral either in overall real economic activity or in the financial structure itself. In the last third of the twentieth century, the major threat to the viability and resiliency of our financial structure lies in the risk of increasing inflation.

The argument has of course been made that modern mixed economies have a built-in inflationary bias, because they are subject to a variety of strong pressures which preclude their staying with the stipulated responsible fiscal and monetary policies. This may well be the case but, *if so,* the resulting distortions in the balance sheets of financial institutions and the resulting strains in financial markets must be attributed to the lax and inflationary fiscal and monetary policies of government, not to the financial markets per se—and, if so, the most important item on the agenda for ensuring the future strength and resiliency of our financial environment is to develop a stronger, firm democratic consensus in favor of such noninflationary fiscal and monetary policies.

Happily, there is evidence that such a consensus is emerging from our recent traumas. *If* such a consensus can be maintained and strengthened so that we succeed in holding to fiscal and monetary policies that do not generate or contribute to protracted and substantial increases in inflation in future years, *then* it is my judgment that the endogenous normal market behavior patterns of financial institutions and the financing activities of nonfinancial corporations will *not* lead to ever-increasing fragility or to financial strains and distortions of unmanageable severity.

George M. von Furstenberg

From the four papers I am relieved to conclude that we are still far away from Medicaid for financially ailing institutions, since the doctors disagree on the diagnosis of what, if anything, is wrong. While Minsky finds that financial fragility has increased continuously since the mid-1960s both Wright and Kaufman feel that the progress of this disease was checked decisively through the 1974–1975 crisis. As a result of recent object lessons, Wallich is perhaps even more hopeful that speculative excesses have been rooted out of the financial system for some time to come. Thus the four authors make different assessments of the outlook for the remainder of this decade.

Some of these differences can be traced to the underlying models on which judgments are based. Wallich and Wright believe that money managers learn from experience and that those factors that make for increasing financial fragility, such as tax features encouraging excessive reliance on debt financing by corporations, can be neutralized through institutional change. Minsky, however, claims that "the incipient financial crises of 1966, 1969–1970, and 1974–1975 were neither accidents nor the result of policy errors but the result of the normal functioning of our particular economy." Furthermore, "success in aborting an embryonic financial crisis leaves a residue which virtually ensures that a period of accelerating inflation will follow." This presages even greater instability in the future.

Minsky's disequilibrium analysis is difficult to assess, because he does not reveal the equilibrium system relationships against which a disequilibrium can be measured. He does, however, present several partial hypotheses and pinpricks designed to puncture elements of the conventional analysis based on stable behavior functions. One such assertion is that the demand of cash kickers and liquid assets shrinks when business is going well and losing caution. Minsky wishes no truck with Friedman's or a more innocent demand for money functions. Yet he clearly makes implicit statements about such functions and changes in the demand for near monies, and these statements ought to be tested. After all, intracyclical studies of velocity have been conducted for some time, but the explanatory power of permanent income and expected wealth (or expected real balance) explanations of intracyclical movements in velocity has not been very high. Hence there may be room for Minsky's notion that businesses will cut it closely in expansion phases, and perhaps households will too, thus setting themselves up for a subsequent fall in velocity.

Even if such reversals in the behavior of desired velocity are laid in store during good times, quite a few other pieces would be required to make this amount to a theory of the business cycle. Minsky has speculatively and perhaps Ponzifinanced businesses dump assets in the scramble for liquidity. He holds that, after the price of real assets has been knocked below the cost of producing them, investment becomes discouraged. If this is the way business cycles go, turns in fixed investment and in inventory growth should lead a downturn. In fact, however, there is not a single postwar cycle in which this has occurred. Thus Minsky's needles contain several interesting drugs that should be tested not just on the reflexes of laboratory animals like Keynes and his critics, but also on the real world.

The Wallich, Wright, and Kaufman papers contain a less systemic view of financial instability, and all are more hopeful that financial excesses have been purged for some time. I have only a slight and tangential disagreement with some of the historical tables used in Wallich's paper in which he intends to show true retained earnings, cash flow, and the composition of external financing. He correctly takes out purely nominal or inflation-induced inventory profits and adjusts book profits for underdepreciation by using replacement cost depreciation. However, he deducts the entire amount of net interest payments, including the inflation premium.

If net interest-bearing liabilities are denominated in nominal dollars and the principal is not indexed, one can presumably refinance the inflation premium in interest rates year after year without a rise in real indebtedness. In addition if one, correctly, ignores inventory profits and underdepreciation in deriving one's true measure of corporate profits and retained earnings, one must still write up the book value of assets to current dollars through imputing nominal capital gains before one can strike meaningful balance sheet ratios. Because the revaluation of assets and stockholders' equity proceeds more or less automatically under steady inflation, while the inflation premium in interest rates must be refinanced explicitly through new debt issues, comparing the composition of net external funds raised across periods with different inflation rates may be potentially misleading. This, however, is a fairly minor matter which does not weaken the overall thrust of Wallich's paper or the need to reduce both the size and variability of inflation to enhance financial stability.

Endangered Financial Markets: Short-term Markets for Debt

ARNOLD W. SAMETZ

The papers in this part of the book deal with particular endangered financial markets.[1] Attention is thus drawn away from general or overall crisis and aggregate economic-financial policy to the strains, say, in the commercial paper market in 1970 and to the particulars of cure as well as cause. While the spread of crisis conditions from one market to another is not precluded, neither is it assumed. And while the central role of aggregative inflationary pressures as a basic cause of a particular market's difficulties is not denied, emphasis is placed not on national antiinflationary policy but on coping—given inflationary pressures—with the results of pressures in *particular* financial markets.

This is not to say that explosive national financial crises are "unthinkable." It is simply a matter of probabilities and priorities. Indeed, a book on crises should deal with (unanticipated, irregular) inflation as the progenitor of crisis conditions,[2] and with national policies, including national financial planning[3]

---

[1] Of course, Minsky and Sinai favor a more systematic view of the crisis process and its prevention.

[2] Both the existence of inflation (which impairs the financial environment) and antinflation policy actions (which may trigger financial crisis) are involved.

[3] Elements of this policy decision come up in the preferences expressed for increasing flexibility of regulation versus ceilings and floors as anticrisis therapy; and on whether bail-out of failing business and their claimants or letting the losses run is the better approach.

211

(i.e., direct credit controls), to cope with virulent inflation and a deteriorating financial environment.

Noyes sets the theme firmly in stating: "There is not and cannot be, an *overall* problem of rollover in the short-term money market. . . ." But of course there can be, and there have been overall problems of *expansion,* as noted in the previous articles; this group of papers demonstrates that there are problems of rollover in *specific* short-term markets or so-called flights to quality.

Wojnilower draws the moral firmly in concluding his paper: ". . . The fragility of financial structures is little more than the frailty of human resolve under stress and temptation." The principal need is for a "body of financial regulation" to frustrate that irresistible urge toward perennial overreaching in financial dealings. So much for sole reliance on free-swinging competition or stable money supply growth to preserve the viability of financial markets and institutions. See Sherman's third point in this regard.[4]

In the other chapters, financial practitioners relate some hair-raising details of the perils involved when a series of short-term financial markets were endangered. But in no case was a general spread of the stringency to other markets threatened. "Leaving aside an idiotically inappropriate monetary policy . . . [The chances of] a good old-fashioned money panic . . . are very, very small." (Noyes). The problem of short-term debt rollover was confined to particular firms or governments and usually with respect to particular forms of short-term debt.

According to Aloi, Franklin National Bank's managerial difficulties led, via unsuccessful speculative activities, to failure without really threatening to pull the banking structure down. But more importantly, its successive frantic efforts to save itself endangered the market for certificates of deposits; but here too the disease was isolated; sequential deterioration was avoided by appropriate regulatory activities and wisely discriminating behavior by private financial marketeers.

The commercial paper market was more threatened by the collapse of Penn Central than the certificate of deposit markets were by the collapse of Franklin National. Timlin's authoritative account shows what actually happens when the Federal Reserve operates as a lender of last resort. Although there was a shift of several billions of dollars out of commercial paper and into bank credit in under a month, shifts in Federal Reserve credit and regulations managed the massive shift without recourse to direct Federal Reserve loans to business corporations, for example, to Chrysler Financial, although the Federal Reserve was prepared to do so. Note too that the market for this sensitive, impersonal, nonmarketable, unregulated instrument revived rather quickly; within 6

---

[4] What we need, perhaps, is an early warning system to alert us to the dangers of monetarists as financial policy makers and regulators.

months of Penn Central's failure the outstanding volume of commercial paper reached a new peak though selective problems continued, namely, REITs, W. T. Grant, and so on.

The crises in the markets for Eurodollars and short-term municipals, reviewed by Hutchins and Gerard, respectively, differed from the certificate of deposit–commercial paper crises mentioned above in that they centered on public or governmental management, but were similar in that the crises in the short-term market were symptomatic of deeper and longer-term financial problems and in that the crisis was contained in the sense that it did not spread to all municipalities or less developed countries (LDCs) much less to other financial markets.

Furthermore, both of these markets were stabilized in part by official assistance to weak borrowers; the object, both internationally and locally, was to ease the short-term rollover problem to allow time for the underlying problems of shrinking revenue sources and rising expenditures to be set to rights. One interesting contrast, however, is that the risk differentials between high- and low-quality loans, which widened hugely (and perhaps excessively) among municipals, widened hardly at all between prime and marginal risk LDC loans.

Most importantly, although the market for New York City securities closed down completely in March 1975, the market for the securities of other municipalities did not. The final group of articles indicates that the New York City problem is symptomatic of a significant part of the market for municipals and has significant impacts on the rest of the market, that is, the high-quality sectors as well.

10. The Overall Problem of Rollover

GUY E. NOYES

One way to deal with this topic is to say categorically that in the absence of a purposefully engineered liquidity squeeze on the part of the central bank there is not, and cannot be, an *overall* problem of rollover in the short-term money market. I daresay few would challenge this position. It has excellent intellectual credentials in the writings of both market participants and academic observers. Even more important, it is supported by an overwhelming historical record. Liquidity problems, when they have arisen in the last 40 years, have invariably been associated with rapidly expanding markets, not markets that were just rolling over. That is to say, if borrowers had been content simply to roll over their outstanding obligations, rather than expand them vigorously, there would have been more than enough lenders to go around. Even in 1974—the year of Franklin National and Herstatt, and of all the tiering—negotiable bank certificates of deposit outstanding expanded by over $25 billion or 40 percent, and commercial paper by $8 billion or 20 percent. It is difficult to even characterize the financial crisis of the early 1930s as one in which markets encountered an overall rollover problem. U.S. Treasury bills were, after all, rolling over at a zero interest rate and prime commercial paper at between 1 and 2 percent. In fact, one might say that the demand for high-quality money market instruments far exceeded the supply. Hence, even at that time rollover problems, though numerous, were specific rather than general. Having worked my way back over that hurdle, I find it fairly easy to move to the conclusion that the last truly overall rollover problem was in 1907. But the interesting thing is that, while no one may be willing to challenge this wisdom and historical fact, no one will quite believe the conclusion either. The suspicion seems to linger in some dark corner of everyone's mind that there will be a cold winter morning when all the sellers of federal funds and all the buyers of top-tier certificates of deposit, commercial paper, and even U.S. Treasury bills will simply disappear from the face of the earth. Their telephones will go unanswered.

Since this fantasy—or nightmare—persists, perhaps I should explore several possibilities, although there is little new that I can add to conventional wisdom.

I have already alluded by exclusion to one way in which an overall rollover problem can arise. A central bank can always create one. It has become increasingly difficult for a single central bank to do, but there is no doubt in my mind that the Federal Reserve could still manage it with an all-out effort. Central banks can create liquidity, and they can also destroy it—and if they destroy enough of it, fast enough, they can certainly produce a crisis. There is no reason to dwell on this prospect, except to say that we all assume that the Federal Reserve has little appetite for this form of self-immolation.

Leaving aside an idiotically inappropriate monetary policy, what would have to happen to create an overall rollover problem in money markets? One thing that would do it would be a runout of all types of short-term money market instruments into currency. A run into gold is now also a legal possibility but not really a practical one. Even if the Federal Reserve fully offsets the reserve impact of a run into cash, there would be a major financial crisis. But under the circumstances that would produce a run out of prime short-term paper, demand deposits would already be long gone, and the Dow would be at 50 and falling, so one might say that the rollover aspect of the problem could be compared to mosquitos buzzing around the head of a person sinking in quicksand. No one can say with complete assurance that a good old-fashioned money panic can never occur again in the United States. However, the chances are very, very small.

Another specter that has attracted some attention of late is the possibility of a runout of dollars into some other currency or currencies. A favorite scenario is a politically motivated transfer to Arab reserves out of the U.S. money market and the Eurodollar market into, say, deutsche marks or Swiss francs. No one knows just how much the total short-term U.S. dollar-denominated money market investment of the Arab countries amounts to, but $30 billion is in the ballpark. Say, something like $5 billion in U.S. Treasury bills and $25 billion in private paper of all sorts, mostly Eurodeposits and large certificates of deposit. That is a lot of money, even by today's standards, and if it were literally run off and converted into other currencies, it would cause a lot of trouble, in both exchange and money markets. As a practical matter, it could not be accomplished unless the central banks of the countries on the receiving end were prepared to take in the dollars. With conversion to gold by central banks no longer an alternative, they would presumably have to return the funds to the dollar money market, either U.S. dollars or Eurodollars, so that the aggregate funds available to the markets would still theoretically remain unchanged.

But it is unlikely that the funds would be recycled in anything like the same pattern in which they were withdrawn, hence a fairly broad market area could experience a general rollover problem. My guess is that it would come in the Eurodollar market. I cannot say with certainty that this could not happen either, but it seems most unlikely. It would be a fantastically expensive exercise for the perpetrators, so costly that it is difficult to imagine that they would even consider it. Certainly all the evidence to date suggests that the OPEC reserve accumulators are handling their funds in traditional central bank style. Again, one has to assign a problem from this source a very low probability.

Beyond these two remote possibilities, conventional wisdom holds up very well. In the absence of central bank intervention, there will always be sufficient funds seeking investment in short-term money market instruments to roll over the outstanding volume. This is not to say that the size of the market is in any sense fixed, or that it is a closed circuit, as some oversimplifiers imply. It can expand or contract at the expense of other segments of the total credit market. But in fact this expansion or contraction takes place at the initiative of the borrowers, not the lenders. It expands when borrowers are prepared to pay a higher rate—relatively but not necessarily absolutely—compared to other interest rates, and it contracts when their needs diminish and they are not prepared to bid so aggressively. In practice lenders tend to try to run to the short-term market, not away from it, in times of trouble.

It is a rather fine semantic question as to whether a widespread flight to quality credit is an overall rollover problem or just a credit problem for those from whom credit flew. Under other circumstances I might have decided to define it into, rather than out of, the title assigned to me. I am sure that if I did I would conclude that it can be and has been a serious problem under whatever heading you classify it. But it would be difficult to even scratch the surface of this complex phenomenon. Moreover, I am certain that the problems that arise when a single failure or series of failures casts a shadow over a whole category of money market instruments will be fully and interestingly dealt with by the papers immediately following. Hence, I have elected to leave it to them, and conclude that the theory of the perpetuity of the short-term money market is almost, if not quite, a tautology.

11.
Case Histories:
Introduction

EUGENE J. SHERMAN

There are three points to bear in mind in reviewing specific case histories. First, the problem of rolling over short-term debt by itself is not cause for alarm. The problem arises out of the growth of reliance on short-term debt and the impact such dependence has on specific firms. The case studies show that the problems grew out of growing dependence on short-term debt, which was itself a manifestation of weakness elsewhere within the firm. Since tight monetary policy made it increasingly difficult for firms to capture short-term money, the need to replace maturing debt and capture new money became the cutting edge of deeper-rooted problems of firms that ran into difficulty.

Second, the authors point out, where appropriate, when the problem of rollover or additional short-term borrowings became a problem. Obviously it was not a problem until it was perceived in the market to be one. At that point the market stopped making additional monies available to the firm in difficulty. Eventually diminishing amounts were made available, which ultimately led to the bankruptcies.

Third, it is appropriate to note that a monetary policy in which monetarism is a major force had to make special contingency plans and develop procedures to deal with the very real and immediate institutional problems that arose when the strict application of monetarism led to financial crises. Theoretical monetarism clearly does not give us any guidance for dealing with market crises in what we may regard as an acceptable environment. In other words, we regard it as unacceptable to allow chain-reaction crises and failures to develop.

12.
Foreign Exchange
and Other Problems—
Franklin National Bank

ANTHONY F. ALOI

Franklin National Bank of New York ran into difficulty as a result of basic philosophic and management problems which only culminated in foreign exchange speculation. In the first instance Franklin National was a regional bank which chose to expand into the highly competitive New York City banking community. To do this it had to offer concessions on the lending side and be extra competitive in bidding for funds. Thus loans that were not of prime quality were assigned the prime rate. Eventually this caught up with the bank. At the same time it consistently had to pay above the most competitive rates in the certificates-of-deposit market. This put a squeeze on earnings, particularly during periods of credit stringency. To cover these problems the bank became increasingly aggressive in seeking earnings in speculative activities. It sought to improve its earnings through active bond market trading. This of course is a risky business. When things go badly they go very badly. Eventually the problems of earnings were exacerbated by speculation that went amisss.

This approach to improvement of earnings through speculation extended to the foreign exchange market. In August 1971, when currency started to float, the opportunity for speculation in foreign exchange markets broadened enormously. Evidently the bank looked to the potential earnings that could be

218

realized through profitable foreign exchange speculation as a panacea and a potential bonanza. Here, too, when things go badly they go very badly. So it was. The key point is that by the time the bank sought salvation in the foreign exchange market the coffin was already well constructed. The losses through speculation in that market represented the final nails in the coffin.

The markets perceived the bank's problems gradually. Banking departments became wary when they started to find loans that had been turned down or bid on in spreads over prime going to Franklin National at prime. Dealers and money market specialists became wary when it became obvious to them that the bank had become speculative in its bond dealings. The market of course is aware in a general sense of speculative positions at various large institutions and whether or not the firms benefit or suffer from these positions. As the markets lost confidence in the bank, federal funds lines were cut back and certificate-of-deposit yields offered by the bank had to be increased substantially over the certificates of deposit of more highly regarded banks. Finally, the foreign exchange market became concerned, owing to the speculative positions the bank was taking in currencies. Lines were cut back and dealings by Franklin National bank became more difficult to accomplish.

In summary, we can see that the problems arose out of management decisions to move aggressively into a highly competitive area and to become a major factor in a short period of time. This led to unforeseen costs and shortfalls in earnings, particularly during periods of tight money. The bank then looked to speculative activities as a panacea. Eventually the whole thing got out of hand.

13. Commercial Paper —Penn Central and Others[1]

THOMAS M. TIMLEN

Penn Central—the name brings to mind not only a railroad but also one of the nation's largest bankruptcies and perhaps the greatest test the commercial paper market has had. This article focuses on the dramatic impact of the Penn Central bankruptcy on the commercial paper market, as well as more recent difficulties experienced by other companies and industries in the commercial paper market. Let me start, however, with a brief commentary on the nature of commercial paper and the commercial paper market.

COMMERCIAL PAPER—THE INSTRUMENT AND THE MARKET

Broadly speaking, commercial paper is a corporate IOU, that is, an unsecured promissory note, in bearer form, issued by a business firm, such as a finance company or a bank holding company. Maturities on commercial paper are generally short-term, ranging from a few days to 270 days, with a large amount of commercial paper having an initial maturity of less than 30

[1] The views expressed herein are solely those of the author and do not necessarily represent the views of the Federal Reserve Bank of New York or of the Federal Reserve system.

days. The smallest customary denomination of commercial paper is $25,000, but notes of $1 million or more are not uncommon.

Since commercial paper is unsecured, the credit-worthiness of the issuer of paper is particularly important. Moreover, an issuer of commercial paper is usually expected to have a backup line of bank credit equal to its outstanding commercial paper. Nonetheless, as the experience of the 1970s has shown, backup lines of credit have not infrequently been substantially less than total outstanding commercial paper.

A variety of parties, including trust departments of banks and pension funds, hold commercial paper, but most often the buyers are corporate treasurers for whom the appeal is short maturity and a rate somewhat higher than the yield on U.S. Treasury bills or other such instruments. There is no active secondary market for commercial paper, as for many other short-term money market instruments. Moreover, the commercial paper market is quite impersonal, with the result that holders of commercial paper feel no restraint about demanding payment at maturity. In fact, some holders are not reluctant to ask for payment before maturity.

During the years immediately preceding the Penn Central bankruptcy in June 1970, the volume of outstanding commercial paper grew tremendously. In 1965, $10 billion in commercial paper was outstanding (double the amount outstanding in 1960). By year end 1969, outstanding commercial paper totaled almost $32 billion, with almost $11 billion added during 1969 alone. By May 1970, $40 billion in commercial paper was outstanding, quadruple the amount in 1965. This very rapid growth during the late 1960s and early 1970 was the result of several factors. They included heavy demands for funds related to the booming 1960s, the inability of banks to acquire funds since they could not pay competitive interest rates on large certificates of deposit because of Regulation Q, and the generally lower cost of commercial paper relative to bank credit during much of the period.

PENN CENTRAL—THE BANKRUPTCY AND THEREAFTER

It is against this bankground of rampant growth in the commercial paper market that the difficulties of Penn Central—ending in its recourse to the bankruptcy court in mid-June 1970—took place. During the year or so preceding Penn Central's demise, many corporations, including Penn Central, were experiencing earnings problems and, as these problems became more widely recognized, holders of commercial paper began to look more carefully at the credit-worthiness of the issuers. Penn Central, with about $200 million in outstanding commercial paper, was facing market resistance after reporting a 1970 first-quarter loss of $63 million. As the railroad's situation became well-known, it was no longer able to sell commercial paper nor roll over maturing issues. Its backup lines of bank credit were exhausted, although a large amount of commercial paper was due to mature in June, July, and August, and the remainder of 1970.

By early June 1970, Penn Central's creditors would not extend further credit to the railroad without a 100 percent government guarantee of the loaned funds and, as a result, on June 2, a group of banks submitted to the Federal Reserve Bank of New York an application for a 100 percent government guarantee of a $225 million loan to the railroad. We all knew that without the loan, Penn Central would be forced into reorganization proceedings under Section 77 of the Bankruptcy Act.

Nonetheless, the Federal Reserve review of the feasibility of a government guarantee of a loan to Penn Central indicated that Penn Central's needs for cash during the succeeding year or so would be enormous—in excess of $0.5 billion and probably more. As a result, the Federal Reserve Bank (FRB) of New York concluded that it could not assure the government that it might not experience considerable financial loss were it to guarantee such a loan. And, in the end, on Friday, June 19, 1970, the bankers were informed that the administration had decided not to go through with the guarantee of the loan to Penn Central.

The immediate concern of the bankers was how to protect their interests in the light of this news. At the FRB of New York the concern was somewhat different. They were concerned as to the possible repercussions of the failure of the largest railroad in the United States and the sixth largest business enterprise in the country—particularly the repercussions in the commercial paper market, because Penn Central still had about $200 million oustanding in paper.

In looking at the major issuers of commercial paper, they were sure that many issuers had adequate backup lines of credit with their banks, so that they could pay off maturing paper, but they also knew that other issuers had only limited lines of credit. Furthermore, there was a record volume of outstanding commercial paper, much of which had short maturities; for example, outstanding finance company paper had an average maturity at that time of 25 days.

All this meant that the demand on banks for loans could well be enormous if the Penn Central failure led holders of commercial paper to lose confidence in all issuers of commercial paper. In any event, the Penn Central failure would surely lead some holders of commercial paper to appraise carefully the creditworthiness of each issuer and its ability to pay, with the result that some paper just would not be renewed on maturity and that some issuers would probably be unable to sell new paper. And it meant that issuers would probably be turning to the banks for funds. Just how much credit would the banks be asked to extend, and what would the response of the banks be?

The FRB of New York decided that the first means to cushion the possible pressure on the banks would be the Federal Reserve discount window. As a result, during the weekend of June 19th, the FRB of New York spoke with the top officials of large New York City banks, reminding them that, as they extended credit to enable their customers to pay off maturing commercial paper, the Federal Reserve discount window would be available. On Monday, discount officers at the other Federal Reserve banks also spoke with the principal banks in their respective districts, making clear that the discount window would be available to them if needed. The banks were also informed that the System, in conducting open market operations, would take account of the possible need for increased reserves in connection with any such shift to bank credit away from commercial paper.

Since it was estimated that $6 billion or more in commercial paper could be presented for payment within the succeeding 2 months, the Federal Reserve decided that additional safeguards should also be available. As a result, on Tuesday, June 23, the Board of Governors voted to suspend interest rate ceilings on large short-term time deposits in an effort to help banks accommodate whatever unusual demands for short-term credit might result in the aftermath of the Penn Central bankruptcy.

MARKET AND RELATED DEVELOPMENTS

In the 3 weeks following the Penn Central failure, outstanding nonbank commercial paper fell by about $3 billion, with more than one-third of the decline ($1.25 billion) in the paper of two captive finance companies, Chrysler Financial and Commercial Credit. Both these finance companies were particularly hard hit because they had outstanding commercial paper in excess of their aggregate bank credit lines and were controlled by industrial companies that were having earnings problems of their own. It should be added that the decline in outstanding commercial paper continued even after the inital shock, so that by year end 1970 total outstanding commercial paper had declined by about $6 billion, a 15 percent drop from pre-Penn Central days.

As companies found themselves unable to roll over or sell commercial paper, they sought bank credit—more than $2 billion of it. And as the demands on the banks grew, borrowings at the Federal Reserve banks also grew. Discount window borrowings hit a peak of almost $1.7 billion nationwide during July, more than 2½ times borrowings immediately preceding the Penn Central failure. I am sure, however, that some of this borrowing was a test of Federal Reserve willingness "to put its money where its mouth was." Finally, with the lifting of Regulation Q ceilings, $10 billion in time deposits flowed into the banks.

And still there was concern that certain large companies would be unable to obtain financial assistance in the amounts needed from banks or other financial institutions, with the result that the Federal Reserve banks, particularly the FRB of New York, began contingency planning in the event that a major issuer of commercial paper might seek direct assistance from the Federal Reserve. Their lawyers updated forms not used since the 1930s. Fortunately, circumstances never reached the point where it was necessary for the Federal Reserve, as lender of last resort, to make a loan directly to a business corporation.

MORE RECENT DEVELOPMENTS

Following the failure of Penn Central, the commercial paper market slowly recovered and, by early 1974, oustanding paper exceeded $45 billion. During 1974, however, wariness grew again as interest rates climbed to historic highs and banks scrambled for funds. With good reason, investors wondered about the ability of banks to make good on lines of credit supporting commercial paper issues. And there were other concerns, like the growing problems of Franklin National Bank of New York, W. T. Grant, and the real estate investment trust (REIT) industry.

The REITs, for example, had a peak of $4 billion in outstanding commercial paper by year end 1973. As their earnings problems became well known, investor confidence fell sharply, and soon hardly a REIT was welcome in the commercial paper market. As bank loans to REITs soared, outstanding commercial paper of REITs fell to less than $0.5 billion by the end of 1974. Bank holding companies, particularly regional bank holding companies associated with REITs, also experienced difficulties in marketing and rolling over their commercial paper during this time.

Lower-rated utilities and finance companies fared no better. Not surprisingly, firms such as W. T. Grant were also facing serious difficulties in marketing and rolling over commercial paper. W. T. Grant, which had had as much as $450 million in commercial paper outstanding, found itself able to market only about $50 million in paper by mid-1974.

CONCLUDING COMMENTS

The experience of the last decade demonstrates rather dramatically the sensitivity of the commercial paper market to changing market conditions, particularly in periods of tight money. Such sensitivity has periodically led to major difficulties for certain companies and industries, given the size of the commercial paper market and the size of the issues of certain firms and industries.

Major criticism regarding the lack of regulation of the market seems to follow each major squeeze in the commercial paper market. This criticism has resulted in some tightening of procedures by commercial paper dealers. The past crises have made both commercial paper issuers and investors more wary. Hopefully, the experiences of the past will lessen the crises of the future.

14. Problems in Eurocurrency Credits

WARREN C. HUTCHINS

It could be argued that perhaps the most significant question mark overhanging the Eurocurrency marketplace today relates to the substantial amount of maturing debt from less developed countries (LDCs) which is now upon us and on the horizon.

The question is, Can the Euromarkets cope with the obvious necessity for refinancing or will there lie in the possible negative answer to that question the seeds of yet another crisis in our marketplace? That there is such a necessity comes as no surprise to any banker who was really honest with himself in putting on these LDC assets some years back. Of course, the necessity has been made more acute and the refinancing, or in some cases rescheduling, function has become a more forced and therefore less palatable idea because of the so-called energy crisis which began in 1973 at a time when banks all over the world were in full swing, creating new Euromarket loans to the tune of $20 billion and more per annum. Since for many LDCs the only possible source of repayment of their Euromarket debt was recognized at the outset as being yet another credit from some other source, the question really boils down to whether the prospective volume of new credit demand and demand in the form of a rescheduling will cause such nervousness in the international financial community as to make continuing access to credit markets an impossibility. Most analysts now seem to feel that for this year this is really a nonproblem, at least in macroeconomic terms. This is not to say that individual countries and borrowers will not have agonizing difficulties in restructuring their debt or in meeting their current debt servicing burden. Overall, however, the numbers are as follows. In 1975 the current account deficits of non-oil-producing developing countries totaled about $27 billion. These deficits were financed without major upheaval by a combination of credits from international bodies such as the World Bank of about $10 billion, by grants and loans from OPEC countries, by a rundown in the reserve level of the developing countries and, to the extent of another some $10 billion, by loans from international banks. 1976 forecasts are for a decrease in the non-oil-producing LDC's overall deficit from $27 billion last year to about $21 billion this year—a very substantial improvement. Financing of these deficits should reflect an increased availability of official development assistance, particularly as a result of the liberalization of International Monetary credit facilities. The Eurobanks are expected to be called on to provide approximately $6 billion. There are no available statistics to show exactly the amount of bank credit in the Euromarket maturing each year from developing countries. It is possible, however, to arrive at reasonable estimates by taking available data and making some reasonable assumptions as to the typical structure of a developing country Euroloan with respect to final maturity, grace period, repayment schedule, spreads, and interest rate levels. For 1975 we came up with a number of $8 billion, including principal and interest, and for 1976 our estimate is about $6 billion for principal payments alone.

With loan demand still lagging somewhat curiously behind the economic recovery in the United States and other countries, international banks still seem eager to offset the slack domestic loan demand by the aggressive building of Eurocurrency assets. This posture of course makes them more receptive to rollover requirements of LDCs. At the 17th Annual Meeting of the Board of Governors of the Inter-American Development Bank, I recently observed bankers and investment bankers from all over the world enthusiastically wining and dining finance ministers and Central Bank officials from the Latin American countries. It is not difficult to conclude from this scene that there is still a certain willingness on the part of bankers to make funds available to the developing countries of Latin America. Recent experience indicates that, even for countries with very high debt service ratios, or for whom, in absolute dollar terms, the "pryamid of debt towers menacingly" it only takes a slight improvement in pricing to start the money flowing once again. For example, a recent syndicated credit of $300 million for a Brazilian state borrower ran into a certain amount of market resistance and was finally closed with a little difficulty. This was at a spread of 1¾ percent over the London Interbank cost of funds (LIBO). The next Brazilian deal in the market, however, with a spread improved from 1¾ to 1⅞ percent, closed quickly with a very substantial oversubscription, as the banks again demonstrated some enthusiasm for additional Brazilian assets at the slightly improved margin. Presumably the same experience may be repeated in the case of Mexico, where the market's capacity must be nearing exhaustion at the classical Mexican terms of a 1½ percent spread for 5 years. It is interesting to note that South Korea, for example, which had disappeared from the big-ticket syndication market for about a year, is currently, based on favorable economic and balance-of-payment developments, completing a very successful 5-year credit of $75 million, oversubscribed and increased from $60 million. Incidentally, it is worth noting that this deal is being completed at spreads lower than paid by Korea on its last major Eurocurrency financing in early 1975. Southeast Asia, which certainly would have been on any banker's list of Euromarket problems since the collapse of South Vietnam, currently seems to be experiencing a evival; Malaysia apparently is quite popular with lenders, and last year Indonesia made at least major progress in the restructuring of its debt burden.

A problem that seems to persist in our market and to which there may be no solution is a competitive environment composed of about 400 banks which are active in some way or another in the continuing lack of significant differential in pricing and overall compensation to lenders, as between high-grade risks and credits of lesser quality. This has been a feature of Euromarket lending for quite a long time. The differential widens or narrows somewhat from time to time, but basically the range in pricing remains so narrowly compressed as to make nonsense of any kind of normal risk-reward relationship. Considering that the ½ percent difference between a prime credit borrowing at, say 1¼ percent over LIBO, and a more marginal risk at, say 1¾ percent over, means for the lenders only $5000 more income per million dollar of loan, or for most lenders say $2500 after taxes, and considering that even this is gross interest differential before any kind of overhead costing, one has to wonder how bankers really justify the additional risk elements. As inflation erodes the value of even that tiny differential, bankers could find themselves embarrassed at the low profitability of their portfolio. Logically, therefore, one may as a general trend expect to see some movement of this differential toward a more normal risk-reward relationship, unless of course, as has been the case heretofore, the fact of too many banks chasing too few desirable mandates prevents this development. In this case of course, what is good for the borrowers may ultimately call into question the profitability of very important segments of banking activity, with concomitant implications as to the willingness of banks to continue putting up their funds on such favorable terms as have been seen in the past.

This is a book on financial crises. Insofar as the Euromarket is concerned it can be said that it has had its summer of 1974 and has survived wiser and stronger. The market has now emerged from its post-Herstatt cocoon and will now demonstrate, as it has so often in the past, a flexibility and an adaptability ensuring that it will continue to play a responsible and important role in the constructive intermediation of international money flows.

15.
Short-Term Municipals— New York City

KAREN GERARD

New York City's fiscal situation moved into a crisis phase in the fall of 1974. As short-term debt escalated and the market became increasingly wary, New York City's difficulty was first diagnosed as a cash flow problem. As the months went by, it became increasingly clear that what had appared to be a rollover problem was in fact symptomatic of a deep-seated imbalance between city expenditures and the resources to finance them. Although the immediate need was for short-term funds, the situation was long-term in its history and in its solutions.

HOW DID NEW YORK CITY REACH THE CRISIS POINT?

There are two extreme views of how New York City's past led it to a short-term debt crisis and the brink of bankruptcy. The invisible-hand-of-fate view is that the city's situation is the inevitable result of outside events. New York is a victim of forces beyond its control. The inexorable move of population and jobs from the older industrial Northeast to the Sunbelt, aided and abetted by federal policies favoring the automobile, single family home ownership, and so on, has drained the strength of older central cities. At the same time, older cities have become the reservoir for an old and dependent population. Their tax base eroded, but their public service needs rising, older cities have encountered fiscal difficulties which come to a head when a combination of national inflation and severe recession transforms problems into crisis. New York City is unique only in that it got there first, but other older cities facing the same forces can, according to this view, expect a similar fate.

The other extreme thesis is that the crisis was self-imposed—the result of greedy unions and politicians, short-sighted bankers, self-indulgent welfare mothers, liberal bleeding hearts, mismanaged and/or dishonest civil servants—take your pick. With no one to blame but New Yorkers, the solution lies within their hands. And New York stands as a warning to any other city tempted to follow the same path of folly to its doom.

The truth undoubtedly lies somewhere between these two extremes. New York City indeed has felt the brunt of long-term national forces which are eroding the strength of older central cities, but there is also little doubt that, in the conduct of its municipal affairs, it helped to turn a difficult situation into a crisis.

A quick look at the city's expenditure patterns helps to illustrate: New York City in fiscal 1974 (the latest year for which comparative data are available) spent $1645 per capita for all municipal functions. This is *twice* the average for the 10 largest cities. In the common functions—highways, police, fire, and so on—those activities that in all cities are performed by the municipal government, New York City spending per capita came to $259, slightly above the 10-city average.

In what are termed "variable" functions, New York City stands sharply apart. These are functions for which there are large differences in the level of government entrusted with financial responsibility and for which there can be wide variations in the services provided. New York City spent $1382 per capita on variable functions in 1974—nearly *three* times the average for the 10 largest cities. This figure includes New York City's spending on schools, which in most cities are financed by school districts with their own taxing power, and welfare, which usually falls under county and/or state jurisdiction. Furthermore, New York City performs some services that are unique. The city university system, the network of municipal hospitals, and the extensive mass transit facilities are examples.

In short, New York City expenditure levels are high on a per capita basis because the city pays somewhat more to perform the municipal functions common to all cities, because it has greater financial responsibilities imposed upon it by the state, and because it provides services that are not available to residents in other cities.

This characterization of New York City has been true for many years. Yet, New York City only recently moved into a crisis phase. One reason is that the variable functions, such as welfare, have grown far more rapidly than the common basic functions, both in New York City and in other large cities. Another factor is that New York City's economic base only fairly recently took a severe turn for the worse—with a serious erosion of its job base and the onset of a population decline. The process began to feed upon itself—for with the erosion of the economy, the revenue-raising capacity of the city was impaired. Thus as New York City moved through the 1970s, its fiscal situation became more precarious. Taxes were increased, the economic base weakened, and revenues did not rise in pace with expenditures. The balancing mechanism of the late 1960s—large new infusions of federal aid—was no longer increasing fast enough to compensate for the imbalance between expenditures and local tax-raising capacity. The city began to rely more on questionable financing practices. Larger amounts of operating expenditures were included in the capital budget and financed by long-term debt (all legally sanctioned by the state legislature). Revenues were overestimated and expenses were underestimated with regularity (in part reflecting a lack of recognition of how rapidly the city's economic base was deteriorating). Finally, in what turned out to be a precipitating factor in the crisis, an accumulated deficit was building up from receivables (identified as federal and state aid), which apparently there was little hope of ever collecting. The end result was that what had initially appeared to be a cash flow problem arising from uneven patterns in the timing of receipts turned out to be a rapidly escalating short-term debt crisis. It came suddenly to a head, as so often in crisis situations, when everything started to fall apart at once.

In the fall of 1974, the nation was in the throes of double-digit inflation; interest rates were at postwar highs; the recession was entering its deepest phase (even though its existence had not yet been officially recognized). New York City, with its already weakened economic base was coming onto the market for short-term debt in ever-increasing amounts just when that market was drying up. The result was that in November the city had to pay historic rates to finance its debt, and the long, hard process by which the investment community, the city, and the public began seriously to unravel the fiscal situation commenced.

By March 1975, the market for New York City securities had closed down completely. The Urban Development Corporation default did not help matters, but, the deeper the investment community probed into the *city's* situation, the more serious it turned out to be. And it soon became clear that it was not a short-term cash flow problem that had to be staunched, but a fundamental long-term imbalance between revenues and expenditures, which could not be wiped away with a magic wand.

Fitfully to be sure, solutions were sought. First, the creation of the Municipal Assistance Corporation in June was considered sufficient to help bring the city back into the market via a state-created intermediary. But the situation was too serious for this to work effectively. Thus, in the fall of 1975, the package was laboriously put together under which the city is now operating.

The Emergency Financial Control Board was created to be overseer of the city's three-year financial plan, and commercial banks, pension funds and the federal government all became committed to various pieces of the city's short-term and long-term financing needs together with noninstitutional investors in the city's notes involved in the $1.6 billion moratorium. The future will by no means be smooth, nor is success of the plan insured. It is clear to all that New York City's problems will require long-term efforts on a sustained basis before this short-term debt crisis passes into history.

16. L'Envoi

ALBERT M. WOJNILOWER

Sometimes it feels as though my whole professional life has been spent on the issues considered in this book: 12 years in the Federal Reserve, a year in commercial banking, 12 more in investment banking; a doctoral dissertation on the quality of business loans; advocacy of Hunt Commission–type financial deregulation proposals in the middle 1960s when they were relatively novel; learning to understand by 1970 how foolish these ideas were and how they would take us to or over the brink of financial catastrophe; and then watching it happen. During the great crises of 1966, 1970, and 1974, I was privileged to witness the action from a front and center seat. The label "crisis" is no overstatement. In mid-1974, our firm—and quite probably some others as well—came within inches of taking self-protective measures whose market impact might have made it far more difficult for the Federal Reserve to save the situation.

The more I reflect on the intimate details, however, the more convinced I become that this history was part of and can only be understood in a much wider context. It was not only in the field of finance that new attitudes, in particular the seeking of short-range advantage without regard to longer-range costs summed up under the heading "performance," came in conflict with and at least for a time overwhelmed older habits and traditions based on a more cautious view of the world. The hallmark of the last 10 years, in many aspects of life including the financial, has been the trampling of inhibitions in the name of greater individual freedom—"doing your thing." The pendulum of attitudes

234

concerning the eternal antinomy between rights and responsibilities, or between liberty and license, took a great swing. In the arts and entertainment, in sexual practice and narcotics use, and in journalism and politics, many conventional boundaries of conduct were obliterated. Institutions of self-restraint and mutual obligation—religion, patriotism, law abidance, family—diminished in the public esteem. Inevitably, these changes in the temper of the times had their counterparts in economic and financial behavior.

As in other aspects of the so-called "youth rebellion," many of the financial practices that are now deplored (or at least regretted) were in fact promoted and encouraged by officials and academics. They were the outcome of the great thrust toward removing all kinds of allegedly out-moded regulations. The emphasis on uninhibited free-market solutions reflects a modern version of social Darwinism which would relieve individuals of judging whether what they are doing is socially desirable or undesirable, or even morally right or wrong. It represents a throwback to the argument that giving to a beggar is an antisocial interference with the teleological progress of mankind to a Pareto-optimal solution of all its problems. As if a lasting polity ever could be organized around the unifying principle of the lonely greed of the individual economic man!

When I defended my dissertation, in 1960, the first question was, "Why are bank examinations necessary? Won't competition weed out the unsound banks?" Fortunately for me, the answer, albeit in the form of another question, was given by my sponsor, one Arthur F. Burns. "What," he asked, "about the effect on all the innocent members of the community whose lives will be ruined?" And, one might add today, What political retribution might they exact on the system that allowed this to happen?

Much of this book has been devoted to early warning models of financial trouble. These models represent a solid improvement over what we had before. But they will not help unless those in public and private responsibility monitor the models and have the will and authority to heed their message. Many great military surprises and disasters—Pearl Harbor and the Yom Kippur War spring immediately to mind—occurred not for lack of warning but for lack of will or ability to understand and respond. Things are no different in finance or in other aspects of human life. It is human to be tempted to test the codes by which we are said to be disciplined, and also human to be sometimes reluctant to police and firmly enforce these codes, especially when the legitimacy of all rules and all policemen is widely questioned.

In the 1960s, commercial bank clients frequently inquired how far they could prudently go in breaching traditional standards of liquidity and capitalization that were clearly obsolescent. My advice was always the same—to stick with the majority. Anyone out front risked drawing the lightning of the Federal Reserve or other regulatory retribution. Anyone who lagged behind would lose their market share. But those in the middle had safety in numbers; they could not all be punished, for fear of the repercussions on the economy as a whole. Besides, to the extent the mass of banks became collectively more vulnerable, that was a macroproblem for the Federal Reserve and not a reason for concern by any individual bank. And if the problem grew too big for the Federal Reserve and the banking system were swamped, well then the world would be at an end anyhow and even the most cautious of banks would likely be dragged down with the rest.

I had the temerity to send these ideas to a distant relative I have never had the privilege to meet—the distinguished economic scholar, Jack Hirshleifer. His response was cool. Later, after happening on some early work of his relating to civilian preparations for the eventuality of nuclear warfare, I undertood why. Let me take the liberty of summarizing as follows:

> On the micro-level, it doesn't pay anyone to build shelters, store food, and so forth, because the chances of surviving a nuclear holocaust are slim in the best of circumstances. But—from a macro-view—if no one builds shelters, then surely none will survive.

The same relation between individual viewpoint and aggregate result holds with respect to financial crises. Unless financial institutions are compelled to build shelters, periodic total destruction is assured. Banking history, I believe, bears out this conclusion.

Wise men of an earlier generation invented the Federal Reserve to counteract these historical tendencies of banking competition. But almost by definition, if the Federal Reserve is to be a credible lender of last resort, not just to individual banks but if necessary to the whole banking system, its own ability to create money and credit must be seen as virtually limitless. Indeed, restraints on money-printing powers incorporated in the original Federal Reserve Act have had to be largely attenuated or eliminated. The clear and everpresent danger is thereby raised, however, that commercial banks may become—organizationally, politically, and most relevant, ideologically—masters of a vastly more prolific money-printing machinery than they ever commanded before. Given the headstart of a Federal Reserve committed to ensure their solvency, the backing of federal deposit insurance, a virtual monopoly over the checking account business, the absence of meaningful restrictions on borrowing or leverage, and growing freedom to invade new lines of business in competition with others lacking these special endowments, the major banks would have to be run by people of superhuman self-restraint to avoid the trap of overreaching themselves. We have had a taste of the consequences. I hope it will discourage repetition of the experiment.

It is precisely in the illusion that government insurance or backing can somehow make the world riskless that the gravest danger lurks. Life always was and always will be full of unavoidable risks—wars, earthquakes, crop failures, embargoes and, most reliably, human error and mismanagement. No amount of innovation, whether in the form of indexation, futures markets, countercyclical fine-tuning of government policy, or long-range economic planning, can change that reality. Indeed, to the extent that such measures prevail against small disturbances, they tend to generate a complacency that renders the big shocks all the more dangerous. There has not been a fire in our neighborhood in years; why should we pay insurance or maintain our fire department? Undue good fortune can make people careless.

A durable system therefore is one that allows room for small but significant setbacks, so as to keep alive the resilience to cushion the unexpected major blows that might otherwise be mortal. And just as even schools built with fireproof construction "waste" student and faculty time on fire drills, so our financial practices and institutions need to be structured as though the government backstops on which they rely may sometime falter. Perhaps there is an analogy to the immunity that people gain by being exposed to certain diseases in childhood or, where the disease is contagious, through compulsory vaccination with a weakened form.

To argue that even the best conceived measures to shore up the financial system may sometimes fail—indeed, possibly because of having succeeded too well—is not to be a pessimist or an advocate of passivity. Although the Federal Reserve for a while poured oil on the fires of our recent difficulties, in its absence the world's financial structure would have collapsed. Our predecessors learned from their experiences and were able to conceive new institutions like the Federal Reserve and deposit insurance which have helped us avoid catastrophe. We, too, can learn.

The principal need, I believe, is for a body of financial regulation based not solely on economic logic, which can always be put in doubt by a new model or compromised in favor of some presumed higher social or political goal, but one rooted more deeply in the common sense and value structure of the society. We need, as it were, a set of financial rules analogous to the ten commandments, which however often breached do not thereby become subject to calls for repeal, usually not even on part of the transgressors. To some extent, usury laws and interest rate ceilings, whatever their defects, performed this function in the past; possibly, stringent capital requirements may do so in the future. Whatever proposals are offered, however, they must be judged by their relevance to the main theme, to the moral of the sermon to be forgotten only at our peril. This essence is that the fragility of financial structures is little more than the frailty of human resolve under stress and temptation.

Endangered
Financial Markets:
The Market for
Municipals

ARNOLD W. SAMETZ

Burkhead and Campbell, in their thorough survey of the macroeconomics of state and local governments, demonstrate that the macro data do not reveal the existence of state and local difficulties, much less evidence with respect to the causes—"... the state surplusses of Texas and Oklahoma are somehow not transferred to the empty coffers of New York and Connecticut"; nor do rich suburbs share their wealth with poorer suburbs, much less poor cities. Whatever the micro causes of state and local government distress—as classified by Lindsay to include on the supply side mismanagement and changing needs, and on the demand side changes in commercial bank purchases and personal income taxes—it is clear that on the macro side the accelerating inflation of 1966–1975 increased expenditures more rapidly and easily than revenues, as did the migration of people and jobs. The macro policy alternatives seem limited simply to fiscal retrenchment downstream or fiscal support upstream at the state, regional, and federal levels.

The other authors concern themselves with more micro aspects of the problems in the market for municipal debt. Lindsay concentrates on the need to set debt limits if New York City's and New York State's problems are to be significantly resolved. Lissenden shows how difficulties spread and cause problems for managers of sound municipalities. And Klein, looking at municipals from the

239

marketplace and the Securities Industries Association, sees some important irreversible effects from past municipals troubles even if future troubles are kept in bounds.

Lindsay stresses the importance of establishing controls over, and accountability for, the size and rate of growth of a government unit's indebted- ness. Using New York State as an object lesson, he demonstrates the shocking lack of accountability at all levels of government and the need to establish con- trol mechanisms that "span all government and government agencies within the state's geographical boundaries," owing to the interconnectedness of expenses, revenues, and debt liabilities.

The penumbra of financial crises seems to be well exemplified by the story told by Lissenden concerning the postponement of a $25 million AA general obligation bond by Richmond, Virginia, in December 1975. "It was a trau- matic moment. With a AA rating, a history of fiscal responsibility, having made the fullest disclosure ever made by a municipality on a general obligation issue, we could not sell our bonds at a reasonable price."

Less than 2 months later, with almost no change in the instrument, the bonds were sold 103 basis points below the one bid offered in December. The uncertainties, instabilities, and injustices of financial markets in crisis is well illustrated by this example of how contagion spreads from diseased to sound segments of the market.

Klein's pessimistic view that "they'll never be the same again" is based pri- marily on the recent impairment of confidence on the demand side of municipals through actual or expected disregard of contractual obligations; for example, moratoria have been declared and tax exemption may be altered via minimum tax rules. To these increased risks Klein adds factors causing increased supplies of municipals (e.g., pollution abatement issues) and other factors causing reduced institutional demand for municipals. The consequence is a level and variability of interest rates that seems unbearable. It is under just such conditions that innovation, private and public, is stimulated. But this in turn—while it offers future balm—increases short-term market uncertainties and thus likely renewed turmoil.

Returning from active engagement on the municipal reform front, both Hempel and Petersen suggest that, insofar as crises are prerequisite to real reform in such inert fields as municipal finance, the worst is well over. However, both caution that fiscal conservatism is not enough to remove public concern about the large urban areas and some of the Northeastern states. Both define crises in these markets more broadly than simply in terms of default on debt payments; a financial crises also occurs in municipal markets when the governmental unit can no longer perform its current levels of services because of inability to pay current payrolls and other bills.

17.
The Overall Problem

ROBERT LINDSAY

It is not likely that anyone needs convincing that the markets for state and local government debt have seen some turbulent times. Nor is there likely to be much disagreement that turbulence of the sort we have had is something to be avoided. It is an economic activity that (1) uses up resources (energy, ingenuity, reputations), and (2) creates a lot of negative output, particularly the fear that the market in question will impose these kinds of costs in the future on anyone who participates.

What is perhaps less agreed-on, and less clear, is why the turbulence has occurred, and how much it can be expected to recur in the near future.

Most of the answers offered for these two questions can be grouped under four headings:

1. One of the most prominent explanations of the recent troubles is mismanagement, or incompetence, or worse, on the supply side of the market. This includes fiscal gimmickry, accounting tricks, and some just flat-out telling of lies. Whether this mismanagement is to be expected also in the future may turn on one's views about the perfectability of humankind.

2. A second set of answers, concerning both what has happened and what will happen, focuses on the changing economic needs and abilities of state and local governments—the fundamental fiscal health of suppliers in this particular

debt market, and not just in the aggregate, but also in the disaggregate, as it were.

3.   Basic changes have occurred on the demand side of the market, weakening the underlying interest in these debt instruments, even if there were no questions about their *quality*. These changes include the shifting role of commercial bank demand and changes in the personal income tax system.

4.   Some of the responses to problems created by the first three groups of changes are beginning to create problems of their own, for example, the rapid escalation of disclosure requirements, and possibly some overreaction by rating agencies, other investment counselors, and investment committees.

The basic system of control of, and accountability for, the *size* of a government's indebtedness is an additional problem that merits attention. As it happens, I am especially aware of the problem in New York, because of a recent association with the Moreland Act Commission on the Urban Development Corporation (UDC) and other state finance agencies. The implications of the New York experience, however, reach well beyond the borders of New York. To begin with, much of the turbulence in the markets has sprung directly from the troubles of New York paper—city and state. In addition, the volume of debt with the New York name is a significant fraction of all state and local government debt and will be for some time. Finally, the problems of New York are far from being resolved.

The problem of the optimal size of debt really has two parts. (1) how to keep debt from growing too fast, and (2) how to cut it back after it *has* grown too fast. New York City and New York State will be occupied with the second part of the problem for some time to come, but I would like to discuss briefly how to keep debt from growing too fast.

First, it should be clear that, in the New York case, *state* debt, including state level authorities, has grown much faster than *city* debt. In the decade 1964–1974, city indebtedness rose from $7 billion to $13.5 billion, an increase of about 90 percent. Over the same period, the state debt started much lower at about $4 billion, but grew to same level as the city debt, $13.5 billion. The state increase was thus almost 250 percent. Even in concentrating on more recent years, the half-decade 1969–1974, the rise in city debt was 63 percent and in state debt 98 percent.

Second, it should also be noted that the state level growth in debt was very largely the consequence of special authorities, not the central government of the state. Some of them used straight revenue bonds, but a lot of the borrowing was done with moral obligation bonds, which legally were treated as revenue bonds with some promise of state budget help if needed. The MO agencies also issued a large volume of short-term notes.

As a consequence, the debt of all state and local government entities in New York not only grew faster than state and local debt in the rest of the country, but also, in the 5 years after 1969, grew faster than personal income in New York State. In the rest of the country, in contrast, debt was growing *less* rapidly than personal income. And, to repeat, this rising debt burden in New York was very heavily dominated by what at the federal level would be identified as off-budget borrowing.

Without detailing the argument, let me just *assert* what I conclude from these events—and let me do this as an indication of the issues that need to be addressed in designing institutional controls for managing the *size* of public debt below the federal level.

First, new control mechanisms are clearly needed in New York State, and very probably in several other states. In particular, it is important to increase the visibility of *decisions* to create debt, so as to have as much *accountability* as possible. Note that:

1. *Constitutional requirements* that state debt be approved by voter referendum did not prevent the rapid runup of debt.
2. The *market* did not, until very late in the day, send any signals to slow down.
3. The comptroller issued his early and repeated warnings about moral obligation financing—and took such a high moral ground in doing so that he had almost no effect whatsoever on the growth of moral obligation debt, and thus on state level debt in general.
4. The *rating agencies* did not, until late in 1973, emit any serious warnings about moral obligation indebtedness.
5. The *accountants* were willing to give only a qualified opinion to the UDC, but that this had very little effect on the UDC's borrowing and, one must add, on the market's willingness to lend.
6. The *disclosure* of the very grave financial condition of the UDC in its bond prospectus in the spring of 1974 deterred neither borrowers nor lenders, nor did it stir any watchdogs in state government to do more than cluck their tongues.

My second major conclusion from the New York experience is that a new control mechanism must span *all* governments and government agencies within the state's geographic boundaries. There is a basic "seamlessness" in the *ability* of all these entities to support debt. This view rests on the following kinds of webbing, as it were, that makes each of these governments a part of each other:

1. The interconnection of *debt liabilities.* For example, moral obligation bonds give some independent authorities a strong claim on general state

revenues. And now New York City debts have been, in a sense, assumed by state level agencies in the form of Big Mac.

2.   The interconnection of *operating expenses*. For example, the Dormitory Authority receives SUNY student tuition and fees for debt service, but the general budget of the state must absorb any overruns in SUNY operating expenses.

3.   The interconnection of *revenue sources*, whether taxes or user fees.

a.   Local governments depend heavily on local assistance appropriations from the state government, and this assistance is in turn a very large chunk of the state budget.

b.   Local governments also collect taxes from their own residents that could be collected by the state but are left to local use (e.g., the power to levy sales taxes was all local before 1966 but since then has been shared between the state and the local government).

c.   Some independent authorities collect revenues that the state itself could collect (e.g., thruway tolls) but instead leaves to the use of the authority.

d.   In sum, the underlying economic base of New York State can be made to generate some finite volume of payments for public services, but whether it takes the form of (i) local taxes or (ii) state taxes or (iii) user fees to independent authorities or (iv) user fees to regular line agencies, it all comes from essentially the same economic base.

Those, then, are the two major conclusions I suggest from the recent New York experience. There is much more to be said on these and other inferences from that experience, and much more thinking to be done.

18. The Macroeconomics of State and Local Governments

JESSE BURKHEAD
ALAN K. CAMPBELL

This paper is partitioned into four sections. The first examines the macro versus the micro dimensions of the current state-local fiscal crisis. The second section attempts a brief look at supply-side and demand-side variables that affect the fiscal health of the state-local sector. The third proposes a taxonomy for the analysis of specific metropolitan areas, and the last suggests a limited number of unrealistic policy options. The pervasive mood is one of pessimism.

IS THIS MICRO OR MACRO?

The macro dimensions of the state-local fiscal malaise are indeed obvious. They start with the failure of national stabilization policy, and the resulting unholy combination of inflation and unemployment that accentuated and in many cases precipitated the budget difficulties so many states and cities are now experiencing. Neo-Keynesian demand management served well for many years; whether it is now completely bankrupt is a most significant issue, but one that lies rather far beyond the scope of this paper. In any event, real gross national

245

Table 1   National Income Accounts, State and Local Sector, 1970–1975 (billion $)

Year	(1) GNP	(2) State-Local Goods and Services	(3) Ratio: (2) to (1)	(4) State-Local Transfers	(5) Ratio: (4) to (1)
1970	982.4	123.2	12.5	14.6	1.5
1971	1063.4	137.5	12.9	17.2	1.6
1972	1171.1	151.0	12.9	18.9	1.6
1973	1306.3	168.0	12.9	20.3	1.6
1974	1406.9	189.4	13.5	20.0	1.4
1975	1499.0	207.8	13.9	22.5	1.5

Source: Economic Report of the President, January 1976, p. 251.

product (GNP) declined seriously in 1974 and 1975, while the GNP deflator in 1975 was 26 percent above 1972 levels, and unemployment grew to 8.5 percent.

1976 has brought the appearance of a healthy recovery, with a real GNP growth (annual rate) of 7.5 percent and an increase in the GNP deflator of a modest 4.8 percent (annual rate). Unemployment has receded, but remains above 7.5 percent. However, the significant point is that, even if this recovery proves to be persistent, the evidence indicates that large portions of the state-local sector will continue to be in serious jeopardy, as is argued in greater detail below.

An examination of the *aggregates* of state-local activities, however, does not reveal a state of jeopardy. Table 1 shows the state and local sector in the

Table 2   State-Local and Total Nonagricultural Employment, 1970–1975 (millions)

Year	(1) State-Local	(2) Total Nonagricultural	(3) Ratio: (1) to (2)
1970	9,830	70,920	13.9
1971	10,192	71,222	14.3
1972	10,656	73,714	14.5
1973	11,075	76,896	14.4
1974	11,453	78,413	14.6
1975	12,023	77,668	15.5

Source: Economic Report of the President, January 1976, p. 203.

Table 3   Surplus and Deficit, State-Local Sector in the National Income Accounts, Selected Years

Calendar Year	Surplus or Deficit (billion $)		
	State-Local Social Insurance Funds	Operating Account	Total
1960	2.3	−2.2	0.1
1965	3.4	−3.4	0
1970	6.8	−4.0	2.8
1971	7.5	−3.8	3.7
1972	8.1	5.6	13.7
1973	8.8	4.1	12.9
1974	9.8	−1.7	8.1

Source: Special Analyses, Budget of the United States Government, Fiscal Year 1977, p. 265. The operating account includes capital outlay typically financed by borrowing.

national income accounts. Between 1970 and 1975 the ratio of goods and services expenditures to GNP increased slightly. The sector exerted a very mild stabilizing effect on the economy as a whole. Transfer payments in relation to the GNP were wholly stable over the period.

Similarly, between 1970 and 1975 state-local employment increased as a proportion of total nonagricultural employment. The stabilizing effect on total employment was stronger, particularly in 1975, than the stabilizing effect on the GNP, as Table 2 shows.

Moreover, when state-local social insurance funds are counted in, the fiscal picture through 1974, the last year for which data are available, looks positively rosy. There were surpluses in the 5 years 1970–1974, as shown in Table 3. Specifically, the surpluses in the operating account in 1972 and 1973, attributable largely to revenue sharing, appear to be quite adequate for offsetting any deficits that may appear in 1975 and 1976.

These aggregates, unfortunately, are seriously misleading, as are any projections that depend on them.[1] It is one of the peculiarities of our federal system that the state surpluses of Texas and Oklahoma are somehow not transferred to the empty coffers of New York and Connecticut. And the Connecticut town that builds bridle paths with its general revenue-sharing money somehow does not yield up this largesse to the state of Connecticut.

---

[1] This is the difficulty with the optimistic 1972 projection of the Tax Foundation (*The Financial Outlook for State and Local Government to 1980*, New York, 1972).

It is only when one examines the micro or the disaggregated dimensions of the state-local sector that a realistic picture emerges. As is commonly known, the states and cites of the Northeast and Midwest are in more difficulty than those elsewhere, but even within this large territory there are many degrees of crisis and the crisis takes a number of forms. Idiosyncratic factors are at work. In some cities the crisis is one of immediate cash flow, and some cooperation from banks and employee pension funds may provide a breathing space to work through. In other cities the problem looms in the near term because of unfunded pension obligations. In other states and cities the economic base is so eroded that any optimism whatsoever must be rejected.

None of this can be isolated from the present prevailing political mood which, if those running for elected office in 1976 are correctly reading the public pulse, is as antigovernment as any time in the last 40 years. Once dedicated and underpaid public servants are now the taxpayer's enemy. They are lazy and unproductive. Their fringe benefits are too large. Their unions have too much power. The sheer size of the bureaucracy is dragging us down to bankruptcy, chaos, and ruin. We have already seen and will continue to see the consequences of this mood. Local government service delivery has been and will be cut—usually for those programs and in those neighborhoods where low-income blacks and whites have little political power. Existing union contracts have been and will be broken. Pension promises to current employees will be abrogated. Public sector employees will no longer be entitled to cost-of-living adjustments.

Aside from the distributional inequities all of this engenders, there is one unfortunate macro consequence. The near-term reduction in rates of growth in the state-local sector are likely to reverse the stabilizing experience of 1974–1975.

Employment comparisons on a quarterly basis are somewhat hazardous, but it appears that between March 1975 and March 1976 the rate of growth in state-local employment was lower than in any previous year in the 1970s. Public employment declined 15,000 in New York City during 1975.[2] Recovery from our most serious postwar recession can be dampened by state-local contributions to unemployment. And, perhaps even more seriously, at the micro level the cutbacks in local government services will contribute further to the nonviability of the economic base of at least some cities, reducing their attractiveness as places of employment and residence.

[2] U.S. Department of Labor, Bureau of Labor Statistics, Middle Atlantic Region "1975 Year-End Report on Employment, Prices, and Earnings in New York City," *Regional Labor Statistics Bulletin,* No. 39, January 1976.

SUPPLY AND DEMAND

If the public sector could easily be subjected to systems analysis, there would be fewer difficulties in understanding its behavior and in prescribing appropriate remedies. The private service sector is difficult enough to analyze in the absence of invariant units of output, but at least there are some price tags. In the public sector there are very few output measures and there are no price tags, since almost all government goods and services are subject, to some degree, to nonexclusion and nonrivalry. The public goods that A is willing to pay for are made available to B without cost to him, and thus B will not reveal his willingness to pay—he becomes a "free rider." All of this is familiar to those who have struggled through the intricacies of neoclassical public goods theory, but the implications are not generally understood. In the absence of an ability to measure discrete units of public output the tools of public sector management intended to improve the effectiveness of government service delivery have very often broken in our hands, and currently the efforts to increase public sector productivity rest on a most infirm conceptual basis.

The same kinds of difficulties are encountered in any effort to separate the demand side from the supply side of the current state-local fiscal situation. Have the costs of local government increased because factor supply prices have increased or because, until recently, citizen-taxpayers have been willing to pay more for a larger quantity and a higher quality of state-local services? Has the very large increase in federal grants to the state-local sector encouraged that sector to overspend, in some sense, or have federal grants tended to reduce the rate of increase in state-local taxes? Is the citizen-taxpayer receiving more or less for his or her tax dollar now than at some time in the past? These are significant questions, far easier to pose than to answer.

There are a few points, however, that can be made with assurance. The supply of taxable resources available to a jurisdiction is most evidently a function of the economic activity that occurs within its boundaries and, when that activity declines, fiscal problems increase in intensity. In an examination of New York City conducted by the Metropolitan Studies Program of the Maxwell School, Syracuse University, it was estimated that in 1970 each job carried with it $820 of city government tax revenue.[3] If employment in New York had grown at the national rate between 1965 and 1974, the city would have had 1.03 million more jobs—25 percent more than it now has—and $800 million in additional revenue in 1974. If the employment decline is extrapolated to 1980, there will be an additional revenue loss of $225 million in that year.[4]

[3] Roy Bahl, Alan K. Campbell, and David Greytak, *Taxes, Expenditure and the Economic Base: Case Study of New York City* (New York: Praeger), 1974.
[4] See Roy Bahl, Bernard Jump, and David Puryear, "The Outlook for State and Local Government Fiscal Performance," Testimony, Joint Economic Committee, January 22, 1976.

Unfortunately, there are no annual data on employment trends by cities; the only employment information available is for cities that are coterminous with their county boundaries, and there are only 10 of these. For these, in the 1965–1972 period, only three—Denver, Nashville, and Jacksonville—had employment increases that exceeded the national average. Important to the growth in Nashville and Jacksonville is that both are post–World War II city-county consolidations. Three—New York, Philadelphia, and St. Louis—experienced absolute declines in employment. The remaining four—Baltimore, Indianapolis, New Orleans, and San Francisco—had employment growth rates below the national average.[5] The suburbanization of employment and residence has surely continued in the last 3 years, even at reduced levels of total economic activity.

In some cases the employment will not return, at least not to the same industries. In New York City public and private construction was a significant source of employment in the 1950s and 1960s; this experience is not likely to be replicated.[6] Similarly, Atlanta is not likely to construct 10 more new hotels in the next decade. Neither can some of the fiscal maneuvering be recycled; Cleveland cannot again sell its sewer system to Cuyahoga County and put the proceeds in its operating budget.

There are other supply-side variables at work. The growth of the state-local sector in the last 20 years has of course been a growth in the number of employees—this is a labor-intensive industry. Making comparisons of relative wages and salaries in the state-local sector and the private sector is most hazardous. The average pay in the state-local sector exceeds slightly that in the private sector, but the absence of detailed wage and salary data by job type means that it not clear whether pay for comparable jobs is better in the state-local sector than in the private sector or merely that state and local governments have higher proportions of more skilled jobs. Comparisons should also attempt to control for differences in the composition of the labor force—education, sex, age, and experience—as well as differences in the type of compensation. This should include fringe benefits, the cost of early retirement, and the cost of pensions. Available data do not permit such comparisons to be made with accuracy, never in the aggregate and seldom for specific states or metropolitan areas.

Table 4 exhibits some relevant data, very much subject to the foregoing limitations. Average annual wages and salaries in the state-local sector are higher than in the private sector, but the percentage differentials are narrowing. In 1950 state-local compensation, measured in these terms, was 10 percent above that in the private sector, and in 1973 it was 2 percent higher.

[5] *Ibid.*
[6] For an examination of the political dimensions of New York City's construction experience see Jason Epstein, "The Last Days of New York," *New York Review,* February 19, 1976, pp. 17–27.

Table 4 Average Annual Wages and Salaries per Full-Time Equivalent Employee, 1950–1973 (dollars)

	1973	1970	1965	1960	1950
All industries	9,106	7,571	5,705	4,743	2,992
Private industry	8,900	7,471	5,706	3,890	2,536
State and local government	9,425	7,818	5,592	4,550	2,786
Public education	9,624	8,140	5,846	4,752	2,794
Federal general government (civilian employees only)	12,984	10,519	7,605	5,895	3,494

Source: Survey of Current Business (selected July issues); U.S. Department of Commerce, *The National Income and Product Accounts of the United States, 1929–65, Statistical Tables,* A Supplement to the *Survey of Current Business* (Washington, D.C.: U.S. Government Printing Office), 1966. (From Bahl, Jump, and Puryear testimony.)

The supplements to wages and salaries—social security and retirement benefits, health, hospital, and life insurance, paid vacations and the like—have grown as a proportion of compensation in both the public and the private sectors. Relative growth is very much affected by the choice of the base year. It can be generalized that between 1950 and 1973, for example, supplements more than doubled in both the private and the state-local sectors. But state-local supplements, over this 23-year period, appear to have amounted to about 80 percent of those in the private sector. The value of the state-local supplement is about 11.5 percent of average annual wages.[7]

These aggregate compensation data hide a great many specific instances of the kind that command newspaper headlines. Retirement benefits for New York City and San Francisco policemen and firemen may indeed be excessive in some sense, but it is most difficult to arrive at an objective definition of that which should be deemed excessive. The same considerations apply to public and private sector occupational wage rate comparisons. Cities where public employee unions are very strong, as in Detroit, pay hourly wage rates in some occupational categories 50 percent greater than their private sector counterparts. Detroit taxpayers may view this as excessive. Detroit city employees may have a different view of the equities. And whether a file clerk is the same occupation in both the public and the private sector in Detroit is a further consideration.

Demand-side variables are even more difficult to quantify than supply-side variables. Given the peculiar nature of the demand for state-local services, as noted above, perhaps the only concept that is operational is "tax willingness" as expressed in state-local tax collections. Appropriate data are exhibited in

[7] Data from Bahl, Jump, and Puryear testimony.

Table 5. In the late 1960s and until 1971 both state and local taxpayers were willing to divert an increased share of the GNP to the state-local sector. State taxpayers continued that willingness into 1972. Local taxpayers began to feel more reluctant in 1972. Not until 1973 did both sectors hold their growth below the GNP growth rate. Property taxpayers lost their tax willingness in 1972-1974 but recovered that willingness, however reluctantly, in 1975.

Indeed, the taxpaying pattern in Table 5 shows a kind of seesaw effect in recent years. When the state sector expands most rapidly, the local sector expands less rapidly, and vice versa. This underscores the point that there is a state sector, a local sector, and a combined state-local sector.[8]

Inflation works on both the demand and the supply sides of the equation— adding to both revenue and expenditure in the state-local sector. The Metropolitan Studies Program has developed a set of inflation indexes to esti- mate the impact of inflation on the revenue and expenditure of both state and local governments. The highlights of these findings are that in the 1967–1972 period one-fourth of the increase in state-local expenditures was attributable to inflation, and in the 3-year period 1972–1974 another one-fourth of the expenditure increase was attributable to inflation.[9]

The impact of inflation on revenues varies greatly from jurisdiction to juris- diction, depending on the elasticity of revenue, which in turn is controlled by the nature of the tax bases utilized. In general, inflation has a greater impact on state-local expenditure than on state-local revenue. When these two are net- ted out, it is possible to estimate the combined effect of inflation on revenue and expenditure. These estimates can then be translated into changes in effective demand or purchasing power. For the period 1972–1974 it is thus estimated that the states alone lost $6.6 billion—an amount that exceeded their gross revenue-sharing entitlement. In the same period counties, municipalities, and townships lost an amount of effective demand equal to about 80 percent of their gross revenue-sharing entitlement.

These forces that have caused a larger and larger portion of the GNP to be devoted to the state and local sectors of the economy—the taxpayers demand for more and better public services, increases in the number of public employees, continuous improvements in employee compensation and fringe benefits, and inflation—will determine in part whether or not the pattern of the past will extend into the future. There is evidence that the rate of growth in state-local public employment is declining. The annual rate of increase since 1950 has been 4.2 percent, but in 1973 it dropped to 3.7 percent and in 1974 to 3.2

---

[8] The authors are indebted to Seymour Sacks for the compilation of the data in Table 5 and for this interpretation.

[9] David Greytak and Bernard Jump, *The Effects of Inflation on State and Local Government Finances, 1967–1974,* Occasional Paper No. 25, Syracuse Metropolitan Studies Program, 1975; see also, Bahl, Jump, and Puryear testimony.

Table 5 State, Local, and Property Tax Collections, 1967–1975

Calendar Year	State Collections (billion $)	Percent Change	Local Collections (billion $)ᵃ	Percent Change	Property Tax Collections (billion $)	Percent Change	GNP (billion $)	Percent Change
1967	33,353		30,989		27,686		796.3	
1968	38,940	16.8	34,254	10.5	30,687	10.8	868.5	9.0
1969	45,059	15.7	37,767	10.3	33,556	9.3	935.5	7.7
1970	49,202	9.2	42,376	12.2	37,502	11.8	982.4	5.0
1971	54,081	9.9	46,643	10.1	41,306	10.1	1063.4	8.2
1972	64,198	18.7	50,387	8.0	44,103	6.8	1171.1	10.1
1973	71,404	11.2	54,044	7.3	47,244	7.1	1306.3	11.5
1974	77,362	8.3	57,976	7.3	49,343	4.4	1406.9	7.7
1975	82,864	7.1	64,131	10.6	54,290	10.0	1499.0	6.5

Source: Compiled from Bureau of the Census, Census of Governments, *Quarterly Summary of State and Local Tax Revenue.*
ᵃ Includes property taxes.

percent. The growth decline in large cities has been even greater. Public employment in the 19 largest cities grew at an annual rate of only 2.3 percent from 1967 to 1974 and, of these 19 cities, 7—New York City, Chicago, Dallas, Boston, St. Louis, New Orleans, and Phoenix—had employment declines in 1974, and 9, including 3 of these 7, declined in 1973.

These differences in the behavior of large cities compared to other parts of the state-local sector suggest another useful way to examine subnational fiscal behavior. The metropolitanization of the country since the end of World War II has resulted in analyses that emphasize central city–suburban disparities.

METROPOLITAN AREAS: SIMILARITIES AND DIFFERENCES

These central city–suburban disparities have dominated metropolitan analysis over the past decade and a half—disparities in socioeconomic characteristics, in fiscal effort, in the distribution of resources between education and municipal services, and in rates of economic and population growth. It was believed that these characteristics were sufficiently similar for all metropolitan areas to justify generalizations about metropolitanism and to base public policy recommendations on them.

For many metropolitan areas, particularly the larger ones, and especially those in the northeastern and north central parts of the country, these generalizations were accurate enough. The population migration from countryside to city and from city to suburb, and the movement of economic activity, particularly manufacturing and services, from city to suburb all contributed to the creation of urban problems. These included a concentration of social problems in central cities, often exacerbated by racial tensions, a central city tax base unable to keep pace with either increased service needs or higher pay and fringe benefits for public employees, and intergovernmental flows of funds which responded more to the growing political strength of the suburbs than to the growing needs of the cities.

The products of these forces included racial revolts, skyrocketing crime rates, violence in the public schools, and the reality, if not the technical condition, of municipal bankruptcy. Suggested solutions have ranged from the restructuring of government in metropolitan areas to major shifts in federal policy, including both the redirecting and increasing of federal aid to cities and the assumption of full responsibility by the federal government of welfare financing.

Although these characteristics and resulting problems were never typical of all central cities and metropolitan areas of all sizes and in all sections of the country, the extent of what commonality there was is declining rather than increasing. This shift away from similarity is a product of birthrate decline, a shift in migration patterns, and growing differentials in economic growth rates for different parts of the country.

A most dramatic general change has been the decline in the growth rate for metropolitan areas in general. Since 1970 metropolitan population has increased by only 3.4 percent. This 0.8 of 1 percent annual increase contrasts with an annual rate of growth for metropolitan populations of 2.5 percent for the period 1950–1966—three times greater than the 1970–1974 rate. Equally important, nonmetropolitan areas have grown since 1970 more than metropolitan ones: 5.5 compared to 3.4 percent, that is, a 62 percent greater growth rate in nonmetropolitan areas.[10]

The other significant change is the great population growth occurring in the southern and southwestern regions of the nation—the so-called Sunbelt—a movement primarily from the northeastern and north central regions. The 1970 census hinted at this change and census estimates since then have documented it. Further, this migration is much different than the 1950 to 1970 movement of people from countryside to city, a movement of people with less education and lower incomes than that of the people already living in the communities to which they moved. Just the opposite is true of those moving from the northeastern and north central sections of the country to the South and Southwest. They possess, on the average, higher incomes and more education and are younger than those who are remaining in the areas from which they are moving, and by the same measures exceed the averages of the population in the region to which they are moving. This movement therefore weakens economically and socially the areas being abandoned and strengthens the receiving areas.

In sum, these changes are reinforcing the decline in the population and economic vitality of many of the nation's large cities, a phenomenon that fits traditional metropolitan analysis but does not fit the decline of entire metropolitan areas. During the decade of the 1960s, only one of the large metropolitan areas, Pittsburgh, lost population, but from 1970 to 1974, 8 of the 15 largest SMSAs are estimated to be losing population. In fact, a total of 37 SMSAs have lost population since 1970. And, as a group, SMSAs with over 2 million population have experienced no growth during the past 4 years.

Even in the metropolitan areas that have experienced some growth, the central counties (the county in which the central city is located) have lost population. This extension of the central city decline to the county surrounds it is further evidence of the weakness of central cities spilling over into the suburbs.

These changes have produced metropolitan areas across the country with quite different characteristics and, instead of one model fitting all areas, there

[10] Bureau of the Census "Population Estimates and Projections," *Current Population Reports,* Series P-25, No. 618, January 1976.

have emerged at least three general types of areas:

1. Declining central city–county and declining metropolitan area (most northeastern and north central metropolitan areas)
2. Declining central city–county and stable or moderate growth metropolitan area (some southern, mid western, and western metropolitan areas)
3. Stable or moderate growth central city–county and a growing metropolitan area (most southern and southwestern metropolitan areas).

The federal government responded to the problems created by the movement of economic activities and people in two general ways: first, by requiring areawide planning and interlocal cooperation as conditions for the receipt of such functional aid programs as airports, urban renewal, transportation, water supply, and waste disposal, and second, by targeting federal dollars to specific social problems, such as labor, housing, and education. The first approach was aimed at reducing friction and duplication among local governments and encouraging metropolitan wide planning. The latter approach sought to meet individual human needs, rather than to improve the state-local jurisdictional system.

During the liberal administration of the 1960s, the maldistribution of wealth and opportunity was clearly recognized and explicit, and national goals were set to deal with the gulf between rich and poor, black and white. Federal initiatives were launched under the Great Society program to assist the disadvantaged populations living in both rural and urban ghettoes. The main effort was focused on the central city, because that was where many needing assistance were concentrated. The social programs that comprised the war on poverty effort were targeted toward individuals—the aim was not to help local or state jurisdictions but rather to help the people who lived within them.

The programs in fact often exacerbated the fiscal consequences of the movement of people and economic activities out of central cities by forcing the cities to meet the matching requirements from local taxes in order to receive the aid. Further, and even more devastating, as federal programs were cut back or eliminated, the city became heir to them with their citizens expecting or, better said, demanding their continuation.

In fact, the vitality, or continued viability, of urban jurisdictions was not perceived as a salient issue. On the contrary, federal poverty programs often were designed consciously to work around established local political units. Community action and model cities agencies were created as para-governments on the premise that conservative local officials would undermine or stall the accomplishment of national goals.[11]

By the end of the 1960s, national policy was reversed by the new Republican

[11] James P. Sundquist and D. Davis, *Making Federalism Work* (Washington, D.C.: Brookings Institution), 1969.

administration. The great social experiment was termed a failure by some, although revisionist views of this verdict are beginning to appear;[12] but whatever their success, it was argued, the nation could no longer afford their cost. The fiscal dividend on which economists Pechman and Heller predicated their support of revenue sharing was absorbed by the Vietnam War and, following that war, economic prosperity faded into a recession combined with inflation (unpleasantly labeled "stagflation"); and the resultant decline in the growth of government revenues coupled with rapid increases in public sector expenditures and rapid decline in public sector purchasing power resulted in tight budgets at all levels of the federal system.

The Kennedy-Johnson policy of an active, dominant national role in domestic social issues was rejected by the Nixon presidency in favor of a radically different philosophy of government which came to be known as "the new federalism." Key to this new view of American government was the devolution of responsibility to state and local jurisdictions—decisions were to be made at the level closest to the people. The manifold social problems the Great Society program attempted to solve were now to be the province of state and local politics.

The original new federalism envisioned not only the transfer of responsibility to states and localities but the shift of funds as well. General Revenue Sharing (GRS) was the sole survivor of that early philosophy, and its impact was negated by corresponding cuts in other federal assistance programs and in its even-handed distribution, which meant the resources were not concentrated in the jurisdictions with the greatest needs.[13]

Accompanying the new federalism was increased federal support for the establishment of councils of government (COGs). Depending on one's views of these organizations, they can be seen either as supportive of the current local jurisdictional system or as a step toward metropolitan government.[14] COGs are viewed by many of their supporters as a device for local officials to cope with their regional issues and to coordinate federal grants which flow into their region. The growth of regional planning agencies or COGs has been a very recent phenomenon. In 1960, only 56 regional councils were in operation but, by 1970, the number had risen to 476. Most COGs are voluntary associations

---

[12] For a favorable account of the accomplishments of the social programs of the 1960s see Sar A. Levitan and Robert Taggart, *The Promise of Greatness* (Cambridge, Mass.: Harvard University Press), 1976.

[13] Revenue sharing has produced more studies, reports, articles, and books than any single government program in recent memory. For a good summary of the issues surrounding this program, see Subcommittee of the Committee on Government Operations, U.S. House of Representatives, *Hearings: Fiscal Relations in the American Federal System* (Washington, D.C.: Government Printing Office), 1975.

[14] M. M. Mogulof, *Governing Metropolitan Areas* (Washington, D.C.: The Urban Institute), 1971. Also by the same author, "Federally Encouraged Multi-Jurisdictional Agencies in Three Metropolitan Areas," Chap. V, ACIR, Vol. 2, *op. cit.*, pp. 141–197.

of elected officials created ostensibly to increase coordination and communication among units of local government.

Federal policy toward COGs is stated positively through the Office of Management and Budget (OMB) Circular A-95 which requires that over 100 federal grant programs be subjected to review by a regional agency and by HUD's 701 planning assistance program which has been the mainstay of financial support for regional planning staffs. While both continue, they have received only lukewarm support, as evidenced by the failure of federal agency heads to pursue compliance with the A-95 review process and by recent attempts by OMB to reduce the 701 annual funding level from $75 million to $25 million. This federal ambivalence is seen further in the continued reliance on, and promotion of, single-purpose areawide agencies for economic development, mass transit, and health planning.

Despite the mixed signals from the federal level, it remains doubtful that voluntary regional agencies composed of elected officials who represent local units can pursue policies that will advance regional goals, especially when these policies may undercut the short-term advantage of individual localities. One of the most distinctive characteristics of the Minneapolis Metropolitan Region Council is that the members of its governing board do not represent jurisdictions but are appointed by the governor. Not being required to represent a local jurisdiction, as is the case with those on COG boards, they are more likely to view issues on a regional basis.

On balance, federal government policy has contributed more to perpetuation of the local jurisdictional status quo than to movement toward a system that would relate local jurisdictions to areas of socioeconomic interdependence. This policy direction probably reflects accurately the distribution of political influence in the country. Efforts to accomplish metropolitan-wide approaches to major social problems—housing, integrated education, social services—have met stiff, and by and large, effective suburban resistance.

The combination of forces currently influencing fiscal behavior in the state and local parts of the governmental system makes projecting future behavior difficult. The pressures for increased expenditures, particularly in the northeastern and north central regions, will necessarily ease somewhat, there will be increasing regional differences caused by population and economic shifts, and central cities will experience the most difficulty in matching revenue to expenditure needs.

POLICY OPTIONS

What are the policy options that can be chosen in light of these conditions.

The first is fiscal retrenchment and adoption of no-growth budgets. Recent trends suggest that the national economy will have to adjust to a slower rate of growth, but, since core cities are growing slower than even the national economy, they are doubly damned in that their budgets will have to reflect an even more stringent measure of control than those of other governments. For many cities, this will mean postponements and reductions in capital expenditures—the first to be cut back will be less essential projects, such as municipal auditoriums, public buildings, and recreation facilities, but there will no doubt be a necessity to curtail other kinds of capital improvements, for example, new school buildings and sewer systems.

Since most public services are labor-intensive, a no-growth city budget will have a substantial impact on negotiations with public employee unions. In many cities, it is not difficult to foresee reductions in the number of public employees, either through attrition or layoffs, as have already occurred in New York and Detroit.

Such cutbacks are bound to affect the level and quality of services. Not only is this likely to weaken the already deteriorating economic base of some jurisdictions, but additionally it will particularly hurt that part of the population dependent on public services. As illustrated by New York City, it is social services that suffer the most when government retrenches—day care centers, services for the elderly, job training, housing and so on.

A second policy option is for financially troubled jurisdictions to shift responsibility for services to a higher level of government, a county government, a regional agency, or the state. This option is of course not a new one; functional consolidations between city and county have been going on for some time, and a few states have assumed greater responsibility for the financing of education and social services. The adoption of regional financing mechanisms has had less precedent. The Minneapolis–St. Paul regional tax-sharing plan whereby 40 percent of nonresidential tax base growth is shared on a formula basis among all jurisdictions in the region is unique. To be optimistic, continued severe economic and fiscal pressure in some of the metropolitan areas may hasten efforts to implement such regional tax plans and may lead to an increase in the number of functional shifts to higher levels.

Despite the frequent suggestion that the total state-local fiscal system could be greatly improved by states playing a larger role in that system by assuming greater responsibility, change in functional assignment has been minimal. One means of measuring the amount of responsibility and the extent of its change in the state-local system is to calculate the assignment of revenue and expenditure responsibilities by measuring the proportion of total state-local revenues and expenditures that are the responsibility of the state level of government. Examined in this way, state governments increased their revenue responsibilities by only 2.2 percent from 1967 to 1972 and, in the case of expenditure responsibility, the median increase was only 1.3 percent. These changes appear to be generally representative of all states. There were only four states in which the state assignment of responsibility for raising revenue increased by more than 6 percent: Nebraska, 8.4 percent; Illinois, 7.3 percent; Florida, 7.1 percent; and Mississippi, 6.1 percent. In the case of expenditures there were also four states that experienced a change greater than 6 percent. Two of these—Alaska (6.9 percent) and Arizona (6.6 percent)—had a reduction in their proportionate responsibility, while two—Hawaii (6.3 percent) and Massachusetts (14.0 percent)—increased their responsibilities. The change in Massachusetts resulted primarily from the state assuming what had been a local share of the cost of welfare services.

The difficulty with state assumption of services is that it requires a search for new resources, since costs increase—a leveling up of services is much more likely than a leveling down. Another major problem with this option is that, unless the proper choice of tax instruments is made, unfavorable income distribution consequences may result, that is, if sales taxes are chosen as the financing mechanism over the income tax alternative, tax burdens on the urban poor may rise as a result of state assumption. State assumption may be an advantage to city governments but a disadvantage to city residents.

The third option is for a more realistic new federalism with national assumption of the financing of services now considered primarily the responsibility of states and localities. Full federal assumption of welfare costs would be a first step in this direction. An increased and realistic allotment of revenue-sharing monies, but under a formula that recognizes the particular problems of central cities, would be a second element of such federalism.

Perhaps more important is the need for federal policies that recognize the changing distribution of wealth and income among regions of the United States and between the core jurisdictions of our metropolitan areas and their suburban fringe. A recent *New York Times* series on the Sunbelt region[15] highlighted the irony of a federal policy which pumps money into the region of the country that is growing fastest and gaining most in economic strength.

> But perhaps the most striking factor of all is the dramatic ability of the region as a whole—the vast southern rim, sweeping from Virginia to Southern California—to extract far more money from the federal coffers than its taxpayers contribute. For three decades, the Sunbelt has been first in line at the pork barrel, amassing vast sums for defense installations, space exploration and technological development.

> In 1974, the region managed to collect $13 billion more from Washington than it paid in federal taxes.

It seems clear that unless the decline of the older metropolitan areas is to be allowed to continue, a drastic realignment in federal spending policies will be

[15] "Sunbelt Region Leads Nation in Growth of Population," *The New York Times*, February 8–13, 1976.

necessary. Considerations of regional economic viability will need to replace those of the political pork barrel, if the deterioration of the economic base in many central cities is to be reversed, or if the social consequences of that deterioration are to be ameliorated.

The restructuring of local government could make a significant contribution to easing the fiscal problems of many central cities, although the contribution will vary among different types of metropolitan areas.

Among the metropolitan areas that are losing population and suffering a decline in the economic base of the entire region, a trend toward centralizing the financing of services at a regional level may occur in order to spread the burden as widely as possible and to achieve whatever cost economies, even though marginal, are possible. Reform efforts in these areas may be stimulated by a fundamental motive of survival. Still, metropolitanization of a structural character will offer small relief for those areas where decline has spread from city to suburb and affects the entire region. Their salvation must come from state and federal levels.

In metropolitan areas that are in the traditional pattern of central city decline with stable or growing suburbs, increasing regional responsibility for the financing and delivery of services would greatly advantage core city residents, but such assistance could come at the expense of suburban residents. Such a change however, might contribute to the continuing economic viability of the whole region. If Indianapolis and Jacksonville, for example, had not regionalized their governments, their central cities would today be experiencing severe financial problems.

In metropolitan areas, most of which are in the South and Southwest, where the entire region enjoys economic health and fiscal vitality, the issue of reform is not likely to be high on the public agenda for two reasons. With both city and suburbs experiencing economic growth, fiscal problems are not likely to be severe and, more important, the disparity issue is practically nonexistent because many of the cities through annexation have captured a substantial portion of their suburbs.

If past actions are a guide to future policies it is not possible to be optimistic that any of these policy options, separately or in combination, will be generally adopted. A few local areas will reorganize their local governments and will benefit from it, and a few states may follow Minnesota and develop state policies relevant to their local government needs, but massive action at either the state or local level seems highly unlikely. Federal action is even less likely if the current presidential campaign is an appropriate guide to the policies which will be followed after the election. The issues covered in this paper are at best dimly visible in that campaign.

19.
Municipal Management: Disarray in the Marketplace

H. JACK LISSENDEN

The financial problems of New York City and several other United States cities have created a whole new ballgame for those responsible for the financial operations of our nation's cities. The recurrent fiscal crises, and the series of revelations of the financial shell games played with the New York City budget and other budgets have created a lack of confidence in city government which has rubbed off on the financial administrators of other jurisdictions. Local tax-payers are now questioning the capability and integrity of their own city officials. This is not all bad. In localities where legislators and administrators have been something less than fiscally responsible, or where there has been some hanky-panky with budgeting or reporting, there is some fast scrambling going on to put the house in order. Thus the New York debacle is eliminating administrative sins that should have long ago been attacked by state governments and lending institutions. The other side of the coin is that city officials who have lived up to high standards of financial administration now find themselves wasting time and resources defending themselves, time and resources that could be better spent carrying out their normal operating responsibilities.

There is, however, a much more critical and visible fallout from the New York situation than the discomfort of local officials. Access to the money market, for many jurisdictions, has at best been seriously curtailed and in many cases has been denied. Many cities and counties, because of their small size, do not have a credit rating. Others, because of political, economic, or demographic problems have poor credit ratings. These people are having great difficulty selling bonds and, if they can sell them at all, must pay unbearably high interest rates. Underwriters and their customers have all participated in what is now described as "a flight to quality."

Another fallout of the various municipal fiscal crises is the new disclosure requirement of the Securities Act Amendments of 1975. For years, municipal bonds were sold with minimal, if any, disclosure of financial matters—and no disclosure of socioeconomic or demographic data. Underwriters relied, almost exclusively, on the rating services and the fact that there had been minimal defaults on municipal bonds since the Great Depression of the 1930s. In the few months since December 1, 1975, when the new regulations became effective, we have seen many full-blown "prospectuses" with page after page of statistical tables and financial statements and reams of text material describing the city government, environment, history, and much more. City officials are now spending weeks and months preparing for bond sales which in former years would have been handled in days. It is a whole new ballgame.

RICHMOND, VIRGINIA

The easiest way for me to convey what I believe city legislators and administrative officals must do in these apoplectic times is to describe what we have done and are attempting to do in Richmond. Our city is a relatively cosmopolitan, old southern city with a history of good, clean government and fiscal conservatism. Since conversion to the council-manager form of government in 1948, the city has had a general fund surplus at the end of each and every year. This has been true even though we are surrounded by bedroom counties and, as a core city, have become a center for the very poor, the very black, and the very old. Our economy is extremely stable; our metropolitan unemployment rate is currently slightly above 4 percent. We have had and still retain an AA rating from both Standard and Poor's and Moody's. How we achieved this posture and what we are doing to retain it can be described together.

Budgeting

The cornerstone of fiscal responsibility is the annual budget. Our city charter, like the city of New York's, requires a balanced budget. There the similarity ends, for our budget is truly balanced—with no hidden deficits. The city council and the administration jealously guard the integrity of the budget by maintaining tight control over expenditures on a daily basis. Before a purchase order can be issued, the finance department must certify that an unencumbered appropriation is available. Every month, before the tenth work day, each department head is advised of the status of his appropriations and, on a quarterly basis, each work program is reprojected to the end of the fiscal year and any apparent excess appropriations are administratively reduced. For example, we started the current year with a $1.5 million budgeted surplus; at the end of the first quarter, appropriations were reduced and projected surplus was adjusted to $3.4 million—a similar, exercise, after the second quarter, projected surplus as $6.1 million, and current estimates are for almost $8 million. This surplus will be used as a source of revenue in next year's budget.

If at any time during the fiscal year it appears that expenditures will exceed annual revenues, the city manager is required by charter to cut expenditures by eliminating positions and reducing other expenditures. The city, on occasion, has made such cuts and we have *never* had a deficit at the end of a fiscal year.

Accounting

Such budgetary control presupposes an adequate accounting system. Our present system is, at best, adequate. We are presently installing modern, computerized systems for payroll, personnel, encumbering, accounts payable, accounts receivable, purchasing, inventories and general ledger. These new systems will not only tighten our controls, with fewer employees, but will also expand our cost-accounting capabilities and further develop the management-by-objectives program installed this year.

Our reporting to the taxpayers is considered outstanding. Each year we issue a report detailing the activities and status of each fund, and relating much statistical and textual material on financial, economic, and demographic trends. Our 1974 report was awarded an updated certificate by the Municipal Finance Officers Association, which states that it conforms to the high standards of the National Committee on Governmental Accounting.

Cash Management

Richmond's cash management program has been rated as very effective. In line with the conservative fiscal posture described, the city's ratios of debt to fair market value of real estate and debt service to total budget have remained well within acceptable limits. Bonds ae issued *only* to finance capital expenditures. Safeguards against promiscuous borrowing are provided by law. No bonds may extend beyond the life of the asset, and in no case may they extend beyond 30 years. Administratively, the council requires at least a 10 percent cash paydown; Just twice in the past 25 years has the city resorted to temporary borrowing. In 1971 and 1972, the city issued bond anticipation notes when construction projects came in faster than anticipated. We do not borrow for general fund expenditures. As a matter of fact, we realize a $2 million to $3 million interest income each year by keeping all excess funds fully invested.

THE DISCLOSURE DILEMMA

In spite of the formidable credit qualifications just described, Richmond still had to postpone a bond sale last December 10. Finance officers now find a new hurdle to clear before they can sell their bonds—that new bogie man called disclosure. Our problem, as it turned out, was not too little disclosure, but rather too much too soon. The Securities Act's Amendments of 1975 became effective December 1, 1975. During the last week in November, the Securities Industry Association held their annual meeting in Boca Raton, and the program included a lengthy discussion of the liability exposure of municipal bond dealers because of the new disclosure requirements. Once week later, Richmond hit the market with a $25 million issue of general obligation bonds.

We had become aware of the new disclosure requirement in the early fall. Our review of the amendments indicated that municipal issuers were specifically exempted from the disclosure requirement, but we felt that any dealer handling such a large issue would feel required to make a fuller disclosure than we had made in the past. The Securities Exchange Commission (SEC) had not, as yet, issued regulations, and the Municipal Finance Officers Association guidelines were still being prepared. We were flying blind. We had lengthy discussions with our bond counsel and local bond dealers. We put together a 30-page official statement setting forth historical, financial, political, social, and economic data we felt was important to a prudent investor who wished to evalute our credit rating.

On November 28 we distributed the official statement to potential bidders. The very same day the SEC issued its regulations, and the pot started to boil. During the next week there were lengthy telephone calls with underwriting group leaders and their legal counselors, and it was obvious that the underwriters were really wrestling with the mass of data we had supplied. No real pattern developed, and each group raised questions different from those of the others. One was concerned about the possible outcome of certain voting rights litigation that had been in court for 5 years. Another wondered how they could perform "due diligence." A third felt that so many data were presented that the independent opinion of a third party as to the validity of the data in the official statement was needed. It was obvious to us that the underwriters were not prepared to deal with full disclosure—a fact that they confirmed at a later date. On the day of the bid opening, all three groups were disbanded, and the only bid we received was from a splinter group put together during the last hour before the scheduled bid opening. Knowing that the one bid was from a group that knew they would be the only bidder, we were sure that the net interest cost would be exorbitant. We therefore did not want to open the bid and have to reject it, so we postponed the sale.

It was a traumatic moment. With an AA rating, a history of fiscal responsibility, having made the fullest disclosure ever made by a municipality on a general obligation issue, we could not sell our bonds at a reasonable price.

During the ensuing weeks we again met with the underwriters and their counsel. The changes required in the official statement were minimal and pertained principally to procedural matters. We provided for "due diligence" by our bond counsel, added the opinion of the city auditor on the financials and a comfort letter on the official statement by the city attorney, the city manager, and the director of finance. The only change of any significance was the addition of a short paragraph on the estimated effect of the possible loss of the voting rights litigation. With those changes, we returned to the market on February 11 and sold the bonds at 115 basis points below the bond buyers average and 103 basis points below the one bid offered in December. In a news article in *The Wall Street Journal* on the day following the sale our official statement was referred to as a model of full disclosure. As a matter of fact, the mockup official statement used by the Municipal Finance Officers Associaiton in disclosure seminars being held all over the country is copied so closely from ours that in many cases only the names have been changed. We must have made a full disclosure.

The city of Richmond really "lucked out." During the 2 months of the postponement, the municipal bond market improved dramatically and, when the bonds were sold, the net interest cost to the city was almost $3 million below what we would have paid in December; however, the fact that we *had* to postpone the sale spotlights the chaotic condition of the market at that time. It has settled down a lot since then, but there are still many uncertainties that must be clarified if it is to achieve normalcy.

WHERE TO FROM HERE

Two clear definitions must be developed to remove the present uncertainties in the market. The first will specify what comprises full disclosure. The second will spell out the relative liability of bond issuers, brokers, and dealers. Neither can be brought forth until significant obstacles are overcome.

In contrast to corporate entities, no two governmental units are exactly alike. They differ in form of government, service delivery requirements, taxing authority, accounting and reporting policies, and so on. Any definition of full disclosure that would be applicable to all jurisdictions would, of necessity, be in such general terms that it would be almost meaningless. The definition is further complicated by the case of characters trying to get into the act. The Municipal Finance Officers Association has a proposed set of guidelines; the SIA is considering working on some; Congress has appointed a municipal securities rule-making board; some legislators want the SEC to take complete control of the municipal market. Evidence of this confusion is the multiplicity of bills before Congress. The Van Deerlin bills call for the repeal of that section of the Securities Act of 1934 that prevents municipal security registration. The Eagleton-Crane bills would require full registration of new municipal offerings. The Williams-Tower bill would not require registration but would establish a degree of disclosure for municipal securities issued in amounts above a specified minimum. And so on *ad nauseum.*

Municipal dealers know that they have a new exposure under the 1975 Securities Act amendments. The Dealer Bank Association and the SIA would like a federal law requiring municipalities to disclose more information. Mandatory disclosure would make them more comfortable. They would be even more comfortable if the suggestion of Wallace O. Sellers of Merrill Lynch were followed. He told the Williams Subcommittee that bond underwriters should not be liable for misstatements of municipal bond issuers. Here we find the ultimate liability being pushed back to the local jurisdiction, and yet the local jurisdiction administrators cannot get a definition of what they should disclose. At this point, it looks like a Gordian knot.

CONCLUSION

It is obvious that great changes must be made in the conduct of the municipal market. Everyone agrees that full disclosure is needed, but we are far from a consensus as to what that constitutes, let alone how and by whom it might be effected, and even further, who would review and regulate it. Jean J. Rousseau, in an article in the February 23 issue of *The Weekly Bond Buyer,* stated the problem well:

> In order to avoid stumbling at the outset of this most important work, everyone—issuers, underwriters and prospective regulators—must first agree on a general outline of the problem and its best resolution. If, by a minor miracle, the underwriting community agreed tomorrow on adequate disclosure standards, its work would scarcely have begun. If, by another miracle, the issuers collectively accepted the underwriters disclosure standards and undertook to comply with them, it would only set the stage for a true test of the standards.

The change in the marketplace will not come easily. It will require much patience, understanding, and cooperation from all involved, if we are to restore an orderly market where issuers and underwriters together can operate with a reasonable expectation that an inadverdent error or omission will not jeopardize their future.

20.
The Future of
the Municipal
Securities Market

ROGER KLEIN

By some standards the municipal securities market performed its function very well in 1975. In spite of an environment that can best be characterized as a continuous state of financial crisis, the municipal securities market raised $60.6 billion for state and local governments. This was a record level of financing and exceeded the level of financing in 1974 by $6.7 billion or 12.4 percent. It exceeded the volume in 1973 by $11.9 billion or 24.4 percent.

This volume of financing was not accomplished without significant costs. During 1975, interest rates on municipal securities stayed at very high levels, while interest rates in other markets came down substantially from their 1974 peaks. The result was that the ratio of tax-exempt yields to yields on taxable securities rose considerably. Thus far this year, interest rates on tax-exempt securities have fallen relative to interest rates in other securities markets. And, for awhile at least, everybody is breathing a lot easier. It is likely, however, that the municipal securities market will continue to be under enormous pressures. It is instructive therefore to examine this market, the factors that impacted it in 1975, and what they are likely to do in future years.

THE MUNICIPAL SECURITIES MARKET

The U.S. municipal securities market has more issuers and more issues outstanding and is more complex than any other securities market in the world. By the end of 1975, for example, there were 78,268 separate issuers of municipal securities (there were only 33,465 issuers of corporate securities) and 1,381,062 separate serial maturities of municipal issues outstanding (there were only 64,486 different corporate issues outstanding).

In recent years, the volume of new issues in the municipal securities market has grown rapidly, from $36 billion in 1970 (including $18 billion in long-term issues and $18 billion in short-term notes) to $60.6 billion in 1975 ($30.7 billion in long-term and $29.9 billion in short-term), a compound annual growth rate of over 10%. Funds from long-term issues have been used to finance educational facilities, hospitals, transportation facilities, public housing, public utilities, and facilities for public services such as fire, police, and sanitation. In 1975, for example, 23.8% of long-term financing was used for utilities and conservation, 15.3% for education, and 14.3% for social welfare projects such as public housing and hospitals. General obligation bonds comprised 52.4% of all long-term new municipal issues in 1975. The balance consisted of revenue bonds of various types. (See Table 1.)

The tax-exempt security developed through constitutional interpretation under the doctrine of reciprocal immunity to protect state and local governments' independence of action. Through it state and local governments have raised massive amounts of funds to provide services and facilities for the public good. The tax-exempt security has served that purpose well. With massive growth in federal income taxation, it has also become valuable in terms of interest cost saving. On average and in the main it has maintained this interest saving at 30 to 35 percent for long-term issues, and at higher percentages for medium-term bonds and short-term notes. (See Table 2.)

Much has happened over the past year, however, that has altered the market's ability to finance state and local government borrowing at rates substantially below those available in the taxable securities market. There are at least six reasons to be somewhat pessimistic about the ability of the municipal securities market to function as well in the future as it has in the past.

The Abrogation of Covenants and Contracts

An early blow to investor confidence came when the New Jersey and New York state legislatures passed legislation in 1974 abrogating a convenant concerning Port of New York Authority expenditures for rail mass transit. By concurrent legislation in 1962 the two states convenanted with each other and with the

Table 1   State and Local Government Debt Characteristics, Selected Years 1960–1976 (billion $)

	1960	1970	1974	1975
Total long-term	6.81	18.19	24.32	30.65
Total short-term	4.01	17.81	29.54	29.89
General obligation	4.36	11.85	13.57	16.05
Revenue	2.07	6.10	10.21	14.61
Utility	1.79	4.59	6.53	3.13
Special Tax	0.08	0.34	0.46	4.16
Rental	0.19	1.17	3.22	5.66
Education	2.28	5.03	4.73	4.68
Transportation	1.31	3.17	1.71	2.21
Utilities and conservation	1.30	3.47	5.64	7.26
Social welfare	0.60	1.47	4.45	4.40
Public housing	0.43	0.13	1.69	0.65
Hospitals	N.A.	N.A.	0.78	1.96
Other	0.17	1.30	1.98	1.79
Industrial revenue	0.04	0.11	0.50	0.46
Pollution control	—	—	1.71	2.22
Others (general purpose)	1.53	4.20	6.50	9.86
New capital	7.06	18.00	23.51	29.60
Refunding	0.05	0.11	0.73	1.01
Total	7.11	18.11	24.24	30.65

Source: Securities Industry Association.

holders of any affected bonds "that no pledged revenues" would be applied "for any railroad purposes whatsoever other than permitted purposes." At the time the covenant's repeal was under consideration, the Securities Industry Association (SIA) warned that repeal would be followed by extended litigation—which it has—and that it would be destructive of investor confidence—which it has.

The recent New York City note moratorium poses a similar threat to the "full faith and credit" concept. While the reason for the moratorium is understandable, the disregard for contractual obligations has had an adverse impact on the municipal securities market.

On April 8, 1976, President Ford signed a bill to revise the Bankruptcy Act to enable municipalities to apply for bankruptcy with relative ease. The bill had been introduced on October 30, 1975, in response to the financial problems of New York City. The bill further diminishes the "full faith and credit pledge." Specifically, the law now permits any municipality, regardless of size, to petition for bankruptcy. No consent of creditors is required prior to filing and, significantly, the prior position of bond holders is not recognized.

Table 2   Tax-Exempt Taxable Yield Ratio, Annual Averages

		Long Term	
	Short Term	Aaa	Baa
1965	N.A.	74.4	73.3
1966	N.A.	71.5	74.3
1967	N.A.	67.9	69.0
1968	N.A.	68.0	70.3
1969	N.A.	77.5	77.7
1970	N.A.	76.1	74.1
1971	N.A.	70.6	68.8
1972	N.A.	69.9	68.6
1973	50.5	64.4	66.6
1974	50.3	65.5	68.7
1975	53.1	65.4	73.3

Source: Securities Industry Association.

By unilaterally changing the terms of contracts, legislators have substantially altered the security behind municipal debt and therefore increased the level of risk to the holders of municipal debt. The easier it becomes to alter contract rights, the less valuable they become. This is reflected in the marketplace by a rise in state and local government borrowing costs.

Proposals for the Inclusion of the Interest on Municipal Bonds in a Minimum Tax

An investor who buys tax-exempt securities must discount not only interest rate risk, credit risk, and price risk, but also his or her expected tax bracket to determine the advantage of tax-exempt income in the future. If you remove the only certainty—that the interest will not be taxed—the investor has no basis on which to calculate what the tax liability will be. Faced with increased uncertainty the investor will demand a higher yield to compensate for the greater risk. This uncertainty will be magnified in the longer end of the municipal securities market. The ratio of tax-exempt interest rates to taxable rates in the long-term market is already much higher than in the shorter maturities. Any tampering with tax exemption will further hurt long-term borrowers.

When Congress considered in 1969 the imposition of a minimum tax on tax-exempt securities, a new uncertainty for investors was created. Faced with this additional uncertainty, they demanded compensation, resulting in high borrowing costs for municipalities. In their 1969 testimony before the Senate Finance Committee, the SIA pointed out that the mere discussion of a minimum tax and the uncertainty the discussion created in the minds of investors increased the borrowing costs for municipal issuers by approximately ½ of 1 percent.

The Senate Finance Committee has recently held hearings on inclusion of the interest on state and local government securities in the minimum tax. Consequently, it seems that the attack on the tax-free status of municipal bond interest income is still strong.

Record Demands on the Municipal Securities Market

The municipal market absorbed a record volume of financing in 1975. A significant portion of that demand was to finance the facilities not of cities and states but of private, profit-making organizations. Following a rapid growth of such securities in the late 1960s, Congress in 1968 wisely limited the use of tax exemption for industrial development bonds. However, limitation was not applied to tax-exempt financing of privately owned pollution abatement facilities. In 1975 tax-exempt financing of private pollution control facilities, including private placements, was estimated at $2.5 billion. Together with other industrial development financing, pollution bonds for private firms represent approximately 10 percent of all reported tax-exempt bond sales. This figure is the reported volume. Most market experts believe that a large portion of pollution control financing goes unreported. Peterson, for example, estimates that pollution control and industrial development financing were underreported by at least $1 billion in each of the last 2 years.[1] This type of financing obviously draws important institutional and individual investors away from conventional tax-exempt financing. This reduces access to the market for state and local government issuers, particularly those with medium-grade credit ratings. These issues therefore place significant upward pressure on tax-exempt interest rates. Some market experts feel that, left alone, pollution control financing will continue to grow rapidly through the remainder of the decade. A recent study, for example, estimates that the annual volume could easily reach $6 billion by 1980.[2]

---

[1] John Peterson, "The Tax Exemption Pollution Control Bond," Municipal Finance Officers Association, *Analysis,* March 1975.
[2] *Ibid.*

The Economic and Financial Problems of Our Major Cities

A recent study made at the University of Chicago and entitled "How Many New Yorks?"[3] concluded that New York is "not alone." A study by Peterson and Forbes entitled "Costs of Credit Erosion in the Municipal Bond Market" on the impact of New York City on the municipal securities market, indicated that there was a ripple effect which raised municipal interest rates across the board.[4] The increases were the largest in the northeast and mid-Atlantic states. If similar fiscal crises develop in other major cities the ripple impact on the market should be similar.

A Continuation of a Stop-Go Economic Policy

A long-standing inclination of the Federal Reserve to fight or moderate the rise in short-term interest rates, combined with the fact that 1976 is a presidential election year, is likely to produce extremely rapid rates of monetary growth. The monetary growth rate over the past several years has already produced an underlying rate of inflation in the 5 to 6 percent range. With short-term interest rates now moving up, the Federal Reserve will pump up the monetary aggregates even further. This may moderate a rise in interest rates now, but will lead to even higher interest rates down the road. The go phase of monetary policy is always followed by stop. And when the Federal Reserve does step on the brakes, it has some implications for the municipal securities market none of them very good.

1. *Municipal markets tend to be much more sensitive to swings in monetary policy than other money markets.* During periods of tight money, the demand for municipal securities by banks, the biggest buyers, generally falls sharply. Securities held by banks or securities banks would have bought must now be purchased by buyers with lower marginal tax rates. Since all rates are going up, municipal rates shoot up even faster. Thus in periods of economic instability municipal markets are even more unstable than other markets.

2. *Constant switching of economic policy increases the level of economic instability.* Since 1965, periods of stop and go have occurred with monotonous regularity. This policy approach, however, has not eliminated the problems economic policy is supposed to solve. Inflation has become worse, and the average unemployment rate has moved up steadily. There has been no trade-

---

[3] Terry Nichols Clark, Irene Sharp Rubin, Lynne C. Pettler, and Erwin Zimmerman, "How Many New Yorks?" Research Report No. 72 of the Comparative Study of Community Decision-Making (Chicago: University of Chicago).

[4] Ronald W. Forbes and John E. Peterson, "Costs of Credit Erosion in the Municipal Bond Market," Municipal Finance Officers Association, December 20, 1975.

off. We have more inflation and more unemployment. Moreover, the money and capital markets are devastated by high and variable inflation. Ironically, in fact, high and variable inflation is the product of a stop-go economic policy. Inflation brings with it high interest rates and, with many municipalities operating under interest rate ceiling constraints, many borrowers find their ability to tap the securities markets severely reduced if not eliminated.

3. *Increased volatility leads to higher risk and liquidity premiums demanded by investors.* Liquidity means the ability to sell quickly without suffering a big loss in value. In the municipal market, where a stop-go economic policy leads to volatile swings in price, investors will raise the premium they demand for a lack of liquidity.

The Changing Composition of the Demand for Municipal Securities

In the past, the largest purchasers of municipal securities have been commerical banks, fire and casualty insurance companies, and individuals. (See Tables 3 and 4.) As mentioned before, banks move into and out of the market, depend-

Table 3   Annual Changes in Holdings of Municipal Bonds 1960–1975 (billion $)

Year	Commercial Banks	Fire and Casualty Insurance Companies	Households	Other	Total Change
1960	0.7	0.8	3.5	3.0	5.3
1961	2.8	1.0	1.2	1.0	5.1
1962	5.7	0.8	−1.0	−0.1	5.4
1963	3.9	0.7	1.0	0.1	5.7
1964	3.6	0.4	2.6	−0.6	6.0
1965	5.2	0.4	1.7	0	7.3
1966	2.3	1.3	3.6	−1.6	5.6
1967	9.1	1.4	−2.2	−1.5	7.8
1968	8.6	1.0	−.8	.7	9.5
1969	0.2	1.2	9.6	−1.1	9.9
1970	10.7	1.5	−0.8	−.1	11.3
1971	12.6	3.9	−0.2	1.3	17.6
1972	7.2	4.8	1.0	1.4	14.4
1973	5.7	3.9	4.3	−0.2	13.7
1974	5.5	1.8	10.0	0.1	17.4
1975	1.7	2.1	7.0	4.6	15.4

Source: Federal Reserve, Flow of Funds. *

Table 4   Ownership of State and Local Securities (billion $)

	1950		1960		1970		1975	
	Amount	Percent of total	Amount	Percent of total	Amount	Percent of total	Amount	Percent of total
Banks	8.2	32.6	17.7	25.0	70.2	48.0	102.8	46.1
Individuals	10.0	39.6	30.8	43.5	47.4	32.5	67.5	30.3
Fire casualty insurance	1.1	4.4	8.1	11.5	17.8	12.2	34.3	15.4
Others	5.9	23.4	14.2	20.0	10.8	7.3	18.2	8.2
Total	25.2	100	70.8	100	146.2	100	222.8	100

Source: Federal Reserve, Flow of Funds.

ing upon the phase of the stop-go policy. Over previous business cycles, banks have tended to buy municipals when loan demand was relatively weak and the Federal Reserve was generous in supplying bank reserves—the go phase of economic policy. Alternatively, when loan demand shoots up, the appetite of banks for municipals is reduced. This is a basic cyclical phenomena which has been going on for a long time.

Many analysts argue that there has been a permanent drop in the demand for municipals by commercial banks. This has occurred for several reasons:

1.   The bank holding company vehicle is providing commercial banks with new ways of employing their funds, which compete powerfully in profitability with investments in municipal bonds, and some of these alternative investment opportunities, such as leasing companies, generate large depreciation throw-offs which may substantially reduce the need for tax-exempt income.

2.   The larger banks in the country that have mature foreign branches are now generating large foreign tax credits which also reduce the need for tax-exempt income. This is one reason why municipal bonds are currently a declining proportion of the portfolios of the large weekly reporting member banks of the Federal Reserve system.

The other large institutional purchaser of municipals is also reducing its demand. Fire and casualty insurance companies, which have traditionally absorbed large quantities of long-term revenue bonds, have not needed tax-exempt income. Over the last 2 years, as a group they suffered large underwriting losses which have severely limited the need for tax-exempt income.

Furthermore, we have observed a shift in the kinds of municipal securities fire and casualty companies are purchasing. We have looked at a sample of fire and casualty companies portfolios at various times over the past few years and observed that they now contain more pollution control and industrial aid securities and fewer traditional municipal revenue bonds. If fire and casualty companies buy fewer municipals and change the composition of those they do buy, and the trend of banks away from municipals continues, individuals will have to fill the void. The need to attract lower income tax rate individuals will lead to a further permanent deterioration of the tax-exempt yield relative to the taxable yield.

CONCLUSION

There are some reasons to be optimistic, at least temporarily. The municipal securities market has come through a difficult period. During 1976, municipal yields have fallen absolutely, as well as relative to taxable yields. Furthermore, New York State has once again attained market access. In addition, there are some favorable indications that state and local governments all over the country are more concerned about controlling spending and balancing budgets. In short, right now, the municipal securities market seems to be functioning reasonably well.

Furthermore, the problems described here are already beginning to be addressed. The SIA and other groups have repeatedly proposed the removal of pollution control bond issues from the tax-exempt securities market. Congress has held hearings, and the House Ways and Means Committee has produced a bill that offers municipalities the option of issuing either tax-exempt securities or taxable securities with a 35 percent federal subsidy. The object of the legislation is to broaden the market for state and local government debt. Legislation has been proposed and hearings held on setting standards for disclosure with respect to municipal securities. The need for more information for investors has been made clear by New York City's financial problems. The market by itself is already imposing a much higher standard of disclosure for new issues. Whether or not legislation is passed soon, it is clear that more information on the municipal securities market is and will be forthcoming.

The municipal securities market is obviously on the verge of enormous change. The market for state and local government securities of the future is likely to be only a faint shadow of what it has been in the past.

Discussion

George H. Hempel

Three interesting papers have discussed three important aspects of the markets for municipals: (1) the socioeconomic conditions of borrowing units, (2) management and reporting by borrowing units, and (3) various conditions affecting the demand for municipal borrowing and the marketplace in which borrowers and lenders meet. The dominant theme has been that conditions on both the supply and demand side of the market and in the marketplace have changed rapidly in the last year or so and are continuing to change. I offer two general conceptual ideas stimulated by these articles followed by a brief evaluation of each of the three papers.

While financial crises are basically damaging, they often have the positive effect of leading to needed changes or reforms. Without crises, many basically positive changes would not be achieved because of apathy and inertia. This seems to be a particularly accurate description of the market for municipals. By the early 1970s several conditions seemed evident: (1) the demand for municipal bonds was dominated by one type of constitutional buyer, commercial banks which were taxed at a marginal corporate income tax rate of 48 percent; (2) the umbrella of tax exemption was being broadened to cover the financing of private or near-private projects for pollution control, housing, and so on; (3) reporting by municipal units was usually poor—millions of dollars were often raised on the basis of several pages of unaudited and generally confusing data on the borrowing unit; (4) numerous questions were being raised about the validity of municipal bond ratings; and (5) there was published evidence that some municipal units were likely to face severe financial strain because of poor financial practice and/or economic strains in some municipal units.

278

The last-mentioned condition was clearly described in a report entitled "City Financial Emergencies," which was published by the Advisory Commission on Intergovernmental Relations in 1973. Six early warning indicators of municipal financial emergencies were identified in that book. Interestingly enough, New York City was identified as heading toward a financial emergency by all of the early warning indicators and was particularly criticized for using hugh amounts of short-term debt to finance current operating deficits. Suggestions for improving municipal reporting and for needed revision in municipal bankruptcy laws and procedures were proposed. In addition, the economic decline of central cities in the Midwest and East was identified as a serious problem. The dangers identified in this book were basically ignored (probably because there was no visible financial emergency in 1973 and 1974) until the current financial crisis in New York City was widely publicized. This visible crisis led and is still leading to some needed changes in the market for municipals. Unfortunately, some of the proposed changes were made in a crisis atmosphere and were not as carefully thought out and tested as might have been the case in less hectic times. Nevertheless, changes were achieved that would probably not have occurred had there been no crises.

The second general point is that there is no clearly established definition of a financial crisis for a state and local unit. Default on interest or principal payment is clearly considered a financial crisis; however, such a narrow definition excludes the recent financial problems in New York State and New York City. The definition of a financial crisis is difficult to formulate but seems worthy of further investigation.

To the resident of a municipality, a financial crisis may mean an increase in taxes or a curtailment of municipal services. To municipal employees, a financial crisis occurs when employees are laid off or pay raises are curtailed. To holders of municipal bonds, a financial crisis occurs when the municipality does not pay interest or principal on its bonds. To members of civic organizations or minority groups in the community, a financial crisis occurs when there is a lack of funds to pay for urgently needed programs. And finally, to a politician, a financial crisis is any situation that generates sufficient voter hostility to affect adversely his chances for reelection.

Probably the most popular definition of a financial crisis refers to a situation in which a state or local unit contains a population whose income is so low that it precludes the unit from supporting minimum services without disproportionately high taxes. Such a unit faces a continuing crisis, because it is confronted with either reducing services below a minimum level or increasing taxes beyond a feasible level. A financial crisis defined by this state of affairs depends, however, on two further definitions—what constitutes a minimum level of municipal services and a maximum acceptable tax effort?

Minimum levels of municipal service are extremely difficult to measure by either qualitative or quantitative criteria. Although the National Commission on Productivity is exploring possible methods for such measurements, the only presently available measure is variation in the dollar value of inputs. Variations in inputs may be caused in turn by variations in the costs of the factors of production, or variations in the quality of service provided. Differences in services from city to city and state to state reflect regional and local traditions and legal requirements. Thus the definition of minimum levels of service entails both careful study and value judgments of a major order.

Maximum tax effort as a factor in determining a financial emergency similarly eludes definition. A review of the largest cities in the country indicates that the property tax rate as a percentage of true value varies from less than 1 percent to more than 5 percent. The Advisory Commission on Intergovernmental Relations (ACIR) index of tax effort shows that, on an index of 100, major cities vary from an effort of 75 to 139.

Minimum levels of service are helpful in understanding, but fail to explain, municipal financial crises. Each municipality has its own standards by which it judges its service levels. To the extent that some municipalities have inadequate services or taxes that are high relative to other municipalities, they may in fact be experiencing a financial emergency. But such a judgment suffers from the lack of any means of objective measurement.

Other popular definitions of financial crises have similar defects. My suggested solution is to use two definitions. First, if payment on interest or principal is not made when promised, the state or local unit should be identified as being in default. Second, a financial crisis occurs when a state or local unit reaches the point at which it can no longer maintain existing levels of services because of the inability to meet payrolls, pay current bills, pay amounts due other government agencies, or pay debt service on bonds or maturing short-term notes because it lacks either cash or appropriations authority. Thus a state or local unit may suffer a financial crisis even though it has not defaulted on its debt payments. While these definitions are broader than the definition of financial crises for some of the other sectors covered in this book, they seem appropriate for the state and local sector. I would like to briefly comment on each of the three papers, keeping the above definitional problems in mind.

Lissenden's paper is a case study of how a generally well-managed city was temporarily inconvenienced by the new municipal disclosure rules which became effective on December 1, 1975. Richmond planned to issue debt only days after the new rules became effective. Underwriting groups were uncertain about the disclosure requirements and their liability if these requirements were not met. Consequently only one (very high) bid was made, which the city refused. Richmond was able to bring its debt offering out a few weeks later, and its original prospectus (with only very minor changes) has been used as a model for other municipal units. My only comment on this case study is that changes resulting from crises are often not well thought out in advance. Somebody, in this case Richmond, often has to serve as the guinea pig to understand the true impact of the enacted changes. I agree strongly with Lissenden's conclusions that we must more clearly define who is responsible for disclosure (there is considerable conflict as to whether the borrower unit or its underwriters are responsible) and then establish better definitions of full disclosure, so that the responsible party will know whether or not it is fulfilling its obligation.

Klein's paper provides broader coverage of the developments and changes in the municipal market brought about by the municipal financial crises in 1974 and 1975. I believe he may be guilty of setting up a straw man in a case or two; for example, I disagree with his statement that marketability was a general characteristic of municipals prior to 1974. Many smaller issues have never approached marketability. Nevertheless, I think he does an excellent job of cataloging many significant recent changes—for example, the fact that banks are leaving the market for municipals, and the abrogation of many municipal bond covenants and contracts. I also agree with his predictions that disclosure rules will become tougher and that there is a high probability that we will have the taxable municipal bond option within the next few years.

Finally, the paper by Burkhead and Campbell identifies many dangerous elements which may lead to future municipal financial crises. Basically the Burkhead-Campbell paper concludes that macroeconomic data indicate that state and local units are in reasonably good financial shape. When the data are disaggregated, however, they identify several worrisome financial trends for selected municipal units. These trends involve basic measures of the ability of the municipality to pay for desired services and its ability to borrow. For some cities, particularly central cities in the East and Midwest, Burkhead and Campbell appear to question whether or not the municipal unit can function in an effective manner. Most of the identified negative trends have been examined in previous works, but Burkhead and Campbell do an effective job of selling the severity of some of the basic economic disparities that exist. It should also be noted that they define the term financial crisis broadly—similar to my definition above—rather than solely as default on indebtedness.

I conclude by mentioning a few relatively new sources of information on the municipal market. Peterson has just finished a booklet for the United States Congress Joint Economic Committee (JEC) called "Changing Conditions in the Market for State and Local Government Debt." In addition to "City Financial Emergencies", the ACIR has recently published a basic monograph entitled *Understanding the Market for State and Local Debt.* In addition, the ACIR is considering updating its earlier study of municipal financial emergencies in order to deal with new questions and needs highlighted or caused by the New York and Massachusetts emergencies.

John E. Petersen

The three papers on this subject provide a useful battery of perspectives on the problems of state and local governments and their relationship to the behavior of the municipal securities market. The Burkhead-Campbell paper casts a broad net from the perspective of the economist and political scientist over the fiscal consequences of changing real conditions in the state and local sector and the difficulties of devising policies to cope with or correct them. Klein, in his recapitulation of the changing market for municipal securities, emphasizes the major events of the last few years that have lead to more turbulent conditions in this market. Finally, Lissenden recounts the difficulties of a local government unit selling debt against a backdrop of deep concern about credit quality and about legal responsibilities, investigating and reporting on the risks inherent in investment, an exercise that can generally be captioned as disclosure.

Burkhead and Campbell discuss the real underpinnings of government debtors. The paper goes through several categories of economic and demographic changes that have not only led to a weakening of the financial health of the state and local sector as viewed in the aggregate but, much more seriously, have eroded the position of certain classes of government units. They note that a review of the macroeconomic situation does not raise a great deal of concern among analysts. But the aggregated national income numbers mask serious conditions for many of the component units. The most salient point is the geographic distribution of hardship, which has focused distress in the northeast region and among the major and older cities east of the Mississippi. Such regional differences threaten to be more pronounced, because the services that must be chopped away by governments that have insufficient revenues may also lead to a denigration of the general quality of life, which lessens their competitive appeal against their younger, more affluent, sister jurisdictions.

Public attention has focused on the profligacy of New York City and the difficulties of attempting to put its expenditures in better balance with its receipts. There has probably been insufficient attention given to other cities that have already undertaken serious retrenchment measures in order to balance their budgets. It was not until early 1975 that surveys began to elicit information which revealed the rapid changes in the regional composition of fiscal soundness in the state and local sector. The surplus enjoyed by the sector taken as a whole in the early 1970s, especially at the advent of revenue sharing in 1972, masked serious financial deterioration in certain regions of the S/L sector. We now know, in retrospect, that there was a painful selectivity in the rates of growth in tax and grant receipts, as well as a rapid increase in such items as fuel costs and wage bills, which had their hardest impact on both the economies and the governments of the Northeast and Midwest. Such units as Detroit, Cleveland and, earlier yet, Pittsburgh had been pulling in their belts for some time. It is important that we analyze the future consequences of such retrenchment measures, not only in terms of balancing the budget but also with regard to how they change the competitive ability of these cities to retain or attract economic vigor and stable populations.

Looking ahead, it seems clear that the changes in state and local conditions in 1974 and 1975 have led governments to restudy their philosophies about services growth. Underscored is the importance of budget balancing and reduced expectations. With fiscal conservatism in vogue, the revenue projections now embodied in most municipal budgets probably understate the revenues to be generated in the process of recovery. Thus state and local budgets will begin to move toward surpluses. Steps to put these governments on a sounder financial footing do not reduce the underlying problems relating to their ability to provide satisfactory levels of public service. These problems will intensify even when governments exist on a tight regime with balanced budgets in order to gain acceptance into the municipal securities markets. However, acceptance will never be as enthusiastic as for those that show stronger underlying conditions. Thus it is difficult to see how many of the large urban areas and some of the states of the Northeast will enjoy very rapid recovery. Moves to reduce operating costs and to delay capital improvements will hasten the decay that comes from a lack of capital replacement and vital services. This will continue until there is a new cycle of public concern.

One aspect of the Burkhead-Campbell paper with which I disagree is their analysis of the varying tax willingness of state and local governments. It is my estimation that the revenue increases of the early 1970s were related more to the passivity of taxpayers with regard to increases in tax payments. Such increases were induced by increases in real income and moderate inflation rather than by a positive willingness to buy more services. This passivity was supplanted first by apprehension and then by downright rejection during the hyperinflation and recession of 1973 and 1974, as the taxpayer was faced with rapid reductions in real income. Moreover, one of the legacies of the early 1970s and the fleeting facade of prosperity presented by the surpluses generated with revenue sharing was the institution of certain redistributive policies, which reduced the local property tax base. By the same token, redistributive notions were behind removal from sales tax of food, medicine, and other necessities. Such policies, while of benefit to certain classes of taxpayers, nonetheless had the overall effect of lowering the real tax base of the state and local sector by a few percentage points. Thus, just before the state and local tax system was called upon to generate its greatest growth of revenue to balance surging inflation and expenditures, the tax real base was pruned back, often being replaced by more income-elastic revenue sources.

Klein's paper discusses several of the recent major changes witnessed in the municipal bond market. He points out that the municipal bond market, although under severe interest rate pressure in 1975, nonetheless extended credit at a record-setting volume. The reaction of the market to changing economic conditions was very selective, and certain securities that had once been favored lost a great deal of appeal to investors. In most cases we can find investor receptivity of types of debt instruments or that the indebtness of certain areas was directly related to the financing difficulties of New York City and New York State agencies. The moral obligation bond, which from the very outset had never been more than simply a method of financing off the budget, and outside of debt constraints, lost almost all its support in the market. Moreover, and perhaps with more serious implications for the great bulk of state and local borrowers, there came to be universal concern about the security pledged to the general obligation bond.

An irony of the last year or so has been the preferred position given to those uses of tax exemption often thought of as perversions: the use of tax-exempt bonds to finance industry and, in particular, industry's efforts at pollution control. With the shrinkage in the overall demand for tax-exempt securities in 1974 and 1975, the competition given to traditional types of state and local securities by these various forms of industrial revenue bonds was particularly serious.

Many reasons can be advanced for the investor preference shown for industrial-type securities and revenue bonds based on user charges. The two most important are: first, investors found reassurance in the industrial firm's promise to repay, because it was not tied to a specific location or to a specific population's service needs and, second, the accounting and reporting techniques involved in enterprise operations provided a better means (or at least a better understood method) of evaluating credit quality. The latter point stems from the use of accounting principles by government enterprises that are almost identical to those used in the corporate sector. Government officials are becoming increasingly displeased about the competition from tax-exempt corporate securities and therefore are launching efforts to diminish the growth of bonds sold for these purposes.

Klein is correct in noting that legislation also played a role in the loss of investor confidence in municipal securities over the last year. One of the problems is that some of the legislative changes are poorly understood by investors. In particular the generalization that the recently passed amendments to the Federal Bankruptcy Code put bond holders at the end of the line is not correct. The legislation does not change the priority of claims, but rather creates a procedure that may be used in meeting these claims in the case of a municipal bankruptcy. The exception to the general rule of not changing the order of payments is that expenses incurred in the process of bankruptcy and certain indebtedness that may be created in the process of composition of claims are given a first claim.

My impression is that the market overreacted to the bankruptcy legislation and to the moratorium law passed in New York. Given the vast uncertainties and emotional edginess at the end of 1975, the reaction was to be expected. However, it is clear to state and local governments that the price of revocation of debt or a rearranging of the terms is exclusion from the bond markets and the paying of very high premiums on any possible future borrowing. I do not think that many, if any, general governments will be encouraged to follow such a course of action, which is simply one of compounding economic difficulties in the future and committing political suicide in the present.

Another source of uncertainty that Klein mentions is the present discussion of the federal minimum income tax and its possible application to municipal bonds. A congenital weakness in the municipal bond market has been its extreme sensitivity to potential changes in the tax code. It is true that this is a peculiarly poor time to envision a change in the tax status of municipal bonds. Individual investors are the major net demander in the municipal bond market and the minimum tax is targeted at them.

But before we become too concerned about the municipal bond market's ability to handle shock and its absorptive capacity, at least over the near term, it is important to note that the market has moved to a new high in the annual rate bond sales so far this year. At the same time there was a substantial reduction in interest costs. This very feature of the market, sharp fluctuations in both the dollar volume of bond sold and in interest rates, reflects another problem and cause of uncertainty: its great volatility. The cyclical instability of the municipal bond market will probably remain as long as large volumes of municipal bonds are sold to financial institutions that constantly shift investments in tune with monetary policy changes and fluctuating needs for tax exemption.

A final item that might be noted, and one that Klein does not address directly, is the compositional nature of radical adjustments in the debt policy of state and local governments. Most, but not all, of the serious debt problems are found in the Northeast and, most particularly, in New York. The first quarter of this year saw massive refinancings of short-term debt to long-term security. Particularly in the case of Massachusetts and New York, large amounts of floating debt have been funded. This should ease many of the liquidity problems for these governments, albeit at the cost of exorbitant rates of interest. It should also relieve the pressure in the short-term municipal financing. With the relatively strong demand of banks for short-term municipal securities this year, this has led to a relaxation of pressure in the short-term market. We see steep yield curves, with the differential between short-term and long-term debt of equivalent quality being roughly on the order of 250 to 300 basis points. Although state and local governments have perhaps decided that too much short-term debt is a bad thing, such a steep yield curve may once again encourage a large amount of short-term borrowing in order to reduce interest costs.

Lissenden's paper addresses on a blow-by-blow basis the difficulties experienced by borrowers at the time of the great disclosure crisis during the latter part of 1975 and early 1976. As he points out, many of these worries are now at a more subdued level, since both underwriter and issuer seem to have a better notion of what is needed in order to meet requirements for information. Approaching such an agreement has not been any easy task, but much cooperation has been accomplished with reassuring speed.

Like motherhood, all favor full disclosure by state and local governments of their financial dealings and fiscal conditions. But, how this can be best accomplished is far from clear. Generally, there are two polar views.

One is that adequate disclosure can be developed by market forces and voluntary efforts. This is because of the competitiveness of the market, the public nature of the issuers, the superior risk record of municipal securities, and the existing liabilities under the antifraud statutes. The degree of legal exposure is uncertain, but all market participants will minimize the risk of fraud by exercising greater care providing information, just as investors will demand more before they buy bonds.

The opposing view holds that the federal government should establish concrete disclosure standards and regulate the market to ensure that they are met. This group also argues that the current uncertainties with respect to the liabilities of various participants must be clarified by federal statute, otherwise there may develop a messy ad hoc system of disclosure based on court decisions and individual legal actions by the Securities Exchange Commission.

Whatever the outcome of this debate, it is promising that many in the municipal bond market are working on disclosure standards and procedures. Without federal legislation, such efforts will generate improvements in informing the market. With legislation, such efforts should help make a mandated system more suited to the realistic needs of the investor.

Index